oyster

oyster
A World History

Drew Smith

The
History
Press

First published 2010

The History Press
The Mill, Brimscombe Port
Stroud, Gloucestershire, GL5 2QG
www.thehistorypress.co.uk

British Library Cataloguing in Publication Data.
A catalogue record for this book is available from the British Library.

ISBN 978 0 7524 5734 5

Typesetting and origination by The History Press
Printed in Great Britain

Contents

Author's Note

For Warwick B., Jeremy R., Peter G. and Caroline W. To Oliver and Grace, of course, and thanks to Beatrice for her continual support; and in memoriam to my cousin Raymond, who first introduced me to oysters on the beach at Cap Breton and was cameraman to Jacques Cousteau before becoming a dentist, and to my father Frank, both of whom died during the course of writing this book. Thanks also to Abbie Wood for publishing it and everyone else who has contributed in different ways.

A note on the recipes: By and large I have tended to leave the recipes as I found them, so as not to disturb the historical archaeology with a personal slant or editing.

There is a companion website to the book, found at www.oysterstew. wordpress.com, with up-to-date news, addresses, information on festivals, more paintings and photographs and yet more cooking.

The Craic

The Celts did not hold with writing things down; they saw it as weak-minded. The proper storyteller should remember. He should remember things from his father, that came from his father, and from his father … if he could imagine that far back – all the way back to New Grange Barrow, on the River Boyne 3,400 BC, perhaps, and probably before that, as if there existed some perpetual line of Druid storytelling that would stretch so far.

The Celts were not the only people in this story who were disadvantaged by not writing things down. So let us tell it as if we are moored on a packet boat on a Cornish creek, as the swell of the tide lifts us off the mud; or on a warm Louisiana bayou, drifting, waiting for the wind to get up; or we are waiting to dive from a galley in the Red Sea …

Waiting, yes, oysters are good at waiting.

PART I

Ancient Times

Our shells clacked on the plates
My tongue was a filling estuary
My palate hung with starlight ... alive and violated
They lay on their beds of ice
Bivalves: the split bulb
And philandering sigh of ocean.

Seamus Heaney, *Oyster*, 1979

In the Beginning

The Palaeozoic Ostrea – The Holocene Era –
The First Knives, Forks, Votes & Boats – The Treasure of Varna

The Palaeozoic Ostrea

The oyster is older than us. Older than grass. It was here at the start of civilisation, at the start of the world.

Oysters are found in the late Palaeozoic. They were abundant in Jurassic and Cretaceous periods. To put numbers on that, the Palaeozoic was 542 to 251 million years ago. They were found in the Cambrian period 545 million years ago – that is four billion years after the origins of the earth, and 3.3 billion years after the origins of life. The Palaeozoic is what science refers to as the start of visible life. By any criteria, the oyster is an extraordinary survivor.

Scientists trying to date the earliest known humanoid skeletons of Omo I and Omo II, discovered at Kibish in Ethiopia in 1987, used the oyster shells buried in the volcanic ash with them to set a date around 195,000 years ago. Before men were men, oysters were oysters.

Oyster fossils can be seen in Portland stone in Dorset, which formed in the Jurassic period. In Peru giant oyster shells have been found 2 miles above sea level in the Andes and dated back 200 million years. Whatever the precise numbers, oysters have been around for a very, very long time.

Prehistoric kitchen middens have been uncovered around the world. At Kattegat in Denmark the shell mounds included mainly oysters, cockles, mussels and periwinkles. Similar finds have been made along the west coast of Ireland, while at Brittany, at St Michel-en-l'Hern, the shell banks were 700yd long, 300yd wide and stood 15ft above the marsh. Archaeologists have found other huge caches at Mycenae in southern Greece and in Japan and Australia. Much of what we know about Native Americans derives from the study of the early oyster shell middens they left behind along the east coast from Mississippi to Maine.

The discovery of a fossil reef on Africa's Red Sea coast in 2000 showed that early humans had taken up coastal life at least 10,000 years earlier than previously believed. In the reef, near Abdur in Eritrea's Gulf of Zula, were found two-sided stone hand-axes and flaked obsidian blades. Nearby were fossil bones of large land animals, including elephants, antelopes, rhinoceros and hippopotamuses. There were also oyster shells.

These first men seem to have driven the animals towards the sea and killed them there to have some meat in their diet. This tribe probably lived in a relatively warm interglacial period between ice ages, or had migrated when inland areas froze. The find confirmed not just that Africa was the original home of humanity, but also that migration followed the coastal routes north and north-east to Europe, and east to the Middle and Near East 100,000 plus years ago.

If you follow the evidence of shell middens then the world would seem to have been populated not as is usually expounded in European centric texts – east to west or north to south – but from Africa perhaps east, to India certainly, possibly on to Japan or south down the Pacific coast. Men were in Victoria, Australia, by 40,000 BC. Modern coastlines probably did not stabilise until around 7,000 BC so it is plausible that migration moved along different patterns. The earliest pottery yet found in the western hemisphere was excavated from a prehistoric shell midden near Santarém in the lower Amazon, Brazil. Radiocarbon dating estimates these shards and evidence of civilisation to be 8,000 years before the present. There are other sites in Peru and Columbia. A frieze sculpted 5,000 years ago was found at Vichama, 120km north of Lima, and shows a hand holding an object like a knife or a spindle. By 4,000 BC Indians had certainly migrated north as far as modern-day Georgia, USA. All of this pre-dates the building of the pyramids by a long, long way.

The oldest skeleton found in Britain, the so-called Red Lady of Swansea Bay, was laid to rest inside a cave in a cliff face in the Gower some 24,000 years ago. She was surrounded by oyster shells. One of the oldest settlements found in Britain is a submerged village, and probably a boatbuilding site, over what are today the oyster beds of the Solent and the Isle of Wight. The date is 6,000 BC.

The Holocene Era

The genetic history of mankind currently dates to a drought in East Africa around 75,000 BC, at which point people started to migrate. Modern history is defined these days from the emergence of farming. The climate in Europe grew suddenly warmer some 15,000 years ago. Climactically, we still live in that Holocene era that came after the last ice age.

Stephen Oppenheimer, in his book *The Origins of the British*, used DNA data to propose that these people congregated in two parts of Europe to shelter from the cold – around the Ukraine and around the Basque Country – as havens warm enough to survive an ice age. As the climate eased, Europe, he argues, was populated from these two families. From the Basque enclave they travelled north along the coast, and when they reached the Channel some turned east and would have gone up as far as modern Scandinavia to become north men, Vikings and Saxons. Others stayed west and colonised Wales, Ireland and Scotland. Thousands of years later, their descendants were to be called 'the Celts' and romanticised as a race of that name by scholars and writers over the last few hundred years. But it was certainly not as simple as that; there were without doubt other peoples further south who would have moved north, and probably some of the Ukraine enclave would also have moved north across land. However, if you lay the map of Megalithic monuments in Europe down, you will find it overlaps precisely with the locations of the oyster coves of the time.

The first farmers, DNA now tells us, arrived in Britain around 4,000 BC from Brittany. The populations quadrupled in 400 years, which is a clear pointer to the arrival of settling communities and disowns the idea that hunter-gatherers slowly converted new areas. These first Europeans moved by boat, exploring tentatively cove to cove, secure in the knowledge that each inlet was a larder. The first settlers in America talked of the fish being so plentiful around oyster coves that the noise of their splashing kept them awake at night.

Travellers could secure a safe settlement around an oyster bed and move on. As their boats got bigger they could travel further, hugging the coast and keeping sight of the rocky edges of land where there was safe and easy-to-grab food. Oysters were so abundant that a man just had to drop over the side and prise a bunch of shells off the reef, shuck them open – if he had iron – or just throw them in the fire to roast and open easily in the heat. Both in Mexico, where Cortez recorded it, and later in the South Seas and Australia, the first western travellers refer to oysters lying around 'carelessly' on the beach.

The oyster reefs were a navigable highway to uncharted lands. Journeys inland held no equivalent reassuring promise. Ironically, in the light of what was to happen millennia later, oysters were safe food too. Their existence was a clear signpost to settlers that this was a place of clean water; an area where it would be secure to stay. The oyster meant rich fishing and the promise of calm inland waters with easy prey.

With settlement and farming came the need to organise, to write things down, to make laws to instill social order, to have ownership and kingships and all the trappings of what is taught in school as history. From this we call the world affectionately the Earth, but the land only accounts for one-third of the planet. In another perspective we might better call it the Rock. Textbook history tends to be obviously land-centric. Oyster history is essentially submarine, or at least coastal. These first explorers were obviously not farmers at all, not even cavemen, but covemen moving slowly around the coastlines, hugging the shore and settling for short times in the most fertile estuaries which inevitably meant oyster coves. These first civilisations, or perhaps more appropriately cultures, moved by sea, not by land and were anything but unsophisticated.

Oyster shells are used in archaeology for carbon dating. They are a constant in our history and where we might not have all the formulas classified, we can see that very often the equations and outcomes must have been the same in different parts of the globe at different times in our past. If history is usually comprised of archaeological finds, language, written records, and now carbon dating and DNA science, the oyster lends another fixed, incontrovertible dimension.

To a naturalist, the oyster is one of the most successful species on the planet ... or it was until we came along.

The First Knives, Forks, Votes & Boats

To early men oysters were essential. In the Neolithic the oyster was more than a source of food. The shells might have been the first knives and spoons, even digging implements; certainly they were used for decoration and artefacts of worship. The luminescent inner coating of mother-of-pearl was lovingly cut out and fashioned into ornaments for the first artists to adorn the first religious icons; the rest might have been broken down and mixed with sand for cement for building. The oyster was traded for flesh and for shell and, most coveted of all – the pearl.

They were also a pointer to another crucial discovery for early man – salt. The shallow bays and inlets where the oyster flourished were necessarily tidal. The oyster's sensitivity to the level of salt was a clear clue that here was man's first preservation material for his own salvation. The ability to salt and preserve foods lent coastal towns a commercial sway and influence denied anywhere inland. The oysters might also have been read as a flag pointing to the presence of other essentials, especially minerals like zinc and copper, which could have been nearby.

The oyster was an early article of trade going right back to Phoenician times and earlier into the Megalithic. It was a token to attract taxes, levies, rents and other impositions, not just in Europe but by the natives of the South Sea Islands too. More recently, in Long Island, Chesapeake, and before that in London, Amsterdam and Rome, the cut and thrust of hiring men, pricing a catch, getting it to market, wholesaling and retailing would have been a commerce that informed the trading cultures in pure city capitalism.

The oystermen developed their own necessary lingua franca of bushels, pecks, gallons and quarts, not to mention barrels and baskets to determine (or often, in the oyster's case, not to determine) weights and measures. In New York in 1858 it was laid down that a cart man could charge 31 cents for a load of oysters, against 25 cents for bricks and 75 cents for furniture.

The oyster infuses the very language we use. The Greek word *ostrea* means to leave out. In Greek society shells were used as ballot papers for elections; voters etched their mark on the mother-of-pearl shell, from which act of choosing one faction over the other derives the word *ostracism*. The word for an estuary has its own regional declensions around the globe from bayou to creek to sound to inlet to lagoon to bay, a firth or a fal, depending where you are. The boats built for oystering are not boats at all but arks, scows, smacks, yarls, bisquines, bugeyes, borleys, catboats, sharpies, shallops, sloops, skiffs and skipjacks. New York oystermen talked of an oyster spitting, as in releasing its seed, hence spat.

First-generation politics was born on the waterfront and developed its own raft of edicts, laws and pronouncements from kings, councillors, captains and anyone who deemed they had an authority to challenge the ownership of the bounty of the seabeds. Some of this was petty, parochial or pious, but nevertheless defined the relationship between state and county, county and port, enfranchised and disenfranchised, landowner and boatman, all of which was a rich school of learning for the would-be lawyer and litigator. Disputes between barons, councils, corporations, fishermen in Essex, England, date back to the Magna Carta and were – and possibly still are – a dress rehearsal for litigants in the Chesapeake and Hudson rivers.

In gastronomy the oyster is pre-eminent. There are as many recipes for cooking an oyster as there are for preparing eggs. Usually, today in Europe, the oyster is served fresh on the shell, which is in part to do with its increased scarcity, but few foods can claim to have been lavished with such culinary guile in surprisingly different ways around the world. The canon of American oyster recipes is one of its great culinary legacies.

The imagery of oysters is entrenched in national consciousness. In England the smacks lined up beside Billingsgate fish market, the costermongers treading the streets selling to the rich and poor, are a postage stamp of Victorian London; in France the oyster has for centuries been a source of Gallic defiance, first against the Romans and then against the dangers of the Atlantic. For the Romans it was associated with both lasciviousness and omnipotence; in America it became an icon of the American dream, and the way it was traded forged the ideals of the American way. In Japan there is supreme elegance in the way it is prepared, as if the oyster was the highest of social mores. Farming artificial pearls was one of the first harbingers of the Asian boom in mass production for sale to the west.

In the Old World it was the pearl from the Persian oyster that was prized more than gold. Wherever you go in history, wherever there are oysters, there are the guts and bones of our own history.

The great seafaring nations – Britain, France, Spain, Portugal, Japan and America herself – have all enjoyed an oyster culture. This is not completely unconnected. Oystermen needed boats and wherever there have been oysters aplenty, there has quickly built up a trade in shipbuilding around it, often distinct and individual according to the needs of the oystermen, or indeed the needs of the sailors for whom oysters were a necessary accompanying food with which to travel. Ships then needed sails which led to cloth making, famously in the Middle Ages in Essex trading with Flanders and equally to the seamstresses of the Chesapeake turning their skilled hands to shirts and suits for Manhattan financiers. Originally oystermen were the navy. In France a sailor's pension from the navy could be an oyster bed.

Social classes were set by whether a man made his living on the water, had moved inland to farm or found wealth in trading. There is an uncomfortable irony that many of the towns that were once famous for trading their now redundant oyster beds have become fashionable, exclusive, leisure beach and sailing resorts. Perhaps we too have come to aspire to be like oysters, sitting quietly breathing in the sea air in our retirement.

The Treasure of Varna

In 1972 archaeologists uncovered a cemetery in Varna, now in Bulgaria, which showed the true sophistication of early Europeans; pre-Greece, pre-Romans. It was dated to 5,000 BC and demonstrated that these people were far from living unstructured lives as hunter-gatherers, but had trading networks, art, wealth and religion. Part of their currency buried with them were oysters, in this case from the Aegean. The shells were probably not just currency or decoration, but tokens of esteem and status, or even a mark of trade along a route more than 1,500km long. They were from the spondylus or thorny oyster rather than the edible or pearl-bearing oyster, and were worn as necklaces and pendants and transparently denoted status. The story has eked out slowly from behind the Iron Curtain but it has been confirmed that these people were farmers moving north from Greece and Macedonia into Old Europe, bringing wheat and barley, sheep and cattle. They settled along the Black Sea and traded back south, selling copper, gold and ceramics.

The Varna finds disproved the idea that because early people did not leave high-status architectural remains they were disorganised nomads. The 310 graves are the oldest yet found where the bodies were buried with their gold, their copper weapons, necklaces and oyster shells in abundance. More than 3,000 pieces of gold have been retrieved from just 62 graves. In fact, one grave – not all, curiously, contained bodies – held more gold than had previously been attributed to the entire era around the world. One presumably high-status male had a gold sheath for his penis.

Despite their wealth, these people seem to have lived modestly. It may well have been that copper was the source of their fortune, taken from the abundant ore in Bulgaria and areas of what is now Serbia. Smelting developed around 5,400 BC. Copper, cast as knives and axes and turned into bracelets, has been found along the Volga and would have been a valuable export.

These early people spent their wealth – or perhaps, like some Neolithic Ikea, manufactured for sale – distinctive, almost abstract in a modern sense, figurines of fired clay of truncated but sensual female figures with large breasts and hips; and men in thinker-style poses.

I

Of Pearls & Gods

Capturing Moonlight – Pliny's Big Mistake – The Lure of Luminescence
– The Immortal Maiden – Between the Zenith and the Horizon –
Egyptian Necklaces – Princess of Bora Bora

*The kingdom of Heaven is like unto a merchant man, seeking goodly pearls; who, when
he had found one pearl of great price, went and sold all that he had and bought it.*

Matthew 13:45, 46

*Light filtered down through the water to the bed where the frilly pearl oysters lay
fastened to the rubbly bottom … this was the bed that had raised the king of Spain
to be a great power in Europe, had helped to pay for his wars, and had decorated his
churches for his soul's sake …*

*Kino lifted the flesh and there it lay, the great pearl perfect as the moon. It captured
the light and refined it and gave it back in silver incandescence … on the surface he
could see dreams form.*

John Steinbeck, *The Pearl*, 1944

Capturing Moonlight

In every civilisation there is some pre-history of gods, of legends, of
larger-than-life ancestors, of indeterminate, ghostly pre-life. The oyster has

always managed to associate with such illustrious company. Gods, mighty warriors, heroes, beautiful women, fearsome, lithe, fire-breathing creatures, fantastical epics, glorious kings and queens … the oyster has been an iconic must-have in the myths of great wealth and devil-fearing, in different manifestations whatever the religion, whatever part of the world, whatever the century even, whoever is telling the story. Oysters were in essence an idea. And that idea is most potent with the miracle of the pearl.

Revered across millennia, continents and cultures, the pearl has enjoyed the ultimate social status, notwithstanding, or possibly because of, the enormous cruelty and endeavour associated with its discovery and gathering. Almost of equal significance, and in some cases value, has been the mother-of-pearl from which it is formed.

Gold and silver were of secondary value in the ancient world. It was not until around the 1400s that craftsmen learned how to cut other gems, so the natural pearl was without rival in value. In the Bible the gates of heaven are each made from a single pearl. In Genesis God gives Adam and Eve coats as 'beautiful as pearls'.

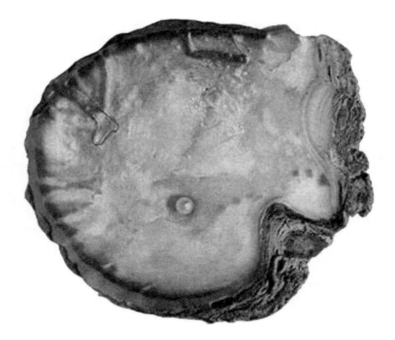

A pearl in its shell from Costa Rica.

The pearl is also enshrined in the Koranic description of Paradise:

> The stones are pearls and jacinths[*]; the fruits of the trees are pearls and
> emeralds; and each person admitted to the delights of the celestial kingdom
> is provided with a tent of pearls, jacinths, and emeralds; is crowned with
> pearls of incomparable lustre, and is attended by beautiful maidens
> resembling hidden pearls.

Much earlier still, the Indian epics Ramayana and Mahabharata both talk
of pearls. The Ramayana tells of a necklace of twenty-seven orbs and says
pearl drillers were drafted in to travel with the army. Krishna dragged a
pearl from the ocean to give to his daughter Pandaia for her wedding.
Another ancient text credited to the second century, in which you would
expect the oyster to appear, is the Sanskrit Kama Sutra. The oyster position
has the man on his knees and the woman in the missionary position,
proffering herself by raising her back, shuck-like.

Further east in China, the earliest of books, the *Shu King*, dating as early
as 2,350 BC, says that in the twenty-third century Yu was given pearls from
the River Hwai. Another source, around 2,800 BC, says pearls came from
the Shen-si province on the western frontier. A man-sized sculpture of an
open-mouthed dragon made completely from oyster shells was unearthed
nearby at a Hou-kang Yang-shao culture site in Honan. It has been dated to
4,460 BC. Some early texts suggest the rich in China paid their taxes in pearls.

Pliny's Big Mistake

An ancient Arab poem said pearls were created by the oyster sipping
the moonlight dew off the surface of the water. Pearls were often kept
in rainwater so as not to break the spell with anything that had touched
the ground. This beautiful literary myth assumed plausibility in early texts,
and it carried into the middle of the second millennia. The Roman savant
Pliny, in his *Historia Naturalis*, repeated the notion as if it was scientific fact.
He even suggested the colour of a pearl was down to the weather:

> If the dew is pure and clear, then the pearls are white, faire and orient … but
> if grosse and troubled, the pearls likewise are dim, foul and duskish.

---

[*] The jacinth is red or purple stone.

No one seemed to want to contradict him for 1,500 years. Middle Age manuscripts followed this idea unquestioningly, which perhaps is a sign of the cloistered distance between the learned and literate and those who lived their lives by the water. It was the first Europeans exploiting the oyster beds of the Americas who realised that it was 'some old philosopher's conceit', as Richard Hawkins put it. Scientifically, Anselmus de Boodt was the first to argue in 1600 that the pearl was generated from the nacre inside of the shell. Even this would have to wait a further century before the physicist Réaumur could prove it satisfactorily with the advent of the microscope.

The misconception is strange because pearls were so obviously valued throughout early history. Maybe associations with wealth and religion allowed their mystery to go unquestioned. Certainly the early Chinese already knew that if they placed beads or tiny figurines of deities inside the soft mantle of a live oyster, the oyster would respond and coat it with the same mother-of-pearl that it used to make its own shell. These beads and carvings were then taken to the temples and offered to the gods in the hope that they would bestow good luck upon the donor. Early Chinese texts said the pearl was formed 'as if by disease', which is a pretty good clue that they realised pearls came from hard objects being inserted inside the shell. A grain of sand is often quoted, but it is usually something larger and less likely to be dislodged. The theory is not dissimilar to the principles that would eventually be adopted in Ayuga Bay, Japan, and patented by Kokichi Mikimoto and Tsauhei Mire in 1906 for the cultivation of artificial pearls.

The Lure of Luminescence

Not all mother-of-pearl is derived from oysters. Of more than 8,000 species of mollusc less than twenty are considered reliable sources for pearls. Some are edible but usually it is flesh or shell. Most molluscs produce nacre (a mix of calcium carbonate and conchiolin) to create their shells – even the humble mussel, which in Mississippi and Birmingham would be turned into shirt buttons right up to the last century. But more usually for workable mother-of-pearl it is abalone oysters, green, paua or red abalone, the silver- or gold-lipped oyster, the akoya oyster or the Ceylon oyster, all of which secrete a more copious and valued fluid. The nacre forms to fight off an invading irritant, such as a parasite or a food particle, by smothering it.

The value of a pearl is determined by the finesse and regularity of the crystals formed in this process. The number of layers formed gives the orb lustre and iridescence. In warm waters – around 30°C – as in the Pacific, the oyster metabolism increases and they grow faster and secrete more nacre. This makes the layers thick and not as translucent, and the imperfect crystal structure results in a dull, less lustrous mother-of-pearl. Therefore, the great oyster-eating areas like the Thames Estuary or Chesapeake Bay in North America have rarely seen a pearl of value formed.

Ideally, when temperatures are lower – around 16°C – the oyster metabolism is slower and it produces the nacre more gradually. These nacre layers are thinner and the crystal structure more even, resulting in an increased translucency and higher value. Even now, dealers will test a pearl by rolling it on their tongue to see if it is real or artificial – artificial pearls are completely round.

The colour of the pearl derives from the shade of plankton that the oysters filter in the water, and so in a way it is a photocopy of the microplankton on which they feed. The Italian director Federico Fellini commented aptly: 'All art is autobiographical; the pearl is the oyster's autobiography.'

You could also say the pearl is mankind's biographer.

The Immortal Maiden

In the east, mother-of-pearl found its way into rings and necklaces, was inlaid into vanity mirrors and brushes, and in later centuries into Chinese and Korean furniture. As Buddhism spread to Korea and Japan – both oyster countries – China became a magnet for mariners and merchants wanting to buy and sell.

In Tao legend, Ho-Hsien-Ku was instructed in a vision that if she ate mother-of-pearl shells she would become immortal. She was said to float from peak to peak until finally she disappeared and hence became known as the Immortal Maiden. She is also that rare species: a woman featuring in an otherwise male-dominated philosophy. For the Tao the ground-up pearl was often seen as a route to fasting and the everlasting. Old potions had them ground with pumice, honeycomb, serpent's gall and malt.

Derivations have seeped through into Chinese pharmacy, where powdered mother-of-pearl is still prescribed to reduce heart palpitations, dizziness and high blood pressure. Very similar ideas have also been found in Peru. In fact, the act of grinding up pearls of lesser value to eat as medicine is found all over the world, from Hindus in India chewing the powder wrapped in beetle leaves to the ancient Greeks, where the first mention of aphrodisia occurs.

Between the Zenith and the Horizon

This account is credited to the seventh century BC from an unnamed Phoenician traveller in Persia who came across fishermen diving for pearls:

> What struck me more in this country is the fishing of pearls. I once had the chance of seeing these pearl fishers at work, off the coasts of the countless islands around the Persian coast. There were at least one hundreds of small boats, each of them carrying 10 pearl divers. They were good divers, capable of staying under water for the time necessary to fill up a bag of oysters, which they removed from the sea-bed with their bare fingers. Then they jumped back onto the deck and started the proceeding all over again.
>
> The owner of each boat opened feverishly the oysters. A swift glance and then he threw them away without even thinking that he could eat them. Unless he found inside a pearl! In that case he removed it gently with the tip of the knife and put it into a bag with a smile as big as the pearl itself. When the sun was halfway between the zenith and the horizon, other boats arrived on the spot with dozens of brokers who chose and set the price for the pearls previously picked, considering their sizes, their roundness, and their light. Those people were the ones that subsequently resold the pearls on the market of Persepolis.

There are illustrations that show divers going down on what must have been wooden ladders into the waters. They would bring up fifty oysters at a time. The early Egyptians traded the oysters from the Red Sea, which even in much later times was known as dangerous water. Divers were often taken by sharks, lost limbs to swordfish or were caught underwater by giant clams. Slaves were brought east from Africa to fish.

These would have been Persian Gulf pearl oysters, the Pinctada radiata, from which mother-of-pearl could be made into ornaments. The word nacre comes from the Arabic word *Naqqarah*, meaning shell, so linguistically, we deduce, oysters and pearls were part of the culture long before Greece or Rome. In Europe the original word for a small pearl, a margaret, derives also from the Persian *Marwari*, being a child of light, and stays with us in Italian as Margherita or Rita, and in French as Marguerite, Margot and Groten; in German Margarethe, Gretchen and Grethel; in English Margaret, Marjorie, Madge, Maggie, Peggy etc.

More recent descriptions show that pearl diving was necessarily a communal activity. When the Portuguese arrived in what was then Ceylon, they imposed a strict sanction on the proceeds – one part for the

Church, one for the king, one part for the soldiers guarding the precious finds, and only then the rest for the fishermen. In the Red Sea Henri de Monfried described how the diver himself was at the bottom of the financial pyramid. He would go out with a guard in a small boat armed with a stick and mask. When he dived his companion used the mask to look out for raiding sharks, or in case he was caught in a giant clam shell and would have to be cut free with a knife. The penalty for trying to steal a pearl was total excommunication, if not worse, or being put out to sea in a small boat without water.

Pearling was a communal activity that spanned the poorest to the richest in a few short days. The harvest of oysters was laid on the port side and all the divers and fishermen gathered around to share in the delight and spoils as each was opened. There was a great sense of joy when one – and it could be one in 300 – produced a pearl. A deputation would then have to go to the middlemen and buyers, usually Indian, to negotiate a value in pounds.

Egyptian Necklaces

Probably the oldest pearl necklace still in existence comes from ancient Persia, from a queen's tomb dating around 2,400 years ago. The Susa necklace (Susa is now Shoosh, 150 miles east of the Tigris in the Khuzestan province of Iran) has three surviving rows of seventy-two pearls each. Originally it may have had up to 500. It was shown for over 100 years in the Louvre Museum in Paris.

In Egypt, mother-of-pearl seems to have been in use as far back as 4,200 BC, brought in probably by the Persians who certainly had easier access to it and used it before then. An oyster shell amulet was a popular ornament in the Egyptian Middle Kingdom – 2,040 to 1,750 BC – usually, but not exclusively, because Tutankhamen wore one in his coffin, they were worn by women. Gold and silver replicas of oyster shells were found inscribed with the name Senwosret I who reined from 1,965 to 1,920 BC.

Egyptian soldiers may have used oyster shells as badges, possibly as a mark of an armed guard, and therefore gold and silver replicas were a significant mark of officer status. Fewer exact examples survive in the Middle East than elsewhere. The acidity of the soil has destroyed the originals but we can trace their usage second hand as representations in art and jewellery.

The shell amulet was thought to promote health – the word *wedja* in Egyptian meant both health (as in sound and healthy) and … oyster.

Copies were fashioned in gold and silver and electrum – an alloy of both – probably for princesses and queens, but shell amulets have also been found in poor graves, beside pottery, at pre-dynastic sites like the Nubian temple excavations at Hierakonpolis.

Senebtisy's burial chamber revealed twenty-five sheet-gold oyster shells, hanging from the lowest of three rows of tiny ball beads of cornelian, feldspar and dark-blue glazed composition, all strung between gold multiple bead spacers. Princess Sithathor wore thirty-one gold oyster shells as a necklace and a larger single oyster-shaped amulet. Queen Mereret owned three large gold oyster-shell pendants, two of them inlaid on the upper surface.

In the 1920s archaeologists excavated tombs near Babylon of Sumerian royalty from ancient Mesopotamia. Part of the treasure included several wooden ornaments and musical instruments inlaid with mother-of-pearl.

The silver lyre of Ur, found in one of the graves, dates back to between 2,600 and 2,400 BC. This predecessor to the modern harp was found in the Great Death Pit, accompanied by seventy men and women buried with their queen. Miraculously well-preserved, the lyre was entirely covered in sheet silver and inlaid with mother-of-pearl patterns. The silver cow's head front has inlaid eyes of shell and lapis lazuli, and the edges, borders and plaques of the sound box are covered in mother-of-pearl.

Sumerian artisans cut a design from the shell, carved the same form out of the wooden setting, and filled the spaces of the engraving with bitumen, which, after acting as glue, hardened to form the background. Inlaying like this was used throughout Asia and Asia Minor up to the time of the Ottoman Empire, and in principle is still practised by artisans in Turkey and Egypt.

Princess of Bora Bora

Appreciation of the pearl is far from unique to European culture. India has long been an important trader and has its own resource and funded commerce with East Africa. Sri Lanka, or Ceylon as it used to be, gave its name to the pearl as much as it did to the tea. There are many examples of early photographs of maharajahs and other nobility – usually men – wearing opulent rows of almost unbelievably fat pearls.

There was an interesting and famously smelly practice recorded in the eighteenth century, probably historic from Ceylon. The oysters were placed in a dug-out wooden tank, covered with matting and left to decompose in the sun for ten days. The maggots ate the flesh and left just pearl and shell. This stinking pile was then washed off with sea water, leaving the valuable shining pearl and mother. Even the fragments were sold to well-to-do Hindus who would ceremonially place them in the mouths of their dead relatives instead of the rice grains used by poorer people.

Around the globe there is evidence of the importance of oysters and pearls. In the South Pacific the black pearl is a pivotal part of the islands' mythology. In Polynesian lore, the iridescence of mother-of-pearl is said to be the reflection of the sky and inspired God to create the stars. He gave pearls to light up the sea. The god of war purportedly filled the lagoon of Bora Bora with pearls as a thank you to the beautiful princess who bore his child.

Millennia later, in the 1920s, the explorers Sperry and Evans discovered one of the last of the more remote islands of New Hebrides, in Papua New Guinea. They were met by a macabre gathering:

> In the opposite corner of the central hut a line of mummies were placed like a barricade … bushy mops of hair still clung to the heads, and their faces wore masks of clay, with huge eyes of mother-of-pearl that shone through the gloom staring at us with an uncanny effect.

These were not ancestral family mummies, but the decorated cadavers of their slain cannibalistic neighbours.

The Austronesians, the Neolithic people from South-east Asia, who appear to have sailed from modern-day Taiwan as far as the Solomon Islands, leave archaeological evidence of their involvement with oysters, with mother-of-pearl inlays in tribal shields and statues of gods. The Solomon Islands were christened by the Spanish explorer Álvaro de Mendaña in 1568, because he saw so many pearls he thought he had found the source of King Solomon's mines.

In Meso-America, probably around the eighth century, the Toltecs, ancestors of the Aztecs, were feared and revered for their military prowess and artistic culture. Among the treasures they left behind were ornamental jewellery and sculptures inlaid with mother-of-pearl, which has been traced back to as far away – not north but south – as the Pacific Rim. There are mentions too of the Mayans and Aztecs using pearls in different manners, which, given the abundance of them which the Spanish would find later around Panama, is logical.

The beautiful thorny oyster – spondylus, although technically now classified as part of the scallop family – is found off Ecuador and seems to have been part of trade inland with Peru, perhaps as early as 2,500 BC. When Caral city in Peru was excavated, the tombs were found to contain fragments of jewellery using mother-of-pearl and fashioned from the spondylus shell. It was dated to 2,527 BC. As archaeology creeps ever further back in time, the oyster and the pearl go with it.

The archaeologist Dr Francis Pryor records first his disbelief and then wonder at discovering how an ancient pot at Flag Fen in East Anglia added an extra 1,500 years to British history in the area:

> In his hand was something I had not wished to see. It was a large piece of hand made pottery, hard and well finished, with a fine almost lustrous outer surface. I snapped a bit off the corner and looked closely at the broken face. The potter had crushed up sea shells, or fossil shells, and added them to the clay … The hardness, the finish and the thorough mixing together of the clay and shell temper led me to believe this sherd was more likely to be Middle Iron Age …
>
> The digger took another shallow scoop and Eb held the bucket in front of me, at eye level. My heart fell. There about three inches from my nose, were two freshly broken pieces of pottery, with their white shell temper shining like so many smiling teeth. One piece of Iron Age pottery could be discounted, but three … Mildenhall pottery belongs to the middle Neolithic.

–≈– **2** –≈–

Biology

Some Unusual Things – The Ecology of the Estuary – Which is Which?
– An Interesting Sex Life – Protandric – Of Pediveligers & Conchiolin –
The Purity of Plankton – Dinoflagellates & Zooplankton –
Some Anatomy & Nutrition

When the sapid and slippery morsel – which is gone like a flash of gustatory summer lightning – as it glides along the palate, few people imagine that they are swallowing a piece of machinery (and going machinery too) greatly more complicated than a watch.

Thomas Huxley

Some Unusual Things

Many things set the oyster apart from other creatures. Most living things are symmetrical. We have two arms and two legs; fish are perfectly aligned left to right; birds have two wings; even most other bivalves have shells that are neatly, roughly equal in size. Not the oyster.

The two sides of an oyster shell are completely different. The top shell is flat, or flatter; the lower side is cupped and sagged because all the conchiolin has leached downwards by force of gravity. And even though an oyster may choose to grow vertically as well as horizontally, the effect is the same. The explanation is simple, but it has no parallel in the universe.

The oyster is the one stable creature in an otherwise completely changing estuary environment. Biology has often stalled on the underlying challenge of it being almost impossible to draw precise comparisons between oysters, even of the same species, raised in one estuary to those raised in another, which is another part of their charming uniqueness. Where everything else moves, the oyster stays still.

To early man the oyster had other virtues. It was portable. Bagged up it could hang off the side of a boat and travel to sea or back home again. Closed up in the shell, the meat stayed fresh and succulent for days. It was wholesome nutritious food too, full of energy-giving minerals: calcium for bones, and vitamins that the early diet would have lacked so badly; a source of nutrition far and away superior to anything else available to wandering Neolithic families.

The oyster was as universal as man, more so in the beginning, whenever that was: Africa, India, South-east Asia, Japan, China, the Philippines, Australia, New Zealand, all the Americas; so long as there was a coastline, where the waters were neither too salty nor too pure, not too cold nor too hot, the oysters spawned. In Europe they clung to the land mass down from Norway along the North Sea, through the Channel, round the edges of the French, Spanish and Portuguese coasts and formed a collar around the Mediterranean. The beds formed a ribbon along the Moroccan coast and penetrated the Black Sea as far as Crimea. They wrapped themselves like a scarf around the coast of Ireland. Britain was encircled by oysters even as far north as Orkney. We can presume that Anglo-Saxons survived and were powerful in part because their home on the Frisian peninsula was also an oyster bay.

The Ecology of the Estuary

The semi-salt waters protect the oyster from other predators, and so long as there is a firm rocky footing to gain attachment; so long as the sea currents are not so strong as to destabilise the colonies; so long as the temperatures are not too extreme; and so long as no hurricane comes to muddy their beds, the oyster thrives. And where the oyster flourishes, so other forms of estuarine life prosper, feeding off the oyster's life-giving habit of filtering the waters, sorting the plankton and turning nitrogen to oxygen.

The oyster is life. Where other creatures feed on each other, the oyster is, to an extent at least, exempt from the life and death struggles of the marine food chain, protected by its rocky shell. Its presence gives the estuary ecology – it is an invisible submarine life-giver, pumping oxygen into estuarine waters; a primeval potentate, an overgrown plankton in itself, surrounded by its family, animatedly filtering the waters around it and spawning in huge numbers. Even the huge quantity of sperm and eggs that do not fertilise and grow to become part of the settlement join the other plankton in the food chain to become valuable nutrients for other creatures, big and small, who in turn attract other predators. These spat form a critical plank in the food pyramid. Those that fertilise and cluster together in their hundreds of thousands, no millions, create reefs that become shelter for other creatures; their hard shells making a stable rock face for plant life to establish and root; their bulk protecting the marsh grasses from the outrageous currents of the seas.

The oyster is not just another marine species. It is the start of life, a benign coloniser, for many other species. Its existence creates if not a marine civilisation, then an environmental parallel. The oyster is the Eden in the estuary. Its presence is a blessing.

Once established, the colony grows in perpetuity. Some oysters might live perhaps to be 100 years old, but even when they finally die, their shells become part of the landscape; the spawning ground for their children and their children's children; the rocks on which the colony can survive; and eventually, even when the incredibly hard shell crumbles, it washes into tooth-like fragments on to the seabed, its multifarious elements broken down into tiny particles that become gravel, limestone and what we just dismissively shorthand as – rock.

Which is Which?

The fabled but now rare European native oyster, to give it its Latin name, is *Ostrea edulis*. The shell is flatter, rounder and usually darker, and more elegantly smooth and sculpted than the craggier invasive crassostrea, often now just called Pacific, from where they originally came, or even just Rock. More meaningful, like with wine, is christening oysters after the estuaries in which they are reared, as in a Colchester or Belon. The important thing with oysters is where they come from.

There are other ostreas like the lurida, native to the west coast of North America, often called Olympia after the City of Olympia on the Puget Sound, Washington, near where they are mostly cultivated, although they have been found from south-east Alaska down to Baja California. These oysters may only be the size of a 50p coin but can still take nearly five years to mature and are held in fond reverence in America's culinary history. There is also a kumamato which was thought to be like other Pacifics but has now been given its own species definition.

Pearl oysters are called pinctada and belong to the other side of the family, more closely related to the scallop and pen shells. The defining difference is that, like mussels, the pinctada attach themselves to stable objects, such as a rope or root in the water, by a filament. The ostrea has an all-important foot which allows scientists to conjecture that early in evolution it might have moved about by itself. The pinctada would always have been sessile. They are known as winged oysters from the Greek *pteria*. Certainly pearl divers ate them, but they are mostly considered not worth cultivating as food.

An Interesting Sex Life

Ostrea are bisexual, in the older terminology, meaning they can change from one sex to the other at will. Hermaphrodite suggests sterility, which oysters certainly are not. They change from male to female and back again seemingly as they like, even during a single breeding season. The female lays her eggs in the shell, the male ejaculates and the sperm is carried to her on a wave of plankton. Quite what makes an oyster change sex is a mystery, although, as in most important events in an oyster's life, a change in water temperature often triggers a dramatic event.

The scientific literature, amazingly, says it was not until 1937 that J.H. Orton in the UK and R. Sparek in Denmark realised that oysters were changing sex at all – although certainly there are other references to the oyster as hermaphroditic before that in literature and less learned journals, so probably science was just playing catch up. During Orton's research, a set of laboratory oysters marked as females started producing sperm. Astounded, Orton drilled holes in the shell. He watched through a microscope as the females changed into males over a few days. It seemed that as soon as the female oyster discharged her eggs, she transformed back into a male quite quickly.

The change from male to female took much longer: weeks, even months, irrespective of the conditions. Technically, this is perhaps unsurprising. Producing sperm is relatively easy and makes fewer demands on the body, while producing eggs and generating enough yolk-like substance to nurture the young is more physically onerous.

Being bisexual makes for easier reproduction. Biologically, the oyster's anatomy is almost abstract. The female has no glands for making albumen or need for a womb to protect the eggs because she has her awesomely powerful protective shell; nor does the male need a penis or anywhere safe to stash his sperm. Nor is there any paraphernalia needed for courtship, which simplifies things even further. There is simply less to get in the way of a sex change than with other creatures. The follicles produce eggs or sperm, or vice versa — a minor issue for a bivalve. It seems usually the young ostrea mature as a male, then slowly change to become female. She will guard the larvae in her shell for twelve days and then release them into the estuary to swim off in search of a safe place to settle.

Protandric

The Pacific crassostrea have no less an interesting sex life, albeit slightly different. They are intersexual; they change sex at will. They will spawn either as a male or produce eggs as a female and the seed and eggs are ejaculated into the estuary to fertilise in the water (unlike the ostrea which lay the eggs in the shell and the female fertilises them). The scientific word is protandric, where the male organs develop first and are then inhibited to allow the growth of the female. They begin life male and then change to females the following season. After that they seem to prefer to stay female most of the time but will and can revert. The older the oyster, the more likely it will be female. The ratios on a bed at any given time vary wildly. One study showed 100 females to 73 males, but in another account it was 133 young males for the same level of females.

Not incubating the larvae means as much as 80 per cent of the crassostrea's bodyweight may be turned to sperm or eggs, which may be one reason for their success.

A male ejaculation in a colony triggers other males to follow suit. The females sense what is happening and immediately start to release their eggs. Soon the whole reef will be covered in white clouds of floating eggs and sperm.

In the context of a single oyster, fertilisation seems almost impossible. How can a sperm find an egg when let loose in the wilds of the river? The answer is that oysters congregate en masse naturally. They spawn across each other. They send out hundreds of thousands of sperm and eggs at the same time, like pollen. The shells of the parents become the breeding grounds for the next generations.

Before the science was better understood, the oysterman never knew when, or if, or critically where, the oysters would spawn at all. They might not spawn for a few years and then suddenly there might be a seemingly spontaneous eruption of breeding, unseen, well out to sea at night. This posed the litigious question as to who actually owned these young larvae. After a fortnight of being battered and carried up and down on the ebb tide of an estuary, an oyster can settle and flourish anywhere. The oysterman might farm one area, and then suddenly his harvest may produce a reef growing in a different place on his neighbour's or unclaimed submarine territory.

The Washington oysterman Earl Newell Steele excitedly described the revelation of the first time he witnessed thousands of oysters suddenly starting to spawn together in Samish Bay in the 1930s:

> I saw a jet of white substance was forced by an oyster into the water with much dexterity; then another and another until the water running over the oysters became white as milk. [He grabbed a bucket and filled it with the milky waters and then transferred some into a glass dish where he could look at it under a microscope.]
>
> It was alive with minute objects. The eggs were much larger than the sperm. The sperm by some force of nature was drawn to the eggs. Sometimes several of them would be attached to one egg. Apparently there was but one entry to the point of fertilization, and there was a struggle between them to get there first. But the instant fertilization took place the others disappeared ...
>
> As the hours went by they came to life. They first developed a number of cilia, or hair-like processes, which they used to propel themselves. They danced around in a lively fashion, reminding one of some of these modern dances.

Huge numbers of egg and sperm drift hopelessly to become part of the estuary plankton. Those that successfully fertilise into larvae will either be eaten by predators or attach themselves to a stationary home on the estuary floor. The tiny larvae are just like any other plankton type being swept up in the currents and offered up to passing predators of all sizes, from jellyfish to the smaller comb-jellies, for dinner.

Of Pediveligers & Conchiolin

Korean scientists estimate a female oyster may release 100,000 eggs at a time and the male even more sperm. An American paper suggests one female might release half a billion eggs in a good season. In Barnstaple, Massachusetts, scientists calculated that they needed 14 million larvae laid out on 1,000 shell bags to produce 250,000 oysters a year.

As ever with oysters, the numbers can be mind-teasingly vast.

Oysters spawn in the spring when the waters start to warm. The young larvae propel themselves along using cilia or hairs. When they get older, and stationary, they will use these same cilia to sort their food. The spat travel quite long distances, perhaps 2 miles up or out of the estuary. After a week they start to sink towards the ocean floor as if some genetic homing device is attracting them downwards. By then they will have started to grow their shell, and under a microscope can be seen to have taken an oyster shape. After fourteen to eighteen days they clasp on to a hard object where they will settle forever.

Unless, that is, man transplants it to different waters to fatten off. Some will take two years to reach marketable size, others five or six years. Left to themselves, oysters can live to be 50 or more. Oysters found in Lake Bras, Canada, have been found to be 100 years old.

Finding something to attach to before giving up their mobility forever is a momentous choice for an oyster. Out of preference it will choose another oyster to settle on. The larvae are, even at this stage, particular about the kind of foods they may eat, which is pretty much an oyster's main activity in life: sorting and filtering what it does and what it does not want to eat. Possibly they are also listening out for the calling of the rest of the colony before committing themselves. There seems to be a primitive communication system which attracts the larvae to settle near other larvae and oysters, as if the gathering of the colony is instilled in the DNA. They cluster one on top of the other to the point where studious oystermen often have to prise them apart before they suffocate each other.

While the infant ostrea are still floating, they develop a pair of eyes – no one is fully agreed on their function – and a foot which they will use to glue themselves to their final resting place. At this stage they are, scientifically speaking, called pediveligers.

If not to another oyster, the young pediveliger will cling to a hard stationary object like a rock, a mangrove tree, the solid bottom of the estuary or the post of a pier. They have been found attached to bricks, boats, cans, tyres, bottles, even crabs and turtles. If they are cultivated they will be ushered on to tiles, ropes, sticks, rafts or bamboo.

Hanging in the water the shell starts to form. The mantle inside absorbs the calcium ion from the seawater; it secretes the conchiolin, which in time becomes calcified, and forms the shell. Since much of the conchiolin secretion occurs around the mantle's edges, the shape and position of the mantle determines the shape of the shell.

The hard shell – which grows in a few short years but survives centuries – is an able defence against most, but not all, predators. A starfish can wrap itself around the oyster and rip it apart. In the Thames there used to be a side industry collecting starfish off oyster beds and selling them on as manure for gardens. An American sea snail, the Odostomia Impressa, is more wily, attaching itself along the outside margin of an oyster shell. When the oyster opens its shell to feed, which it will be doing for nine-tenths of its life, the snail inserts its snout and pierces the oyster's mantle to suck the flesh dry. Another snail – the urosalpinx – wiped out young oysters in the Blackwater estuary in Essex. It is so determined that even if it is moved a few feet away from its prey and tipped on its back, it still returns, like a dog to a bone, many times over.

Similarly, but less instantly fatal, is the tiny pea crab which climbs inside the shell and sets up home along the mantle, grabbing the plankton as the oyster is processing it for itself. The plover-like oystercatcher forages along the low tide mark, slipping its bill inside the shell and snipping the adductor muscle – although the bird seems as happy to eat mussels and limpets, and any other shellfish, despite its name. Crabs can crack open an oyster shell with their claws and stingrays too are partial to oysters.

We are not the only species to covet the flesh of the oyster.

The Purity of Plankton

Although sessile, the world of the oyster is far from static. It lives in a constantly changing flow of plankton rushing through the estuary creating myriad changes of environment and diet, washing the oysters clean as well as delivering the precious algae, which they diligently filter and sort. Like a good mother surrounded by her brood, the oyster is constantly active.

The plankton which feed an oyster are an array of micro-matter, pushed around by tides and winds, replenished by rainfall and washed off the river banks; a living soup held in suspension on the ocean currents, almost a creature in itself: wild, organic, untamed, invisible and highly nutritious.

Professor T. Rymer Jones recorded with some delight in the *Aquarian Naturalist* in 1858 how active an oyster really is – and at the same time managed to produce that rare thing: a grammatical sentence of more than 100 words:

Wonderful indeed is the elaborate mechanism employed to effect the double purpose of renewing the respire fluid and feeding the helpless inhabitant of these shells. Every filament of the bronchial fringe, when examined under a powerful microscope, is found to be covered with countless cilia in constant vibration, causing by their united efforts powerful and rapid currents, which, sweeping over the entire surface of the gills, hurry towards the mouth of whatever floating animalcule or nutritious particles happen to come within the limits of their action, and thus bring streams of nutritive molecules to the very aperture through which they are conveyed into the stomach – the lips and labial fringes acting as sentinels to admit or refuse entrance, as the matter supplied is of wholesome or pernicious character.

We know what an oyster eats. Scientists have dissected the contents of an adult oyster's stomach and found a constellation of tiny plankton that enjoy their own marine biological sub-language – a study as early as 1933 reported the following as an oyster's dinner: algae, dinoflagellates, tintinnids, silico-flagellates, ostracods, eggs and larvae of marine invertebrates, pollen grains from land plants, detritus, sponge spicules and sand.

It is because of this plankton that the oyster is such a valuable part of an estuary ecosystem, and also why it is such a nutritious food itself. In a sense it is pure plankton. The richness of this diet allows it to grow, relatively speaking, spectacularly quickly and to create such a resilient shell in such a short time.

Dinoflagellates & Zooplankton

The micro-universes of plankton are tiny open-water plants, animals or bacteria. The name, like the word planet, comes from the Greek for wanderer. The generic term can mean anything from invisible microscopic bacteria to larger floaters like jellyfish. The numbers here are awesome, literally hundreds of thousands of separate life forms sharing a space of a few cups of water, all of which perhaps have their own roles and identities beyond the edge of our knowledge or understanding, but in this context just form a mass of food, an estuarine forest on which other marine predators can graze. Some are similar to leaves and plants, others are spawn and young fish, others algae and diatoms.

Typically they have no, or very little, ability to swim for themselves, and exist in continual helpless, mutually supportive or predatory flotation. Perhaps they are in mutation on their way to becoming something else and their vulnerability is temporary; but for the moment these are creatures or life forms almost without predetermination, hostage to the movement of water with the only mathematical certainty that some will survive at the expense of the rest. Some will just happen to pass by an oyster bed.

Phytoplankton are plants which flourish according to the levels of light near the surface of the water. They take the energy from the sun and transform it into sugar and oxygen. The chemical equation is six molecules of water + six molecules of carbon dioxide = one molecule of sugar + six molecules of oxygen, which is what we all need to survive. Phytoplankton converts energy from the sun into organic compounds as food. A by-product is the oxygen.

The largest concentrations of phytoplankton occur in the spring when the rain washes the bank and spills its own cargo of micronutrients into the water. When the temperatures rise suddenly, these plankton can multiply too quickly, creating colourful but suffocating blooms of algae. Dense blooms block off the light from the bay and kill the creatures lower down, and eventually they and everything else in the river flow dies. These are what give the estuary waters their colour. When dinoflagellates dominate, a red-tinted bloom, known as a mahogany or red tide, occurs.

Also part of the plankton mass is zooplankton, tiny embryonic fish ranging from microscopic rotifers to macroscopic squids. The smallest recycle the water column and feed off the other plankton, while the larger ones are important because they are a food for larger fish. Much of the zooplankton may be larvae of different fish, including oyster spawn and pediveligers. A gallon of rich estuary water can contain 500,000 different zooplankton.

Within this mass of life is both dinner and those looking for dinner. The largest enemy for an oyster will be the jellyfish; the smallest might be the colourful comb-jellies, sometimes known as sea-gooseberries. These tiny deep-blue creatures have a rainbow-coloured spine and look like they were the inspiration for an Apple computer mouse. They grow to about 2cm long and are effective gelatinous predators, feeding primarily, when they can, on the oyster larvae. Charles Darwin said of them: 'Few things are more beautiful ... they might have been created to be studied under a microscope.'

The main constituents of plankton are diatoms, tiny silica-shelled, one-celled creatures. Looked at under the microscope, they often have floral-like, intricate and beautiful sculpturing. Mostly they are brown or yellow. They carry chlorophylls a and c, and the carotenoid fucoxanthin, and, like oysters, reproduce asexually, but in their case by cell division. There are upward of 40,000 species of diatoms and we are still counting. The living matter of each diatom is enclosed in a shell of silica that it secretes, again not unlike the oyster. When these creatures die, their shells drop to the ocean floor. Deposits of diatomaceous material, formed underwater in past geologic times, are found in all parts of the world. Diatomite is used as an insulating material, in making dynamite and other explosives, and for filters, abrasives and similar products. Most of the earth's limestone has been deposited by diatoms. The majority of the petrol we use is of diatomic origin.

So that is what an oyster eats. Canned sunshine, as one biologist called it. But equally, there is a model here for the start of life that is much older than anything land-borne.

Some Anatomy & Nutrition

Oysters are sensitive. They react physically in the same way that we taste or smell. That is an oyster's essential sense. In case of danger, it closes its shell. They react to light, to levels of salt in the water, to temperature, to shadow and sound. They have complex responses to changes in the environment. Any disturbing change in the water, or even just a passing shadow, stimulates the nerves of the mantle and causes the adductor muscle to close the shells. The inner ridge, the largest of the three, is muscular and mobile. It pumps water in and out of the shell fifteen times a minute, washing the body and keeping it constantly bathed. As long as the shell stays shut and retains this liquid, it can ignore most predators; can survive in polluted waters or exposure at low tide; and withstand the trauma of being transported.

Walk along the beach at low tide near an oyster cove and you can hear – even from quite a distance – a series of short, sharp spitting sounds as the oysters react and close their shells. They are powerful. Canadian trials have shown that it would take a pull of more than 9kg to open up a 10cm mature oyster that has clamped its shell shut.

They breathe like fish, using both the gills and the mantle. A small three-chambered heart lies under the adductor muscle and pumps colourless blood, with its supply of oxygen, through the body. It also has two kidneys to purify the blood. The food is sorted by the lips and passed into its digestive system; then, through a coiled intestine, expelled through the rectal chute.

They continue to grow through their life, although more slowly as they get older. Old paintings by Manet and the Dutch masters show how large oysters were compared to today (see illustrations), but even by that time reports were coming back from America of surprise at how much bigger oysters found on the east coast seaboard were than those in Europe. William Makepeace Thackeray said they were so big 'it was like eating a baby'.

The way an oyster feeds means they are a highly nutritious and healthy food. Dietary textbooks hopefully recommend them for the young, infirm and the elderly and frail. The prospect of granny shucking oysters in her armchair, or a mother slipping an oyster into a sick child's supper, may smack of nutritional hubris, but it was a familiar recommendation from old apothecaries and the analysis is solid enough. The oyster would have been an ideal food for sailors, settlers and early nomadic natives.

A dozen oysters can amount to less than 100 calories but are worth as much in protein as 100g of steak and contain as much calcium as a glass of milk. Unusually for any living animal or marine food, they are also a source of vitamin C. They are low in fat because the fat is glycogen and starch. The glycogen, stored glucose, would have been an important source of energy, especially useful for people facing long hard days of labour building new settlements. The cocktail of vitamins that an oyster provides would have been a viable alternative to fruit and vegetables, and would help stave off diseases like scurvy, particularly for early sailors. Vitamin B12 was thought only to originate in fungi and bacteria, but it is the most pronounced of all the vitamin sources found in an oyster. B12 influences nerve cell activity, the metabolism in general, DNA replication and positively affects your mood. It is often prescribed as a top-up for depression. In lesser amounts, in descending order, the oyster will have vitamin B1 (thiamin), which helps convert the glycogen to energy, vitamin B2 (riboflavin), vitamin C, niacin, vitamin A, vitamin B6 and vitamin E.

The highest quantity of mineral in an oyster is zinc, which protects the immune system, helps to heal wounds and supports general growth, especially in pregnancy and childhood. It is also linked to fertility. Curiously, the next largest mineral is copper. Zinc often inhibits the absorption of copper into the body, which in turn allows the body to absorb and use iron. Iron and selenium are the other main minerals, among a supporting cast that includes magnesium, phosphorus, manganese and calcium.

By instinct, if not perhaps by science, early medicine across Europe, going back as far as the Romans, assigned oysters as therapy against tuberculosis, catarrh, stomach ache, anaemia and for invalids in general. Pliny was an enthusiast and suggested them for improving the complexion. It was one reason that drove oysters inland to cities.

Only liver can equal an oyster in terms of the levels of iron and copper it delivers into the diet. Only spinach has as much folic acid. You do not need to be a forensic expert to deduce from the nutritional breakdown that if any food is likely to be an aphrodisiac, then the oyster is the main candidate.

The high zinc levels are directly linked to the production of good sperm and fertility. The glycogen provides energy. The vitamin B12 lightens the mood. Vitamins C and B2 are antioxidants.

The zinc traces are relevant. A man can lose between 1 and 3mg of zinc when he ejaculates, so possibly, in terms of revitalising himself, the oyster's zinc may be helpful. Low levels of zinc have been linked to impotence and in some cases restoring the zinc level has resulted in a recovery of potency. Even the staid American Federal Drug Administration – staid in the sense that it does not usually give much credence to the benefits of individual foods – has recognised that historically many people might have had zinc deficiencies in their diets and therefore the impact of eating oysters could well have been more marked 100 years ago than it might be today.

The shells, too, have had medicinal and nutritional benefits. They were raw material for lime, they enriched arable land and they were fed to laying chickens to harden the egg shell. The pharmaceutical industry has also used ground oyster shell, incorporating it in pills to prevent osteoporosis because of its high level of calcium.

It is only in the last 100 years that such practices have died out, as we have come to realise that the best use of the shell is to recycle it back into the beds to create optimum spawning grounds and let the oyster breed again.

3

Fabulous Legends: Megaliths, Celts & Phoenicians

Middens: Fragments of Pre-history – The Phoenicians – Jerusalem – Big Stones & Tin – Mother of Europe

The Neolithic people who built Newgrange seem to have belonged to a rich and powerful culture, farming and trading along the Atlantic coastline from the Orkneys to Brittany and beyond.

Simon Bostock, *Celtic Connections*, 1996

At the same time the region had the advantage of easy communication with both the Baltic and the Mediterranean. The Mediterranean was one of the world's most precocious regions of maritime development.

Michael Cook, *Brief History of the Human Race*

Middens: Fragments of Pre-history

There may have been trade in British oysters in Europe before the Greek and Roman eras. The Megalithic map of Europe can be overlaid almost precisely with the geography of oyster colonies. The long barrows and ancient stone tombs are rarely found more than a few miles from the sea, and predictably near to oyster coves. Water was often regarded as sacred. Offerings to gods and goddesses were cast in the currents. The middens near oyster coves might be evidence of larger gatherings rather than just domestic bric-a-brac.

The dramatic burial mound at Newgrange on the River Boyne in Ireland pre-dates Stonehenge and the building of the pyramids. It is thought to have been erected around 3,200 BC as a site of celebration or worship of the winter solstice. The Boyne itself is the site of many other Neolithic monuments and artefacts and was clearly an important community or meeting point in the period. Simon Bostock, writing in *Celtic Connections*, says:

> All that remained of these people at Newgrange were four huge, shallow stone basins on the floor of the alcoves of the inner chamber; some cremated human remains, nine heads and pins damaged from funeral pyres, stone pendants, seven stone balls, fragments of flint tools, animal bones and shells (the remains of ritual feasts, offerings to the spirits or nourishment for the dead) …

A few miles north of the Boyne is Carlingford, still one of the oyster capitals of Ireland. Bostock continues:

> We can speculate that the Celts were the most influential tribes of northern Europe and that their contact with the southern Mediterranean might have been initiated by the seafaring Phoenicians. In neither culture does anything survive of their own histories because the Celts strictly followed an oral tradition of storytelling and opposed the written word; while the Phoenicians wrote on papyrus that did not survive and also as sailors perhaps the water would have destroyed any records. Later, probably between 500–100 BC the Celts introduced money. Previously they had traded in animals and gold alone, but as highly prized mercenaries they needed other currencies to recompense their services. They preferred gold and silver coinage, but had a third denomination known as potin, which was cut in strips and then weighed. It was made from a tin alloy, much of it seemingly coming from Cornwall.

Historical records may not survive. Irish history goes blank for a millennium until St Patrick, but oyster shells point to the fact that there were communities active in this period, or at least the pre-Roman period.

Neither the Greeks nor the Romans had much incentive to aggrandise the cultures of the people they were conquering and colonising. This western alliance was almost certainly deliberately consigned to the very dog ends of history. But there could have been another style of empire, which may have been as important as either the Greeks or the Romans, at least in a practical sense.

The Phoenicians

Donald Harden opens his history of the Phoenicians like this:

> Until archaeology came to the rescue in the middle of the 19th century our
> knowledge of the Phoenicians derived from the writings of other nations,
> notably the Jews, Greeks and Romans, with whom they were from time to
> time in contact, not always on a friendly basis; for the Phoenician literature
> has almost wholly perished. Such a picture was bound to be distorted.

There is a certain irresistible inter-tracing of the Phoenician myth and history tantalisingly close to these oyster communities. There exist fragments of evidence that clearly link all these people, though how structured or dynamic a society is less clear.

One of the earliest settlements so far dated in mainland England is a submerged Mesolithic village in the Solent at Bouldnor Cliff, off Yarmouth, assigned to 8,100 years ago and discovered in 1999. It would have adjoined the Isle of Wight and the mainland then, as the sea level is probably 12m higher today. It was probably – from the cut wooden marks on the remaining timbers and its location – used for boat building. The site is beside a historic oyster bed.

The Phoenicians bartered with the westerly fringes of Britain from an indeterminate point in early history. They wanted tin from Cornwall badly enough to set up and mine for it. There are references to an area being called the Tin Isles and some remnants of mining have been traced back to 500 BC. There is further evidence of trading with Spain and Portugal as far as back as the Bronze Age, 2,100–1,500 BC. Tin was rare in Europe and important. It was needed to make bronze, from which we might speculate that Cornwall, as a prime source of tin on the Continent, may well have been important in its own right. The natural harbour at Falmouth, with its estuarine oyster beds nearby, would have been an obvious choice to land. Another material of interest would have been copper, which was also found in Cornish waters, and in Swansea. And so too Somerset lead.

Swansea may well have been important for similar reasons. The Mumbles area was previously known as Oystermouth and, in its heyday, as Copperolis. Possibly the Swansea connection is even earlier. In 1826 a skeleton of a woman coloured in red ochre, wearing periwinkle decorations, was discovered at Paviland Cave on the Gower peninsula. At first it was thought that she had been ritually buried at the time of the

Romans, but more modern tests found her to be a man – another odd parallel with oysters – and have dated him to 24,000 BC, which suggest that southern Wales may have avoided the last ice age altogether and as such could have been a pivotal community for early trading. The body lay surrounded by oyster shells. Also in the same coves were drawings similar to those found in coves in Brittany. And Irish tin has been found in early Welsh artefacts.

Ireland, Cornwall and South Wales are, or were, all rich in oysters, which would logically have been welcome to the Phoenician seafarers, not just as sustenance but also as another cargo to take back to what is now Lebanon or other ports en route. Any ship captain ploughing the coastal routes north from Africa would have passed oyster reefs along what is now Portugal, Spain and France, and up the Channel, and would hardly be likely to pass up such a ready supply of easily gathered nutritious food. With warships perhaps having as many as 170 oarsmen to feed, the oyster would have been a welcome and essential resource.

The first trading boats could also take another path: the three-river route through France, along the Seine, Saône and Rhône. The Greeks founded the port of Massilia (Marseille) near the mouth of the Rhône around 600 BC to engineer trade between north and south. Oysters on this route could have been valuable and obvious cargo to sell on the way to inland people, who would not have had links to their own coast. Go back even earlier to when England was joined to the European landmass, and the Seine and Saône connection flowed directly into another oyster-rich estuary: the Thames. But perhaps that is another even more ancient story. More recent accounts discount it. Brittany oystermen in the eighteenth century preferred to send their oysters to Paris overland because the sea route was too slow.

Along the west coast of Europe it is easy enough to imagine a community linked by boat to the west coast of Ireland, Wales, Cornwall and Brittany, that traded with Spain and further south – a thesis that in the last few years, through fragments of pottery, linguistic analysis and DNA testing, has been shown to be more than credible. The Brittany tribe of the Veneti could muster more than 200 ships by the start of the first millennium which is a notable navy in any terms. Equally plausible is that the Phoenicians were the agents who facilitated this trade. Fragments of wine and olive oil flasks have been found in Cornwall at Tintagel, Lundy, further west at Glastonbury Tor, and in South Wales, at the Iron Age fort at Dinas Powys. The Isles of Scilly also seem to have been an important trading port as far back as 4,000 BC.

An oyster man ready for work in Brittany, but has time to stop by the photographer's tent.

The name of the Scilly Islands is curious. Possibly it was just one island because a certain Roman account talks of *Scillonia insula*, but the geography may have changed over time. There is an obvious linguistic parallel with Sicily as an island at the boot of Italy, although the Roman occupation of England seems to have stopped largely at Exeter. Recently there have been new finds of three first-century forts in the south-east of the county, at Calstock, Restormel Castle, Lostwithiel and Nanstallon near Bodmin. Each is close to a resource for tin mining and possibly silver smelting. It is the more interesting because Cornwall has obvious advantages for the Romans in terms of climate, resource and proximity to the Atlantic, if indeed that was their preferred route home. There is something not visible here, unless the empire was content to leave the territory to a friendly – or at least not openly hostile – alliance. Equally, there is a similar mystery as regards the transparent connections between Brittany and Cornwall – the former was known as Little Briton up to Norman times, but there appears to be no evidence to explain the nature of the relationship.

The Romans would take slaves from the defeated and colonised tribes and turn them into legionnaires. What they did not do was ever return them home. A surviving legionnaire would be rewarded with new territories, so perhaps they unwittingly caused the spread of Celtic people? Or perhaps the Iberian peoples were more of a community than previously thought, omitted from the Roman world as being too far to the west. The use of the harp and lyre is another tantalising connection between all these people from Ireland and Wales in the north to the Egyptians of pre-history.

Power and community may have been completely different concepts to early Europeans. The historian Sanford Holts gave a paper to the Annual Conference of the World History Association on 19 June 2004, at Fairfax, Virginia. He argued that a lot of the confusion over the might and precise dates of the Phoenicians was down to the fact that their influence came from the sea. They did not, in conventional terms, start to colonise and empire-build in other territories until around 1,100 BC, adding Cádiz, Málaga and Ibiza, Tangier in Morocco, Carthage (Tunis) in North Africa, plus colonies on Cyprus, Sicily, Sardinia and Corsica. But archaeological dating has shown that Byblos (the Phoenician city of Gebal) was founded as a small fishing port in 6,000 BC, and the cedars of Lebanon that grew on the mountainsides provided both wood for shipbuilding and lumber for trade. By 4,500 BC there is evidence of hundreds of houses. Archaeological research and contemporary writings depict the fabled city of Tyre – which at that time was two islands just offshore – as being founded around 2,750 BC.

Underestimating the power and influence of a seaborne community resonates as a constant theme around the world of oyster communities. Their empires were older and all eventually usurped and their stories rewritten, often falsely, by their ultimate conquerors.

Jerusalem

Cornwall has some lush and fanciful legends from this pre-history. One of the most intriguing says that 'Christ came in a ship and anchored in St Just Creek', arriving in St Just-in-Roseland, near Place Manor. Across the estuary, so the tale goes, Joseph of Arimathea and the young Jesus landed at the Strand, now Falmouth town quay, crossed the stream and went up Smithick Hill. In the far west of Cornwall there supposedly were two rich lodes of tin. One was named *Corpus Christi*, the Body of Christ, and the other *Wheal Jesus*. *Wheal* is the old Cornish word for mine.

In Catholic accounts this 'fabulous legend' shows that Phoenician traders were not unusual in Cornwall at the time, and equally that they chose to land at one of the county's main oyster beds in the Fal. There is a further twist. The coat of arms of the town of East Looe, a few miles east, purports to portray a ship bringing Joseph and the young Jesus to Cornwall, or at least two men who might be them. Certainly the legendary Joseph was said to have been a rich trader who may have made many trips to England and even owned mines; which, if true, just supports the importance of the west countries at the time. It is not so much about whether this story is true or not, it is the very fact that it exists at all that is most arresting.

The Joseph in this interpretation could have been an uncle to Mary – he who asked Pilate if he could bury Jesus' body. Then he was cast off without oars and sails as an exile and washed up at Marseille with twelve disciples. He reputedly travelled north and eventually sailed for Somerset. It is said he was already known as a trader in lead, and he was welcomed at Glastonbury, which would have made England the home of the first church in Europe.

Some claim this would have been AD 37, others say AD 63, by which point Joseph would have been quite an old man to undertake such arduous adventures. He is supposed to have laid the Holy Grail – the cup from which Christ drank at the Last Supper – at the fecund Chalice Well in Glastonbury. In the Middle Ages, four church councils – at Pisa 1409, Constance 1417, Sienna 1424 and Basel 1434 – mention that 'the Churches of France and Spain must yield in points of antiquity and precedence to that of Britain, as the latter Church was founded by Joseph of Arimathea immediately after the passion of Christ'. Glastonbury was called Roma Secunda. On all of which is predicated William Blake's inspiration for the hymn *Jerusalem*:

> And did those feet in ancient time
> Walk upon England's mountains green
> And was the holy Lamb of God
> On England's pleasant pastures seen?

Later, around the fifth century AD, there is much written about first Patrick and then other Irish saints coming to Cornwall and then returning to convert Ireland. The Scilly Isles were known as a place of pilgrimage, although it is unclear precisely why because so many legends entwine. But more concrete are the burial sites on the islands, which date back to the Neolithic era, *c.* 2,500 BC, which would also coincide with the influence of the Phoenician empire.

Sensitive issues of faith interlock with legend here, but at heart we are dealing with more evidence of the recognition of some form of community being active and known across Europe. Even if it was applied retrospectively, it still suggests Britain was not an unknown wasteland of heathen barbarians.

The evidence of the burial tombs contradicts much of the centralist north–south thesis. Earlier, perhaps even as far back as 5,000 BC, there were communities seemingly stretching from the Orkneys, Ireland and western Britain down as far as Portugal and Spain. They seem to have shared at least a version of religion, which probably centred on a single female deity associated with the moon.

Big Stones & Tin

However distant, we know that at some point in the Neolithic era, between 5,000 and 2,000 BC, men managed to assemble stones of more than 350 tons apiece and place them upright, for whatever reason. More than 3,000 can still be found around Carnac in Brittany, as they are at Stonehenge and Avebury. Carnac nestles a few kilometres back from the huge oyster beds of the bay of Quiberon. Here is one of those inspiring sculptures of a Celtic goddess, the Giver of Birth, dated 3,500 BC. The Grand Menir at Carnac was erected around 4,500 BC, two millennia before Stonehenge.

The technology to move huge tombstones, some hundreds of tons in weight, could logically have been a development from shipbuilding. At Stonehenge the construction is not thought to have been achieved by stonemasons, but from alternative technologies, probably carpenters, which might also point to shipbuilding and back to the coves.

In Stonehenge's case the blue stones of the Preseli hills in western Wales were taken. If we discount the theory that they were moved by an ice age then most likely they were dragged from the Severn estuary. And if there were religious ambitions here, possibly it was deemed important to show off the endeavours to everyone. The ability to bridge would also have evolved from shipbuilding, which is another link to the oyster coves and coastal communities.

Stonehenge, though, is not a one-off. All over Europe, but especially on the coast, there are legacies of communities dating back to 3,000 BC and older. None of these use Roman vocabulary. A *dolmen* is from Brittany, meaning a stone table; in German it is a *hunenbett*; in Dutch a *hunebed*; in Welsh a *cromlech*; in Cornish a *quoit*; in Portuguese an *anta*, and in Swedish a *dos*.

Another Cornish legend reflects what Hurricane Katrina did to New Orleans and Biloxi in 2005 – which we will address later – and also what happened at the Marennes-Oléron, which was devastated by 225kph winds on the night of 27 December 1991, and even the North Sea surge that hit Canvey Island in 1953. Huge land-changing winds and surge tides are not new. Oysters and hurricanes do not like each other; the Ceylon pearl trade was destroyed by a tsunami. The most convincing thing here is perhaps the more precise dating. It is said that there was a vast area to the west of Land's End known as Lyonesse. It had 140 churches and notable cities, but was overrun by a huge storm on 11 November 1099 and disappeared, leaving only its mountains visible, which are today's Scilly Isles. Only one man, Trevilian, managed to outrun the waves on a white horse and got to the safety of high ground at Perranuthnoe, opposite Newlyn. There are many tales of the church bells from the lost cities being heard in rough weather.

The Seven Stones Rocks to the west of Land's End are linked to a great city referred to as the City of Lions. Old fishermen called it the Town, and it is often retold that they have dragged up doors and windows in their nets in this area. In calm seas it is possible to see walls beneath the water, and possible field boundaries show up at low tide along the sands of the Sampson Flats between the isles of Tresco and Sampson. Some of this has been handed down in notes by the sixteenth-century antiquarian William Camden, so the timeline is not as exaggerated as in some ancient tales.

Wilson Beckles, writing in 1902, pointed out that available tin was not really found in what we now call Cornwall until the mid-1750s, so if there was a trade in tin, the mines would have been amongst the vast lands that are now submerged. He argued: 'Britain became to the Phoenicians what Peru in later years came to be to Spain.' For gold read tin.

The parish council's official guide to the Scilly Isles says boldly: 'The isles were found 3,000 years ago by Hamilco, a Carthaginian of the Silures, a Phoenician colony in Spain.' If it is the same Hamilco, then he is usually thought to have found Britain in 450 BC – 500 years later.

The name Silures is probably Roman. The historian Tacitus called them 'a naturally fierce people' and speculates: 'The dark complexion of the Silures, their usually curly hair, and the fact that Spain is the opposite shore to them, are an evidence that Iberians of a former date crossed over and occupied these parts.'

There has been some conjecture on whether modern-day Welsh people owe their DNA to this tough tribe, of whom Caractacus was one leader; but the same might be said of the early Basques who share the west coast route and have no obvious DNA family either. Roman sailors might well have mixed up all these west coast ports.

Roman writers noted the sophistication of this westerly community. Diodorus Sicilus reported: 'The Britons … live in a very hospitable and polite manner.' He described the way in which the tin was mined, was taken to the islands to be fashioned into ingots and then transported to Gaul and overland on horse packs to Marseille in thirty days. This is an interesting figure because it disproves the thesis that English oysters got to Rome – which they did in big numbers – by horse. An oyster would not survive that long, so there must have been another route. The smarter route to get to Marseille would surely have been by sea to Bordeaux and then across land, but that is still a long way.

Town names, too, owe something to the Phoenician alphabet with endings like *pon*, meaning *pennah* in Phoencian or a hill; and *tre* taken from tiara, meaning town or castle on a hill.

The Greeks seemingly did not arrive in Cornwall until 350 BC, looking for the Phoenician tin treasure trove. They called it Cassiterides, meaning tin islands, although there is some conjecture as to whether that really meant Cornwall or somewhere further south.

Watchet Blue

The Phoenicians may well have tried to keep the location of the tin mines in Cornwall a secret because they were so valuable. They needed the tin and lead to make pans that would not discolour their famous, emblematic purple dyes. Even more emotionally important and quite plausible, and another link back to the oyster areas of the West Country, is that the dye was extracted from the crushed shells of the Muricidae, a predatory snail whose toxins turn purple when exposed to the air. It is a voracious predator to other shellfish and so possibly therein was another trade for which the oyster communities would have been a thankful supplier. The purple dye was so valued in ancient Rome (and before then) because it required huge numbers of snails – maybe 1,200 to dye a single toga. When the snail dies it releases pigmented toxins, so larger molluscs had their shells broken and their veins removed, while smaller ones were ground up. In fact, some of the snails are edible, although some people can react badly to the toxins.

Equally, there were other shells that created the same effects, for example *Nucella lapillus*, the common dog whelk. In AD 1685 William Cole proved that the dog whelks he gathered on the shores of the Bristol Channel could also be a source of dye and showed how exposure to sunlight caused the glands to change colour through a spectrum from light green to watchet blue, and finally to a deep purple, emitting a pungent garlic-like smell.

It is said that a Phoenician captain would have scuppered his ship rather than reveal the location of the tin mines to an enemy boat following him on the high seas. Or the location of his dyes, which would cost considerably more than gold – in some estimates fifteen to twenty times as much.

The Phoenicians settled in Cornwall and intermarried. This may have been peaceful or otherwise. Some accounts say the tin was shipped to France and then taken south to Spain by packhorses, but that does not seem logical. Why risk carrying such a precious cargo over land, where it might be hijacked, when they had ships and boats aplenty to take it more safely on the sea? At the time, the harnessing of horses had not been invented and would not arrive until much later from China. The Romans built roads but only expected a horseman to ride 30 miles a day. And these roads may well have been open to robbers and local barons. If it were tin destined for Spain, then a stopover in France from the West Country is more believable. Or surely, more likely, the tin was manufactured into items for trade on the way.

J. A. Buckley's 1988 account of *The Cornish Mining Industry* (Tor Mark Press) has the tin industry stretching from Dartmoor to Land's End. He writes:

> Historical references … show a well-established and fairly sophisticated tin trade between Cornwall and the Mediterranean by the 4th century BC. There is little evidence that the great events of history – such as the invasion

by the Romans and their subsequent withdrawal 400 years later – did any more than temporarily disturb that international trade.

Again the mystery recurs: why did the omnipotent Romans ignore such wealth and waste their time trying to subdue the north and parts of Wales?

Pytheas of Massalia (Marseille) is credited with circumnavigating Britain between 325–250 BC and reported on the importance of West Country tin; he said the Cornish were 'friendly and civilised' which they had learnt from contact with 'foreign merchants'.

Even earlier perhaps, possibly 2,600 BC, there is evidence of mining for copper at Great Orme near Llandudno on the North Wales coast. Bronze is usually a mix of copper and tin, so to have a bronze age it must have come from somewhere. There is further evidence to back this up – a fragment of a bronze dagger, found at Pelynt, Cornwall, appears to be of Greek design and dates to 1,200 BC.

Mother of Europe

The Phoenicians were principally traders – their original name 'Canaanite' means 'merchant' in Hebrew – and they may have been more advanced and civilising than the empires that were to follow, but much of their wealth and influence stemmed from the sea. At Tyre it is recorded that they traded in slaves, cypress, cedar, oak, ebony, ivory, embroidered linen, purple and scarlet cloth, gold, silver, iron, tin, lead, bronze, horses, mules and other livestock, coral, rubies, corn, wax, honey, tallow, balm, wine, wool and spices. The word cinnamon is Phoenician, as are probably the words cumin, coriander, crocus, myrrh, aloe, balsam, jasper, diamond and sapphire. The Greeks named the North Sea as the Phoenician Star in recognition of their discovery. The Phoenicians were an ingenious and advanced society; their knowledge of the stars allowed them to navigate the oceans, which creates another interesting juxtaposition with early Britain and the Celts, where druids too were supposedly fluent astronomers and read the stars to invoke their knowledge.

The Phoenicians were accomplished textile makers and sought out minerals not just from around Europe and the Mediterranean, but probably circumvented the horn of Africa. This seafaring nation left an immense legacy from the fifth century BC which is still being uncovered. Among other things, they left us with an alphabet. The city of Byblos gave its name indirectly to the Bible; *byblos* in Greek means 'papyrus', hence book, hence the Book. The Tyrian princess Europa gave her name to the continent. They needed this language to communicate with different people around the globe, and although it is derived from Egyptian hieroglyphics, it forms the basis from which both Greek and Latin evolved. Hieroglyphics were important to ancient traders because they could be understood more readily than an alphabet.

The Phoenicians needed language to trade. One graphic yet simplistic early image of trading with new people shows how the sailors would row to the beach and leave a consignment of goods neatly on the sand and then make their way back to the ship. A fire was lit and the smoke would attract the natives who would come down to see what was going on. If they wanted to trade the natives would lay up their own goods next to the first pile and then disappear into the hills or forests. The traders would come back and either take some of the goods or return to the ship and light the fire again to indicate they wanted more. In such early basic trade-offs the use of a symbolic language that could be etched in the sand would have represented something of an advance. Reading the Columbus biography many centuries later, one is struck that hieroglyphics might have worked much better in the sand than an alphabet. Oppenheimer also connects the hieroglyphic language of runes to both Phoenicia and Ireland.

There is another nation on this route which, like the Phoenicians, has little to show of their early history, but geneticists have shown they have a DNA that is unique in Europe and goes back into pre-history. The Basques were similarly great sailors and had the Bay of Arcachon on their doorstep, an abundant source of oysters along the ocean shelf. Their language is unique in Europe, having no apparent connection to any Roman or Greek influence. And they too have their scatter of Megalithic monuments – the Santimamiñe Caves at Kortezubi, near Gernika, were discovered by chance in 1916, a prehistoric sanctuary inhabited at least 13,000 years ago. The walls are etched with drawings of bison and ibex. The caves at Astigarraga in Deba, discovered in 1967, have yielded red paintings dating to 20,000 and 22,000 years ago. Further north, across the border in the Haute Garonne, the Aurignac lends its name to a people dating around 32,000 and 26,000 BC, who had evolved stone cutting, pierced shell jewellery and other art.

The distant evidence is compelling if fragmentary, and sometimes circumstantial. The Basques were shipbuilders, famous traders, and made their own laws. As late, or as early, as AD 1351, it was the Basques who signed the Treaty of Berneo with Edward III of England, which declared the 'freedom of the high seas'. The suspicion is that the Basques may well have been early players in a seaborne republic … as they were to be later.

Ultimately, it seems much more likely that in early history these people were connected, and that connection came not from the land but from the sea.

4

Edible Bones:
Greeks & Romans

The Myth of Aphrodite – The Baiae of Vice – Pearls & Power –
Supper with Martial – The Valiant Veneti – The Rutupian Oyster –
Getting Oysters to Rome – The English Pearl

*He, too, was the first to adjudge the pre-eminence of delicacy of flavour to the oysters of
Lake Lucrinus … The British shores had not yet sent their supplies, at the time when
Orata thus enobled the Lucrine oysters.*

Pliny the Elder

The Myth of Aphrodite

The oyster's association with love and sex traces its route back to Aphrodite,
the Greek goddess of love and sexual rapture. She is so often quoted as
lying on an oyster shell that it has entered common mythology. You could
hardly have a better patron for the connection of love and oysters than
Aphrodite, with her great beauty, fast eye, many lovers and her priestesses
to whom men might make love by way of worship. Her birth alone was
dramatic enough. According to Hesiod, around 700 BC, Cronus castrated
his father Uranus, the father of the gods, and threw the severed genitals
into the ocean which began to churn and foam, and Aphrodite rose up out
of the waves and the surf, borne up on a shell.

A good story, but unfortunately all the paintings depict her clearly arising
in a ribbed, smooth scallop shell. In a terracotta statue dated to the fourth
century BC she is emerging from inside two scallop shells opening up like

wings on either side of her. And by the time she had been adopted by the Romans as Venus, in her most famous incarnation, Sandro Botticelli paints her demonstrably standing in the unmistakeable shell of a scallop (*see plate 14*). In *The Birth of Venus* by William Bouguereau, in 1879, the surrounding men are blowing on conches, not oysters. Pity really. Possibly you could make a tenuous link visually that it was not a scallop but a winged oyster pinctada from which pearls arise, but it was not an edible oyster. Art has been faithless to the oyster's legend in that regard.

As shipbuilders and sailors, the Greeks might have plundered oysters from further afield. By 400 BC they were laying out twigs and pottery in organised shallow ponds to attract larvae. At the time, Taranto – now on the eastern boot of Italy – was a Greek port and is still today an oyster-growing area.

Homer had already observed in Book XVI of *The Iliad*, written some 300 years earlier: 'How active he is and how well he dives. If we had been at sea this fellow would have dived from the ship's side and brought up as many oysters as the whole crew could stomach.'

Aristotle, in the third century BC, noted that oysters would be moved from one bed to another to fatten. The Greeks christened the oyster *ostreum* and from there comes the Latin derivation *ostrea edulis*, literally meaning edible bones. The Roman writer Himilco referred to Brittany as the 'ostrymnian promontory'.

Pliny records the first Roman attempt at oyster culture around the Bay of Naples, probably around the turn of the first millennia:

> The first person who formed artificial oyster beds was Sergius Orata, who established them at Baiae, in the time of Lucius Crassius the orator, just before the Marsic War. This was done by him, not for the gratification of gluttony, but of avarice, as he contrived to make a large income by this exercise of his ingenuity … at a later date, however, it was thought worthwhile to fetch oysters all the way from Brindisium, at the very extremity of Italy; and in order that there might exist no rivalry between the two flavours, a plan has recently been hit upon, of feeding the oysters of Brindisium in Lake Lucrinus, famished as they must naturally be after so long a journey.

The name Lucrinus, it is sometimes said, gives us *lucrum*, or profit, there being a material gain to be made out of the oyster culture, but also with connotations of avarice which in turn was translated into filthy lucre. Pliny's sarcastic quip at Orata has stuck down the years.

A more charitable thesis is that the beds at Lucrinus were being eyed up as possible naval bases and Orata was anxious to save the oyster trade. Orata was a businessman who made other fortunes selling villas and inventing shower baths. His husbandry is still broadly followed today. He cleared the grounds of other marine life, placed seed oysters in their place and checked them constantly to be sure they had enough room to grow to a good size. He sorted them regularly, rid them of pests that attached to their shells and kept them clean of silt. More revolutionary, he arranged stones in a pile under the water and placed the mature oysters on them; he then surrounded them with stakes and faggots suspended in the waters so as to catch the spawn and encouraged them to attach where he wanted them.

The lake at Baiae was also used to farm the admired gilthead bream, which were hand-fed oysters to fatten them up.

The Baiae of Vice

This early cultivation around Baiae lent the oyster two of its more fantastical reputations: first, its repeated association with the underworld and the ancients. The neighbouring semicircular Lake Fusaro was described by the Greek writer Lycophron in 28 BC as a 'billowing and tempestuous lagoon', and later by Strabo as a 'muddy expanse of sea'. Mythology and poetry going back much further place it in the centre of hell, in the area of Tartarus, 'where kings were punished and the righteous passed through on their way to the Elysian Fields'. Righteous or not, it became a fertile and eventually historic oyster lagoon.

Second, Baiae, by association, reinforced the oyster's reputation for licentiousness. It was a popular, decadent seaside town where rich Romans went to take the waters and misbehave. Baiae is now sunk in the Bay of Naples, but at the time was the most fashionable of resorts and home to the imperial fleet.

There are many references to its debauchery. The socialite Marcus Caelius Rufus in 60 BC was accused of living the life of a harlot in Rome and in the 'crowded resort of Baiae', indulging in beach parties and drinking sessions. Seneca the Younger, who died in 65 BC, wrote a moral epistle on 'Baiae and Vice', describing the spa town as being a 'vortex of luxury' and a 'harbour of vice'. Things had obviously not changed much when Sextus Propertius, who died in 15 BC, described the town as a 'den of licentiousness and vice'.

It was also here that Caligula ordered a 2-mile bridge of pontoons to be set across the bay for a stunt, so he could ride his horse across the water in defiance of an astrologer's prediction that he had 'no more chance of becoming Emperor than of riding a horse across the Baiae'. And it was here that Emperor Claudius built a grand villa for his third wife Messalina, who spent her days and nights revelling and plotting to have her husband replaced by her lover, a thought for which she was eventually beheaded.

Messalina alone might single-handedly have been responsible for both Rome and the oyster's reputation for sexual depravity, although her promiscuity and intrigue must have been embellished over time. Married at 15, on the orders of Caligula, to the 50-year-old Claudius, Valeria Messalina was reputedly as beautiful as she was politically scheming and frustrated. She took lovers seemingly as she pleased, and in one incident, so the story goes, she challenged the champion prostitute Scylla to see who could satisfy the most men in one night. Scylla retired before dawn after twenty-five men, but Messalina carried on through the morning. According to Juvenal she was 'tired but never satisfied'. Anyone who spurned Messalina's advances ran the risk of execution. She slept with the handsomest, most powerful and even on occasion the ugliest men in Rome for her own diversion or for political and financial gain.

Apologists suggest a variation where she was the victim of the intrigue: they say her children were fathered by Caligula and that he foisted her into a marriage with the elderly Claudius to save his own reputation. Eventually she fell in love with the consul Caius Silius and determined to marry him, even bigamously. Possibly this may have been part of a wider failed coup attempt, and her real motive was self-protection in a post-Claudius order. Claudius, who, while thought of as a dumb but benign dictator, seems to have been genuinely fond of her at the start of their union. He was coerced into sending soldiers to the wedding feast to kill her. She was 23.

Coincidentally, it was at Baiae that Claudius would be poisoned by his last wife Agrippina, the controlling mother of Nero who wanted to put her son on the throne.

Baiae was just the sort of place, you might think, for a respectable oyster to lodge and find a reputation. The town even had its own well-known stew named after it – a casserole of oysters, mussels, jellyfish, pine nuts, rue, celery, pepper, coriander, cumin, wine, garum, dates and oil.

Much was made of how many oysters were eaten at Roman banquets. The emperor Aulus Vitellius reportedly ate 1,200 oysters at one go. But there would have been a certain practicality involved here. Even with cellars built underneath their villas, each cargo of oysters would need to be eaten while still fresh. The rest would have been sent to the kitchen for cooking or preserving.

Pliny, however, was an enthusiast for the oyster as a cure-all, recommending them poached in wine and honey for stomach ills, roasted in their shells and eaten as a remedy against catarrh, diluted in water against ulcers and a tonic for women's skin. The ground shells he recommended as toothpaste. Many of his ideas were turned into quack medicine down the years.

Pearls & Power

Rome had another aphrodisiac – power. Far more political and persuasive than a few nice titbits to licentiousness, or the idea that these fat potentates needed two days of swallowing oysters to copulate, is the sense of status and power displayed by serving oysters brought from far-off lands. That was Rome's real opulence. It was not just a good taste, it was a taste of a subjugated land and taxes and extreme wealth.

Shakespeare in *Antony and Cleopatra* has Alexas saying:

> Say, the firm Roman to great Egypt sends
> This treasure of an oyster; at whose foot,
> To mend the petty present, I will piece
> Her opulent throne with kingdoms; all the east,
> Say thou, shall call her mistress.

And there was even more status to be had in the pearl. Cleopatra bets Mark Antony she would spend more than 10 million sesteri on a dinner for him. The story has been re-told in different guises, but this seems accurate:

> The servitors set before her only one cruet of sharpe vinegar ... now she had at her ears hanging these two most precious pearls ... as Anthony looked wistly upon her, she took one from her ear, steeped it in the vinegar, and as soon as it was liquefied, drank it off.

Whether the pearls would have dissolved in vinegar is artistic licence, but she could just as easily have swallowed them in wine and recouped them back the next day.

These pearls would have come from Rome's south-eastern borders, the Persian Gulf, the Red Sea and even perhaps as far as Ceylon. For one victory march Pompey himself brought back thirty-three crowns of pearls. For newly empowered Rome, the pearl – the poet Manus called them 'the gems of the sea, which resembled milk and snow' – became the first emblem of power and status. Aristocracy flaunted them: they wore them on their clothes and had them embroidered into their couches; Caligula had a pearl necklace for his horse; Nero made the actors in his theatre wear pearl-encrusted masks.

The sense of envy at this excess survives, even if the artefacts themselves have mostly perished. There is an undertone to the writings of the time. Horace sarcastically remarked that a woman 'loved her pearls more than her son'. Seneca wondered that earlobes could carry so many pearls at all. And possibly there is a political overtone to the much-quoted line that Julius Caesar wanted to invade Britain to find pearls, at a time when other generals and campaigns were doing just that to the south and east.

The value in the pearl was inflationary. It remained a symbol of rank and prestige. Women of lesser rank were banned from wearing them at all – an edict that would be repeated many times in the ensuing 1,500 years. Pearls became so expensive that the general Vitellius, who went on to become the eighth emperor of Rome, raised enough money to pay for a whole military campaign by selling one of his mother's earrings.

The Roman enthusiasm for oysters in general pushed the occupation of France and Britain and the rest of the empire. Suetoneous, the Roman biographer, says Ceasar was looking for 'pearls' which, given the trade that was to develop later, could well have been a factor. But Caesar would also have feared the sea-based might of the Brittany oystermen; coveted perhaps the Cornish tin trade; and was anxious to stop eastern England offering refuge and sanctuary to kindred tribes he thought he had subdued in north-west France and Belgium. Caesar also needed a military triumph to give to Rome.

Supper with Martial

The Romans demonstrably liked oysters. They baked a special bread to be served with them – a forerunner of the American oyster crackers and oyster loaves. Orgies or not, dinner was an important occasion to look forward to for the elite, as this invitation from Martial suggests:

> You will dine well, Julius Cerialis, at my house … The first course will be a lettuce (a useful digestive aid), and tender shoots cut from leek plants, and then a pickled young tuna which is larger than a small lizard fish and will be garnished with eggs and rue leaves. And there will be more eggs, those cooked over a low flame, and cheese from Velabrum Street, and olives which

have felt the Picene cold. That's enough for the appetizers ... You want to know what else we are having? Fish, oysters, sow's udder, stuffed wild fowl and barnyard hens.

Typically, oysters were served on the shell with a dressing, quoted by everyone writing of the time as of pepper, lovage, egg yolk, vinegar, liquamen, olive oil and wine. The Roman sauce of liquamen, like garum, was made from the fermented insides of (usually) oil fish like mackerel and tuna. This was the soya sauce, perhaps more akin to the Thai fish sauce – as common as a seasoning for a poor man's gruel, as a condiment of the richest houses or watered down a drink for legionnaires.

The trade was markedly smelly and undertaken outside of towns. The literature suggests it was originally a poison that evolved into a culinary speciality made in large vats with alternate layers of wild herbs – perm from aniseed, coriander, fennel, celery, mint, savory, penny royal, lovage, oregano, thyme, purple betony and poppy; in fact, pretty much anything that could be scraped off a Mediterranean hillside – fish, more herbs and salt. There were notable sources spread around the Mediterranean that map out the regular southerly trade routes around Arles in France as a distribution point to troops in the north, Baelo Claudia in the Straits of Gibraltar, and Tunis and Lagos in the Algarve. Baelo Claudia would eventually be overrun by 'pirates from the Iberia and Celtic peoples'. In the history of Lagos it is said that Celts were recruited to fight against Rome.

This quote of gastronomic enthusiasm from Mucianus shows how far the Romans went to get their oysters, as well as how particular a Roman could be about his supper:

> The oysters from Cyzicus (on the far side of Greece) are bigger than those from the Lucrine, gentler than those from Brittany, more flavoured than those from the Medoc, spicier than those from Ephesos (near Izmir in Turkey), more valuable than those from Illice (in Murcia), drier than those from Coryplas (possibly Greek or the site of a Greek temple near Rome) tenderer than those from Istria (near Palma) and whiter than those from Circei (near Rome).

The Valiant Veneti

The defeat of the Veneti proved decisive in the fall of Britain. Much of the westerly European trade and culture would seem to have been invested in the main seafaring race of Gaul. The Veneti, or the men of Vannes, lived in Brittany off the Morbihan coast and had intimate dealings with Cornwall and Devon. Without their submission, Caesar faced a sea battle to control the English Channel. That he chose this as his primary military task is a further pointer to the importance of a westerly European seaborne power axis.

The Veneti had developed their own style of ships. Where the English built light curraghs that could skip across the Channel waves and were flexible enough to bend in stormy seas, the Veneti ships were huge, built out of oak, with timbers as much as a foot thick and bolted together with iron pins 'as thick as a man's thumb'. In place of sails they used skins from untanned hides. Everything was built for strength. Instead of hemp cables, they had iron chains for their anchors, something that would not be seen again until the nineteenth century. These ships were obviously built to travel long distances and to handle the mighty swells of the open Atlantic. They had broad beams and shallow keels so they could also nip more easily into tidal inlets.

With these ships, they had tapped the tin trade at its source and established trading posts at Falmouth, Plymouth and Exmouth. From there they sailed by the inland routes with their freight to the Seine, the Loire, the Garonne – probably to Spain too. Devon and Cornwall were in close alliance and seem to have sent auxiliaries to fight against the Romans. The Veneti influence may have gone further – relics of prehistoric boats found in the silt at Glasgow share similar designs.

Caesar describes his struggle with the Veneti and their British allies as one of the most arduous in his Gallic campaigns. At first the Veneti were content to let the legions march into their countryside. They avoided pitched battles. They withdrew to their coastal strongholds and, if a Roman army appeared, they would move everyone by boat along the coast.

The Roman war galleys depended largely on ramming to win their sea battles. On a first sail past, they would pass close by and smash the oars and then come back to board the stranded enemy. The Venetian ships were so solidly built that such attacks were useless. The lofty prows and sterns allowed the Veneti to tower over enemy boats and shoot arrows and drop cauldrons of burning tar on to assailants.

After several unsuccessful skirmishes, Caesar came up with a new plan. He armed his boats with billhooks and instructed his captains to sail past the Veneti boats, ripping the huge leathern mainsails down from the masts so they swamped the boats and gave the legionnaires time to board. He faced a Veneti fleet 220 strong. This was 56 BC.

The Veneti were defeated at the battle of Morbihan Gulf. The mainsails were slashed 'covering the ship as with a pall', hopelessly crippling the vessel, whether for sailing or rowing. The whole Venetian fleet fell into Roman hands. In Gallic accounts the fleet became becalmed and trapped. The men chose to drown themselves rather than be captured. Either way, the strongholds on the coast were then stormed, and the populations either slaughtered or sold into slavery as a lesson to the rest of the confederacy of the fate in store for those who dared to stand out against the genius of Rome. The slave dealers typically were Levantine Jews or Syrians.

Celtic historians point to the sophistication of the Veneti as evidence of a long-standing civilisation. They had soap and bathed regularly. They dressed smartly and their clothes were admired, adopted and traded by the Romans. All of which underlines the point that before Caesar butchered and enslaved them, there was an active cultural and commercial activity between Brittany and Rome. The Veneti, especially, had respect for beauty of the human body; obese men, or those unfit to fight, might be fined.

The women were sexually liberated. Much later, the fourth-century historian Sulpicius Severus reproached the wife of an aristocratic Veneti for the wantonness of Celtic women, but she replied cuttingly: 'We fulfil the demands of Nature in a much better way than do your Roman women: for we consort openly with the best men, whereas you let yourselves be debauched in secret by the vilest.' By that time, the decadence of Rome was rampant; much of the wealth had been acquired by money lenders, so the proud Celt may have chosen her words well.

But it was the same for the British women. The poet Martial much earlier wrote a poem for a friend who married a noble Englishwoman called Claudia, 'a fabulous blue painted savage of the north'. England seemed to enjoy a glamour among Romans for its untamed savagery. Boadicea's atrocities against the Romans were well known and respected. So too were domestic things. The word basket derives from *bascaunda*, an import to Latin through English women who would bring a Sussex trug-style basket to Roman towns in England and which briefly became fashionable in Rome itself.

The Celts had developed a productive level of agriculture. Possibly it was these crops that the Romans were anxious to secure for themselves. Farming seems to have been common in Wales as far back as 4,000 BC. Much of the vision of early Britain, as a nation of cave-dwelling, loin-clothed, blue-dyed savages, stems from Caesar's own chronicles. Where he had the advantage of being a first-hand reporter, he was also a soldier, conqueror and politician. Much of our historical inferiority complex stems from Caesar's opinions. The Celtic vision of pre-Roman Britain being wealthy in trade, sophisticated in its crafts of pottery and metalwork, trading its cloth as far as Rome and being a largely settled agrarian string of communities, would have been a more rational reason for Caesar to invade.

Caesar's invasion of Britain was a serious business. His first essays in 55 BC involved 98 transport ships and 10,000 men. This was repulsed. He retreated to France but the next year returned with no less than 800 ships, 5 legions and 2,000 cavalry. Obviously the resource to find 800 ships was an indicator that shipbuilding itself and the timber to support it was readily available, which is hardly a primitive achievement, and presumably much of it would have been requisitioned from the Gauls. If it is not a spelling mistake or just an attempt at self-aggrandisement, then this was a mighty armada – bigger than William would assemble 1,000 years later for the Norman Conquests. If it proves nothing else, it says traffic.

The Rutupian Oyster

The oyster was not overtly regarded as anything special in England, especially if there was meat about or other foods; although one could say that so little evidence remains of that period that there are very few examples of anything being perceived as special. But the first recorded example of interracial marriage comes from the bodies of a middle-aged couple, she British and he Roman, found at Bridgford, Nottingham. They were dated by the oyster shells with which they were buried; they were almost certainly butchered by Boadicea's troops in retaliation for their collaboration. The oysters could have come easily enough along Watling Street, which was connected to the east coast, but it is still more than 100 miles inland. The date would have been just before AD 61.

To the Romans, the British oyster, especially the Colchester oyster, known as the Rutupian oyster, was a fabled delicacy. Rutupiae was Richborough, the main Roman port from where Watling Street began; the oysters should therefore not be directly associated with the town itself, but that is where the boats left from. Both oysters from around Brittany and England found their way to Rome in what appears to be a regular and well-organised trade and for which the Romans had built ice cellars beneath their villas.

Gnaeus Julius Agricola, the Roman governor from AD 78–85, first sent back quantities of oysters from Reculver to Rome, packed in snow it is said, although that must be fanciful. But it underlines the strength of the seafaring at the time. The distance by sea might have taken six weeks – probably longer than an oyster could survive out of water. Perhaps they were bagged on the side of the boats because they would have been too heavy to transport in large numbers. The presence of the shell also shows the Romans did not want them pickled or preserved, but fresh.

Logic says that there would have been trading points around the west European coast where oysters could be traded, refreshed in new water and transferred to more suitable boats for the Mediterranean. It could also be deduced that this was not just for oysters either, but more than likely was a full-blown trade around the continent.

Getting Oysters to Rome

Historians have glossed over the small technical feat of how Colchester – because it was Essex rather than Southampton or Cornwall, which does not seem completely logical – oysters managed to get to Rome at all. In a straight line it is the best part of 1,500km, so at an average land speed of a Roman carriage that would be fifty days, by which time the oysters would be dead. The sea route is much further; probably 5,000km plus. Even the possibility of offloading the cargo at Bordeaux and taking it the shorter distance overland to Marseille and then back on ship is 600km. And where a Roman war galleon with 180 oarsmen could move at a reasonable speed, a cargo ship loaded with oysters could never attain anything like that pace.

John Morris in his history of Roman London, *Londinium*, notes:

> British oysters were known in Rome in the early empire … and most of them originated in the neighbourhood of London. In Rome oysters were expensive, a dozen cost half a labourer's daily wage. Overland transport across Europe is unlikely, direct carriage by sea from the port of London to the port of Rome probable; and Rome was but one of the innumerable Mediterranean cities whose populations liked oysters.

Transport remains the issue – as it was for another great British export to Rome: Maldon salt. The Essex marshes have yielded up more antiquarian salt pans than any other Roman colony. Salt and oysters probably travelled together.

Some of the practices of the day, as outlined by Morris, may hold an explanation. Sea trade was undertaken by the rich and was high risk but also high profit. These galleons still hugger-muggered near the shore in case of bad weather. Rudders were not invented until the twelfth century so they still used the side oars to steer – hence our word, derived from Old English, *starboard*. Open seas were dangerous.

Morris also suggests that most sea trade, therefore, concentrated on the summer months, which was pragmatic but hardly suits an oysterman whose harvest is at its best in winter. The trade in inland oysters was, says Morris, 'organized on a massive scale'. The oysters were kept in barrels which contained seawater.

It would seem inevitable that these cargoes were not delivered in one journey. London was probably one end of a seafaring chain that stretched around Brittany, sheltered in the Gironde – where the infant wine trade with Britain was already beginning – along to the Tagus, before striking for the Mediterranean. At each stage a consignment of oysters might have been refreshed in new waters, even laid back into the estuary for some weeks or months to fatten up again, and then replenished before the first consignment moved on.

Given the high risks involved, it would also seem likely that traders were happy to pass the risk down the chain. The oyster was worth next to nothing at source and so there was probably enough margin for the journey.

In another possible explanation, a small crew may have kept refreshing the oysters with seawater as they travelled and traded their way around the coast. The rewards would have been greater but equally, the weight of an oyster rules against huge consignments; instead they may well have been special cargo for special clients mixed in among other lighter goods.

To the Roman mind, the idea of bringing goods and foods from far-flung points of the empire back to Rome was more than just ingenuity, or even just commerce. It was a justification of empire. So where the Romans appreciated oysters and would have applauded extreme lengths to deliver them back to the capital of the then civilised world, they might, and probably did, feel much the same about any exotics brought from afar, be that silk from India or elephants and lions from Africa or slaves from Scotland. This was the business of empire. A return cargo of pots, vessels, oil and wine also had an assured market for the intrepid captain prepared to risk the Channel, the Morbihan, Biscay and the western Mediterranean.

In Britain the Romans secured Caernarfon, Swansea, Cardiff and Newport. They made Colchester their base. They set up forts in Dorchester, Chichester, Reculver and round the Thames estuary. And these were not the only settlements; far from it. Neither did the Romans seem to overlook any productive oyster-bearing regions for their settlements and villas. At a Roman camp at Silchester, near modern-day Basingstoke, a million shells have been unearthed. Additionally, shells have been found as far north as Hadrian's Wall.

Even in its collapse, the Roman Empire left us its enthusiasm for the oysters. The trade in edible oysters may have disappeared, but the caches of pearls that the royal houses of Rome had assembled were ransacked and carried away by conquering Goths; they were scattered among the territorial lords of northern and western Europe, always retaining their sense of value, treasure and importance.

From here, in the Dark Ages, the pearl found another expression, this time more pious. They became part of the religious jewellery of the first missals and manuscripts, adorning the covers of sacred Bibles and texts – the pearl had passed from an item of vanity to become a symbol of all that was great in religion, and could be found increasingly on altars, in sacred vessels and as part of priestly sacraments. The empire had fallen, but its wealth was redistributed.

The English Pearl

There is a curious aside to the story of the pearl in England. In one sense Caesar was proved right. Pearls were found in Britain from before Roman times. Morris mentions a trade in 'second grade pearls of British oysters for their wives' necklaces'. But these, like those found in other fast-running streams across northern Europe, were not from oysters, but from mussels. They were probably used in the crowns of early kings.

Agricola declares:

> Britain yields gold, silver and other metals, to make it worth conquering. Ocean, too, has its pearls, but they are dusky and mottled. Some think that the natives are unskilful in gathering them. Whereas in the Red Sea the oysters are torn alive and breathing from the rocks, in Britain they are collected as the sea throws them up. I find it easier to believe in a defect of quality in the pearls than of greed in us.

The Venerable Bede (AD 673–735) lists the things for which Britain was known and writes: 'many sorts of shellfish, among them mussels, in which are often found excellent pearls of all colours; red, purple, violet and green but mostly white.'

The Bishop of Rennes, writing in 1070, declared British pearls as the equal of the orient. By the twelfth century there was a market in Europe for Scottish pearls, although they did not fetch the same prices as those of the east. By 1355 John II forbade jewellers from mounting Scottish and oriental pearls together, except for ecclesiastical ornaments.

In 1521 the Privy Council appointed Pearl Conservators for Aberdeen, Ross and Sutherland to oversee the fishing in July and August, when it was supposedly the best, and to ensure the finest examples were secured for the Crown. Paisley in Scotland and Irton in Cumberland were noted pearling places; the Tay, the Teith and the Eran were as well known in Victorian times for pearl fishing as for salmon.

Writing in 1908, the jeweller George Frederick Kunz said:

> The summer of 1862 was most famous for pearling owing to the dryness of the season and the low water, and unusually large quantities of pearls were found, the prices ranging ordinarily from 10/- to £2 6s. Queen Victoria is said to have purchased one for 40 guineas … a necklace was purchased for £35 in 1863. The value of the whole catch in Scotland in 1864 was estimated at £12,000 to the fishermen.

Much more, of course, to the jewellers and traders. Pearls may still be found in fast-running streams, but it seems they were usually found in older, wizened mussels, and the agitation in the cascading waters might have started the growth whereas they needed time to mature. As the mussel industry moved to coastal waters, the English pearl disappeared.

PART II

Old World

Have you ever tasted a Whitstable oyster? If you have you will remember it. Some quirk of the Kentish coastline makes Whitstable natives, as they are properly known, the largest and the juiciest, the savouriest, yet the subtlest oysters in the whole of England.

Sara Waters, *Tipping the Velvet*

— 5 —

England

The Thames — Good Deeds in Colchester — The Mystery of Wellfleet —
Laws Dissolve in Water — In Defence of English Cooking — Invitations to
Disorder — Smuggling & the Black Economy — Curdley & Nipperkins —
The Literature of Oysters — Oyster Girls — Boom & Doom

The Thames

Faversham, on the inner lip of the Thames in Kent, takes its name from the
Latin *faber*, meaning a smith, and the Germanic *ham*, meaning a homestead.
The Romans actually called it Durovelum, meaning the stronghold by the
sea. It was important enough to christen in both eras.

The town history has it that after the Romans, Jutes and Saxons were
brought over as mercenaries to protect the port. They liked it and stayed.
Its creek was strategic. It supplied shelter from the Channel storms and
deep wells offered fresh water. As early as the eighth century the Dutch
were coming to shelter, trade, settle, buy, raid and smuggle, just as the
Romans would have settled for the same reasons.

King Stephen is buried at the abbey to whom he granted a charter
in 1147; the charter included oyster fishing. But earlier than that, in 930,
Athelstan held a council at the town implying it must have been regarded
as somewhere of import even at that stage. Along with oysters it was
known for its metal work, and especially for shipbuilding. The vessels built
there were called Peter boats, after St Peter, but in design and construction
were informed by Viking long boats, suggesting the Scandinavian contacts
were already well ingrained that far south.

Even if much of the recorded trade with mainland Europe collapsed with the fall of Rome, it would seem that a safe coastal Channel port like Faversham was active and multinational in the so-called Dark Ages.

Fish Days

The recorded wealth of middle Saxon England around 700 BC was based on the undefended seafaring from three ports around the south-east Thames mouth – from London at Aldwych, Ipswich in Suffolk and Southampton – all of which claim clear lineage to their oyster beds and thence shipbuilding.

By the eighth century, and certainly before the Normans, oysters were being sent up from the coasts. This trade did not stop with the departure of the Romans. In part, this was because the Church insisted on fish days, not just in Lent, but on Fridays, Saturdays and sometimes Wednesdays too. Studies of the diets of the time show oysters were commonly eaten across rural areas. Fish days were strictly enforced for a thousand years and it was only later, possibly as a reaction, that the singularly English culinary tactic of pairing oysters with meats – with mutton, with steak in a pie, as a stuffing for chicken, turkey or even duck, or made into sausages with pork – came to the fore with the first printed texts, around the seventeenth century.

Oysters occupied a different position in the trading hierarchy to other goods. This is a medieval edict from Ipswich:

> Concerning oysters and mussels brought by boat to the town quay, for selling, it is ordained for common benefit (of poor men as well of rich men) that such shellfish be sold by the same men who brought them. No one in the town is to meddle with such merchandise contrary to this ordinance, upon pain of its confiscation and 40d.

The same ethic was still afoot hundreds of years later; this edict is dated 1578: 'The bailiff may licence any impotent or lame person to dredge oysters ... provided there be but one person in the boat.'

The local oyster resource was protected as a way of feeding the local poor. When oysters were scarce, the local burghers made sure they had enough for themselves and the town before any were sent away to market. Oysters were not really seen as a trading commodity.

Ipswich had other lively local by-laws to do with food: cooks could be put in the pillory if their cooking was not good enough; so too bakers if they adulterated their bread or cooked anything for which they did not have a licence. The town bailiffs visited the inns and taverns annually to taste the wines to make sure old wines had not gone off and were not debasing the new season's imports. So trade with the east coast and Bordeaux was obviously ongoing.

A town freeman could buy any other cargo brought for sale to the port. Merchants negotiated a price for their goods with the town bailiff and then posted an announcement in the town hall or market square. Local businessmen had first refusal to buy. This trade was a communal activity. If one freeman failed to pay up, the whole town became liable.

On this basis began the East Anglian and Essex trade in wool and cloth. A town that could erect a crane at Hythe – in Old English literally a place where goods are landed – meant it was important. Much of the commercial activity centred on the passage of boats, both local and international, including those from Holland, France and even as far as Italy. Some trades, essentials like coal, could only be pursued by freemen, but others like brewing and baking could be done by outsiders, but only by licence. Herrings were listed as items of trade, but oysters were regarded as essential to the parish and, as such, were set apart. Such administration was a direct hand-me-down from the way the Romans ran their towns, with public office being tied to specific tasks for the general upkeep and well-being.

Awash with Spat

It is often assumed that oysters were not cultivated before the eleventh century. It was presumed that fishermen were just taking abundant oysters from the wild and moving on to new reefs as they exhausted one site. This is probably not true. The Romans could have shown them how to cultivate oysters, if need be, and the presumption smacks of city patrimony.

The nature of the Thames estuary also discredits the idea. The largest and most famous native English oyster beds are at the mouth of the Thames, along the north Kent coast around Whitstable and Faversham, and across the water in creeks at Colne, Crouch, Maldon, Blackwater and Roach, along the coast of Essex.

But Essex can rarely have been self-sufficient in oysters, or never had enough to meet demand. Its tidal creeks opened on to the Thames which would wash away the spat; except at Paglesham on the Roach, where the twin tides around Foulness Island kept the spat inland and made it the natural hatchery. But the other creeks would take in oysters from Kent and further afield to fatten off for market. Quite when this started is not clear, but it was ancient, logical and not always amicable. If we accept that oysters were being ferried to Rome then it is a small deduction to conclude that they were being fattened and replanted in different waters in stages along the way. Moving an oyster from one bed to another was a simple business.

Royal Patronage

The Thames towns enjoyed two advantages over other fisheries. Billingsgate market for London was upriver, which may be why the East Anglian creeks, being that much further north, where they could be used for raising oysters (and still are at Orford), were latterly turned over to mussels instead, which were thought to be an easier sale. But these harbours were also the front door to Europe, to trade and smuggle unseen. And they were a backdrop to an invisible international royal politic.

In the eleventh century the Danish king, Canute the Great, imported shiploads of oysters from England to what is now Germany's north-west coast, which sustained an industry for a millennium. Some of these traders were kings or at least their emissaries.

The oyster towns' closeness to Europe assumed an intimacy with the affairs of state that other parts of Britain could never achieve; or at least not until the industrial revolution and the advancement of the colonies opened up the west coast ports.

English history, in a European sense, was conducted across the Channel between the Thames and the northern coastal towns of the European headland. The oyster folk were their boatmen, envoys and their guards.

The emerging English monarchy encouraged the Kent ports to form the Cinque Ports – originally five but later spread out over twenty-three towns and creeks and extended to include Brightlingsea in Essex. The origins are not precise. Edward the Confessor offered the ports the power to raise taxes and make laws in return for protecting the trading routes with Normandy. (In the complicated affairs of state at the time he had been born while England was at 'war' with the Danes and had a Danish king in Canute. He was a Saxon, so the lawlessness that must have been afloat on the Channel was clear to him.) Edward demanded in return fifty-seven ships, each with a crew of twenty-one men and a boy, for fifteen days every year, should he need them – all of which vessels would certainly have been built 'by nearby coastal and creek-side' oyster towns. That the oyster towns were not directly named suggests they probably had other more important business to be tending to. The charters for the ports were to be administered by the Admiralty.

In the twelfth century Henry II gave Maldon the rights not just to its own creek but also to the now-commuter towns of Southend, Leigh and Hadleigh, where oysters were still laid at the start of the twentieth century, although these are now opposite the oil refinery of Canvey Island.

Maldon also had mysterious sources of wealth. It seemingly had many landowning merchants with no obvious land-based business to go with

them. Further north, Ipswich, which had Felixstowe and Harwich as its
harbours, is rich in recorded laws that denote how merchants should
behave and be treated. Horsey Island, now a bird sanctuary, was well
known as a safe haunt for Thames barges to hide smuggled booty away
from customs. Between the better-known Clacton and Frinton lies
Holland-on-Sea, just south of Great Holland. If a small seafaring town like
Colchester could flourish, by comparison a capital city like Amsterdam,
just across the water in Holland, could boom.

West Mersea claims the oldest charter from Edward the Confessor which
dates to 1046; but for reasons which no longer seem comprehensible,
600 years later, in 1687, Charles II issued a second charter, this time giving
the beds to Charterhouse Hospital in London, which also owns the public
school in Surrey – a legal point which was contested by the incumbent
landlord as recently as 1967.

Similarly, further west, the same kind of royal patronage was afoot at
Abbotsbury in Dorset. Here Chesil Bank and Portland stone have oyster
shell ingrained in them dating back to pre-history. King Canute gave the
Fleet lagoon to one of his servants, Orc, who commented ungratefully:
'there is little fish in the Flete except eels, flounders, and grey mullet, but is
noted for its oyster beds.'

Orc, in turn, passed the ownership to his wife Tula, who bequeathed
it to the local abbey. By 1427 the abbot was demanding taxes on the
fish caught in his waters – two pence for 200 oysters but sixpence for a
salmon. In 1543 Henry VIII dissolved the monastery and allowed one of
his knights, Sir Giles Strangeways, to buy this part of Dorset for £1,000.
His descendants are still there.

Good Deeds in Colchester

Colchester was a notable town as far back as the seventh century. But these
communities needed protection. In the ninth century soldiers from Surrey,
Kent and Essex had to march on Colchester and reclaim it from marauding
Danes. But only 100 years later the same city was wealthy enough to have
its own mint.

The Colne was controlled by the nearby Colchester Corporation in a
charter given to the town by Richard I in 1189; but this charter mentions his
grandfather Henry so the town may have been ennobled 100 years before
that. The Corporation has used this charter to defend its interests, not least
from its own fishermen. Colchester oysters are known worldwide but the

actual beds are further south, off the flatlands at Wivenhoe, Brightlingsea and West Mersea. It was not a right the town was going to forsake. It had a crane.

Colchester demanded that all oysters be sold at the quayside market at Hythe. Anyone selling oysters anywhere or to anyone else, even in their own village, was liable to be imprisoned and to have their boats seized. As early as 1200, court cases were brought against boats for illicitly carrying wool or other contraband that was not offered for sale to the town freemen first.

But these men were also far-sighted in their administration. They seem to have been conservation-minded and philanthropic. They set a closed season for fishing from Easter to Holy Rood Day – 14 September; they licensed and registered anyone fishing for oysters; and they demanded that no oysters be sold on to London unless there was enough to supply the Colchester people first, 'which by that provision were chiefly relieved'.

Over time they went further to preserve the fisheries: no boat was to carry more than two persons or tow more than one dredge of the existing standard size; summer dredgers could only go one in a boat with a mast and sail not more than 7ft high; fishermen were to sort the contents of their dredges at sea and put back all brood and immature oysters; licences demanded that beds be kept free of predatory starfish and tingles.

If there was not full-scale aquaculture then there is, at the very least, plenty of early evidence of advanced husbandry.

The Jolly Freemen

For the men, traders and freemasons of the Middle Ages, drinking and banqueting together was a much anticipated activity. The oyster acquired social status. In Colchester the town accounts were carefully doctored to make sure that the exact quantity of food and drink purchased at public expense did not show up in the books.

Writing in October 1893, the local historian Gurney Burnham reported: 'The sagacious town clerks of the past so compiled their records of Corporation proceedings that one would hardly suspect that nearly all the town's revenues were spent eating and drinking.'

The town had a fair on 9 October for St Denys, going as far back as 1318. The Colchester Oyster Fair still carries on today. Poetically, Denys is the patron saint of Paris. He was sent by the Pope to convert third-century France but was beheaded at Montmartre, the hill of martyrs, where he reputedly picked up his head and walked off still preaching a sermon. Naming the fair for St Denys was a symbolic recognition of events on the other side of the water and that his message carried on.

This was far from being the only feast day. There were to be meals at public expense on the annual election of the bailiff and mayor in August, and then the new mayor had to have a celebration dinner at the end of September. Then there were dinners for quarter sessions, for the magistrates, for the audit (twice a year), and for the opening of the fisheries and the closing. And another for the venison feast, and for the subsidy dinner, and on public and royal holidays and the quarterly allowance day, which was when the rents were paid. By 1520 there were so many dinners and banquets for the oyster traders and freemen of Colchester that nearly all the proceeds of the oyster company were being spent on eating and drinking. In 1563 the mayor tried to put a brake on the flow of funds and ordered that no future election dinner should cost more than 40s, no law dinner more than 20s, and no allowance dinner more than 10s. How much notice they paid to this is anyone's guess.

Lavish menus survive in the accounts, or at least what was paid for the ingredients, which presumably were often supplied by the freemen themselves. In 1617 the freemen bought:

Six sirloins of beef	Twenty shillings
Five fat pigs	Three shillings and six pence
Six coople of rabbits	Six shillings
Four barrels of beer	Thirty-two shillings

Sometimes the oyster purchases were discreetly disguised in the books as 'two goyinges down the river'. Carriage was 'always costly', although it may have been creative accountancy. On one occasion, sending a man and a horse to Brightlingsea for oysters was charged at 4s; on another, to pick up the same amount of oysters, it was 60s.

Another odd item, because oyster knives don't have to be sharp, is:

Grindinge ye oyster knife	Six pennies

At dinner in 1645 they purchased:

Boiled fishe	Three shillings
Green oysters	Six shillings
Stewed oysters	Four shillings
Oyster pies	Five shillings

The Corporation was never ungenerous and through the millennia notes of its gifts, invariably oysters, to the court houses and to kings and prime ministers are plenty. The assizes only had to sit at Chelmsford and the judges were assured of a basket or two. Henry VIII took local oysters to his meeting in Calais with Emperor Charles V; Elizabeth I's ministers were solicited for favours with nipperkins of oysters. Centuries on and Disraeli, as prime minister, received the same gift but had the grace to write and say thank you: 'Your oysters are worthy of Roman emperors ... I am ashamed to add, I devoured most of them myself.'

One senses a society that was emancipated with liberated sources of income. By the seventeenth century Colchester – presumably like cities in Holland – was notably prosperous. A travel writer, Celia Fiennes, described it respectfully at the time:

> It is a large town. You enter the town by a gate. There are four in all. There is a large street which runs a great length down to the bridge; it is nearly a mile long. Through the middle of it runs another broad street nearly the same length in which is the Market Cross and Town Hall and a long building, like stalls, on which they lay their bays, exposed for sale. Great quantities are made here and sent in bales to London. The whole town is employed in spinning, weaving, washing, drying and dressing their bays in which they seem very industrious. The town looks a thriving place judging by the substantial houses. It has well paved streets, which are broad enough for two coaches to go abreast.

The Mystery of Wellfleet

The Wellfleet was one of the most famous oysters of the era, though there is no town called Wellfleet. It was an area of water which produced a green-tinged oyster, reputedly the best in the area, and commanded premiums at the London markets even if no one was too sure where it came from. John Gay, better known as the author of the original *Beggars Opera*, mentions them in a poem written at the start of the eighteenth century:

> Be sure observe where brown ostrea stands,
> Who boasts her shelly ware from Wellfleet Sands.

But writing in 1594 John Norden, an Essex historian, reported:

> Some part of the sea shore of Essex yealdeth the beste oysters in England, which are called Walflete oysters: so called of a place in the sea; but of which

place in the sea it is, hath been some disputation. And by the circumstances that I have observed thereof in my travail, I take it to be the shore which lieth betwene St. Peter's chappell and Crowch the bredthe onlie of Denge hundred, through which upon the verie shore, was erected a wall for the preservation of the lande. And thereof St. Peter's on the wall. And all the sea shore which beateth on the wall is called Walfleet. And upon that shore on, and not elswher, but up in Crouche creeke, at the ende of the wall, wher also is an ilande called commonlie and corruptlie Walled (but I take it more trulie Wallflete) Island, wher and about which ilande thys kinde of oyster abonndeth. Ther is greate difference betwene theis oysters and others which lie ypon other shores, for this oyster, that in London and els wher carieth the name of Walflete, is a little full oyster with a verie greene finn. And like vnto theis in quantetie and qualitie are none in this lande, thowgh farr bigger, and for some mens diettes better.

Doubtless the oystermen knew exactly where the Wellfleet beds were, but were too canny to let on. Dengie 100 is a peninsula to the east of modern-day Chelmsford, bounded by the North Sea to the east, the River Crouch to the south and the River Blackwater to the north. It is recognised in the Domesday Book and has been settled since the Iron Age.

Laws Dissolve in Water

Ownership and administration of the waters and their harvest was complex, vexed and various, and in 2,000 years has never been wholly resolved. Ownership of land, however bloodily fought over, has eventually proved decisive thanks to visible walls and fences, but a few feet, even a few inches, of water is enough to leave any tenure open to perpetual dispute.

A tangle of legalities governed the 'ownership' of the waters, estuaries, sea shores and submerged territories and their harvests. Essex traders thought nothing of using their superior boat building to raid other estuaries in summer looking for spat, although they also demanded protection for their own creeks from marauding Kentish men, French and Dutch boats.

Even in law, the oyster was different. Unlike other fish it could not swim away, so when a new bank was discovered it had potential to attract outsiders looking for a windfall harvest. But equally, oysters do not always grow where they are expected, so a landlord who buys a land site productive in oysters at the time, can find a few years later that they have died out and moved downriver.

The slight adjustments to the laws over the centuries, as vested interests fought for the harvest, became increasingly farcical as lawyers wrestled with problems they did not understand. One decision stated a man could not steal an oyster unless it was labelled, so that he knew he was stealing. Another decree held up in court was that stealing an oyster was not theft because the oyster was not harmed and was going to a better home. The list of misdemeanours was long. Fishermen were accused of summer dredging, using a smack sail instead of a row boat, staking off exclusive beds in creeks, selling oyster spat to foreign traders, exporting oysters, especially to Flanders, and threatening the bailiffs and even the mayor. But the oyster poachers had a reliable defence, declaring simply to the East Mersea magistrates that any offences were committed outside the court's jurisdiction – and they walked free.

Even if the Crown or Parliament could prove exclusive domain over the shores, it could not override the historic claims of fishermen on a particular stretch of water, who might in perpetuity have been awarded such rights by some long-lost agreement. The sea was common ground in common law and so fishing was enshrined in law by the Magna Carta. It was open to all. Many centuries later, in 1886, a Royal Commission was set up to consider the question of ownership of oyster spat that might drift out to sea and beyond the territory of the owners. Canute was proved right, his kingdom really did stop at the water's edge and he could not, and neither could his successors, control such a legal tide.

The situation is the same fudge today, as is neatly summed up by this modern advice from the Crown estate – not regarding the oyster beds but more prosaically the rights to moor a boat:

> Harbour legislation is therefore one factor complicating the legal position on mooring. The other is the issue of long usage. It is a broad principle of property law that, if something has gone on for a long time without objection, whether it be using a right of way or occupying land to which one has no title, the law will eventually recognise the fact and give the person doing it the legal right to continue. Unfortunately, it is very unclear how this principle would be applied by the courts in relation to moorings – the case law is hazy and sometimes contradictory.

If the law is hazy and contradictory today for yachtsmen, it has been the same for oystermen for millennia. Laws, it seems, invariably dissolve in estuarine waters.

Even now, in law, oysters are deemed wild, and neither owning an oyster bed nor having a historical right to gather oysters amounts to ownership

of a given oyster. Theoretically, if an oyster were attached permanently
to the seabed then it could be deemed part of an estate and belong to
someone. But it can always be argued the other way around, that an oyster
is not attached to the ground, but to another oyster, and it is therefore
'moveable property' and becomes the property of anyone who wants to
pick it up. As one legal counsel put it, when asked for an opinion on the
legality of scavenging for wild oysters, as recently as 1993:

> There seems to be some uncertainty in common law about the ownership
> of oysters themselves (as distinct from the right to gather them), which turns
> on the degree to which they are considered to be attached to the substratum
> and, in legal terms, therefore, have 'acceded' to the solum (ground).

In Defence of English Cooking

French dictionaries of gastronomy are dismissive of English efforts with the
oyster, offering an austere view of the cooking of this time. One example
that is sometimes trotted out is this singular recipe for oyster sauce credited
to England. It says it should be served with grilled meats, meat pudding or
grilled cod:

Old English Oyster Sauce
Stir six tablespoons of oyster liquor with twice as much light brown stock,
butter and flour. Season very lightly, bring to the boil and cook for 10 minutes.
Strain, add 12 poached, de-bearded and sliced oysters, and a pinch of cayenne.

That the oysters had to be sliced suggests that larger oysters were sent to
the kitchen, although it is not too clear why they had to be pre-poached
at all. In an alternative version, Larousse suggests you might use milk. Such
sauces seem to be designed for taverns and large-scale events.

But early English cooking offers a better insight into the kitchens of
earlier centuries, and was more of an inspiration to people of the New
World who would become more adept at cooking with oysters than any
people before them.

English cooking was quite showy. The diaries of James Woodforde, the
parson of Weston Longville in Norfolk in the late eighteenth century,
show he entertained seven poor bachelors of the parish on Christmas Day
1788 and gave them 'rost beef and plumb puddings – and after dinner a
pint of strong beer'. But with his friends the parson rolled out the barrel.

On 1 January 1790 dinner for eight was 'Skaite and oyster sauce, peas soup, ham and chicken, a boiled leg of mutton with capers, a rost turkey, fryed rabbit, brawn, tarts, mince pies and etc.'

Oysters featured widely in public cooking in pubs, taverns and larger houses, usually on the shell. There is a pub in London's east end by Liverpool Street Station, Dirty Dicks, which still declares itself as what might have been the oldest of oyster houses, dated 1648, although it has long since lost its sense of history in a series of blatant makeovers. The sign outside survives. The origins of oyster stout are usually credited to the London taverns of this era. The prevailing view is that it was oysters and stout rather than one drink, but microbrewers have successfully thrown oysters and even shells into their mash, and in rural areas it would seem logical to have tried to add more goodness into ale. Another plausible technique was to use crushed oyster shells to filter the beer. The name stout comes from Middle English *estout*, deriving from France and Germany. Guinness has on occasion used the pairing in its marketing, declaring that 'the Guinness makes the oysters come out of their shells'. Marstons make a very good beer called Oyster Stout XXX but it has no oysters in it.

Many restaurants began life as oyster bars and survive. Wiltons, now in Jermyn Street but originally in Great Ryder Street, claims to have first opened in 1742 and supplied Buckingham Palace with oysters for 200 years, from George III onwards.

That most English of restaurants, Rules in Maiden Lane, was originally an oyster shop and fishmonger, founded in 1798. Sweetings seems also to have begun life as an oyster trading room before settling down to become a restaurant in 1840. Wheelers was set up by the captain of a Whitstable oyster smack called Bubbles in 1856, and only moved to Old Compton Street in Soho in 1924 before reincarnating as one of the first restaurant chains. Sheekeys and Bentleys opened later, in 1896 and 1916 respectively.

In medieval banqueting there were a great many complex recipes, for example, oysters with cabbage and fried larks, and fried frogs' legs with oysters. Puddings too were often made up with oysters. Suet pastry parcels were filled with blanched oysters, bacon, onion and parsley and steamed. The liquor from the oyster was mixed with chives and parsley, and thickened with flour and butter to make a gravy. Steak and oyster pie can still be found. Looking back, the pairing of meat and fish seems like a celebration of the end of fish days, or perhaps it was a ruse to circumvent the Church's dietary guidelines – an oyster pie might be acceptable if no one checked that it was filled also with beef.

Making a stuffing with oysters, to cook with a chicken or other fowl, was a common approach emanating from England and later popularly adopted by the early settlers in Canada and America. Presumably, oyster with chicken would have been a special dish which may be why it is mentioned so often; not as today, though, where the oysters would be the expensive ingredient, but the other way round, where the fowl was the prized centrepiece and the stuffing would have been a means of making the meal go further round the table.

Oyster Stuffing for Chicken
Poach oysters briefly in a minimum of water. Pour the liquor over bread to soak. Chop the oysters. Brown some sausage meat in a pan. Mix in the bread, chopped onion, garlic and the giblets from the chicken. Pan fry gently for five minutes. Take off the heat and let cool. Fill the chicken and roast.

On fish days there might have been a simpler rendition of oyster sausages: the oysters poached, then chopped with herbs and anchovies, mixed with egg and breadcrumbs, suet or butter and seasoned with pepper or nutmeg or both; this mix was then fried off by the spoonful.

Another approach widely adopted by the Americans was the habit of scooping out the middle of a roll or a loaf of bread and filling it with a sometimes quite exotic mix of oysters, poached in cream, ale or wine, and sweetbreads or other small pieces of offal, butter and onions, and baking it off in the oven. Rather like pasties and hotpots, this may well have its origins in bake houses and cook shops, and would have been a good way for the baker to use up unsold loaves.

Before the railways oysters were pickled in jars, especially by the Dutch, but notably at Poole in Dorset and at Swansea, and exported often to Spain and Italy and also the West Indies. The practice of pickling oysters still survives in Swansea and they are sold through pubs. This recipe hardly changed through the centuries or around the world, although in American versions they sometimes add chilli or more Tabasco. The wine, vinegar and sherry should be preservative enough to keep it out of the fridge and demonstrates further links between the smaller ports and France and Spain:

Pickled Oysters
Simmer peppercorns, salt, mace, wine, vinegar and sherry over low heat for 10 minutes. Remove and allow to cool. Shuck the oysters and put them, along with their liquor, into a sauté pan. Simmer until they 'begin to curl around the edges'. Put the cooked oysters into a quart container with a lid. Pour the cooled pickling sauce over. Cover tightly.

Escoffer credited just one oyster recipe to England. Over time it has become a cocktail party cliché, but it is easy to imagine the sheer sense of enjoyment and communal spirit – even found in the name – of assembling such a delicacy on an open fire. Some variations suggest the oysters be given a drink of wine first but that seems a very chef-like affectation. Pork and oysters are a common pairing all around the world – a pragmatic reality since the two would have been reared in coastal towns alongside each other – although pairing fish and meats in general is rare enough:

Angels on Horseback
Shuck your oysters. Wrap each one around with a slice of bacon. Secure it neatly with a cocktail stick to form neat parcels. Lay up over hot coals (or in an oven) and grill for two to three minutes, then turn over until the bacon is crisp. Serve immediately.

Invitations to Disorder

How these oyster people thought is in part revealed in a series of petitions to Parliament starting in 1718, at which time squabbles big and small with the Dutch were ongoing. Their presence in the Channel was hailed as an 'invitation to smuggling and disorder'. The Dutch vessels had extra large wells. Contraband could be hidden under a cargo of oysters.

The south coast dredgers complained that cheap imports were threatening their livelihoods. Foreign oysters, they said, were sold at 'low rates and very cheap abroad'. The trade, they said, was 'unfair and fraudulent ... to the great discouragement of your petitioners and to the prejudice, decay and ruin of our own fisheries'. It might be seen as an early argument over free trade versus economic protectionism.

More than 10,000 men at the time were directly employed oystering. And beyond that, they pointed out that the dredgers 'sold to the freightmen who sold to the storers who sold to the marketmen who sold to the retailers who sold to the consumers'. The petitioners also argued that there were other ancillary trades that would be affected, including iron, sail cloth, hemp, pitch, tar, soap, leather and many other 'customable merchandises that are a "public convenience"'.

They pleaded: 'The people employed would all be turned loose on the world ... the building of small crafts will be cast aside ... the crown will lose taxable revenues and government will lose its nursery of breeding up seamen for the service of the royal navy.'

They estimated that the eighteen rivers of the Medway and the creeks of Essex employed nearly 4,000 men. Out of season they would sail around the coast looking for trade, spat and mischief. 'In this part of the trade, many thousands of pounds are expended on the west and north parts of the kingdom for flesh, bread, drink and provisions and necessaries for the people.'

In 1737 Parliament responded and decreed a levy of 2s 2d a bushel on imported oysters as duty. Unfortunately, the winter of 1739 saw a huge frost. The boats were frozen in harbour for three months and most of the oysters died – the patriotic protectionism had proved futile.

Foreign imports were not the only threat. Beyond just trying to protect their own interests, the fishermen often scurrilously accused their rivals of avoiding paying tax. One Thomas Ellis was charged in 1720 for bringing a consignment of oysters from Cancale in France. He declared their value at £5 for customs at the quay but then sold them the same day for £61. And two years later, one John Hoyfield did the same, selling them for £54. The charge was eloquently made:

> It is a well known thing that nowadays he who imports 1400 bushels, Kentish measure, if he thinks fit to make an entry, don't, upon his oath report above 500 and sometimes 400 bushels as the whole of his cargo. And the different ways the entries are made up by the importers as by the bushel, the wash, the thousand and the basket, are contrivances to conceal the true quantities and carry on the juggle of avoiding the proper duty.

The captains argued that they could not tell if the oysters were dead or not and could not predict how many might get to market, so therefore it was right to under-declare. The customs officer complained that even where they suspected skulduggery, they could not impound a boatload of oysters because they were just too big and he would have nowhere to put or keep them; or the oysters would die in his care and be worth nothing. But the oyster cargo was often just a front. The weight of the oysters made them a useful covering to hide contraband like brandy beneath.

At the bottom of this was often the acrimony between Essex and Kent oystermen. The Essex side complained: 'In Kent for the most of them being poor, unruly and incorrigible and violating all orders in dredging on the set grounds at prohibited times … plenty are overgrown with ouse and nothing but muscles where formerly were oysters.' In 1725 a raiding party from Whitstable crossed the Thames and made off with thousands of newly laid oysters from Southend.

The Essex cartel revealed that they had only started to go to Cancale in France to get their oysters because the Kent fisheries had refused to supply them. In return, the Kent dredgers were disparaging in their testimony as far as the oysters were concerned.

The French oysters themselves were unusual and came to be known as Whiteshell, which may well have been another ruse to discredit the Essex importers. They were only sold by the 'meanest of retailers' who would 'disfigure them to disguise them'.

They were usually brought over in March and sold out quickly in August or earlier before the native market opened. They grew very quickly, which it was said meant they were all shell and no meat.

Hector Bolitho reports a more stable imagery of fourteen hoys at Whitstable carrying 1,000 bushels each, which might have been as many as 160,000 oysters 'constantly going to and fro in the Whitstable happy fishers carrying trade', watched over by binoculars by a 'sodden' inspector. Later, the men would all meet in the Duke of Cumberland pub where the proceeds were divided up upstairs.

There was one boon to the Cancale trade and one that shows again that the French and English were already more advanced in aquaculture than other literature has suggested.

Orc's original beds at Abbotsbury in Dorset had died out from a mix of neglect, disease and marauding, but in 1743 the enterprising Captain Lysle bought 30 tons of seed oysters from Cancale in France for £50 6s 6d and planted them in the lagoon near Wyke. Lysle obviously had an understanding of what he was doing and laid the foundations for a business that flourished into the twentieth century. The Fleet oyster even gets an iconic literary mention in the opening paragraph of J. Mead Falkner's smuggling adventure *Moonfleet*: 'The lake is good for nothing except sea fowl, herons, and oysters …'

However well regarded in literary terms, the reputation of the Fleet oyster – and Dorset oysters are often mentioned, and presumably were from here or Poole – survived until 1880 and the building of the Ferrybridge Fever Isolation Hospital which coincided with their disappearance for another century.

Smuggling & the Black Economy

In the 1700s the Whitstable smacks were fully engaged in smuggling. This was not so much a black economy as a full-blown alternative.

Oystermen willingly threw their boats into the illicit trade. Where there was smuggling, there were oysters. The means for one was the means for the other.

Vicious hikes in taxes to pay for the wars in France had made commodities expensive and hard to find. Flushing in the Netherlands (now Vlissingen), Calais, Boulogne, Dieppe, Dunkirk, Nante, Lorient and Le Havre in France all were anxious to sell contraband to their neighbours, officially or unofficially. The Channel Islands enjoyed unrestricted trade. They were used as a staging post until 1767, when the British government stepped in to claim its duties. The French responded by developing the then unknown and unfrequented port of Roscoff into a major depot to supply Devon and Cornwall. In a few years, the port was transformed from cottage settlements to commodious houses and large stores run by immigrants from England, Scotland, Ireland and Guernsey — probably from their geography, they were all oyster merchants.

The smugglers needed to carry small packages. They could not break large illegal quantities down in the ports, where customs could see them. They needed to distribute their goods quickly; a trade to which an oyster smack was familiar and well suited. And there was more money in it.

Some barely needed to sail across the Channel, but would use their sailing skills to hover close to a passing ship and take receipt of a few small cases of tobacco, rum or tea. Or they built rafts a few miles outside the estuary on which they could stash the contraband, mark it with a blown-up bladder and a feather and, using their knowledge of the currents, let it drift innocently and unseen past the customs houses to be retrieved safely a few hours later at low tide in a quiet creek.

On reaching Faversham, Daniel Defoe wrote in his *Tour through the Whole Island of Great Britain* in 1824–26:

> I know nothing else this town is remarkable for, except the most notorious smuggling trade, carried on partly by the assistance of the Dutch, in their oyster boats … the people's hereabouts are arrived to such proficiency that they are grown monstrous rich by that wicked trade.

Faversham's wealth was delivered in the dead of night. But when the oyster harvest was plentiful they must have done very well. The Faversham oystermen ran the fishery as a monopoly between father and sons, which dates back to at least as early as the town charter. In good years they earned good money, as much of the local architecture testifies. In 1703 a wash of oysters (a quarter of a tub) could be sold for £3, and on a good trip a boat might bring back 120 washes. The Dutch paid top prices. And Dutch money did not always attract taxes.

Oysters could also be the booty. George IV tried to pass a law that 'any person that shall steal any oyster brood shall be deemed guilty of larceny'. In 1814 an Essex fisherman was accused of stealing 3 gallons of oyster spat from Chichester harbour. He re-laid them near Colchester. He refused to pay the £10 fine, but on appeal the House of Lords dismissed the case on the grounds that 'his purpose was not to destroy but to preserve'.

The clandestine became a way of life. One Cherbourg house in 1768 was shipping 200 gallons of brandy a month on to English boats. If there was any danger of being caught the kegs were dropped over the side and marked with tubular lanterns to be retrieved later. Once on land, the respectable Whitstable townsfolk showed no qualms in putting one over the Revenue. The port was also busy with coal and many a coal cart had been adapted with a false bottom to move the contraband around inland. Tea was a prized booty due to the high taxes it carried. Ostrich feathers were another lucrative trade. At times it was said there was so much illicit gin in Kent that villagers used it to clean their windows. Anything to outwit customs was fine.

An often retold story recalls how a gang of sailors came to realise that the English guinea coin was worth more in France than in England – 28*s* against 21*s*. They amassed a haul of 300 coins and set sail from Faversham but were intercepted by police. Quickly, they stashed the coins in a pot of tar. Customs found no contraband on board and the men were freed. The ship was impounded for a year after which magistrates ordered it to be broken up and its contents sold. The crew reappeared at the auction and reclaimed their money with a token bid for a seemingly worthless pot of tar ... and so they got their undiscovered guineas back.

Even in war there would have been both camaraderie and closeness among the sailors, on both sides of the Channel, and an easy familiarity with the ways of trading with each other. Allegiance had little to do with land-based politics. Richard Platt, www.smuggling.co.uk, relates:

During the Napoleonic wars the enormous numbers of POWs put a considerable strain on the country's resources, and led to a vast prison building program (including Dartmoor). Many French prisoners lived in appalling conditions in prison hulks – filthy, overcrowded and disease-ridden vessels anchored off-shore. Through an elaborate network of contacts and safe havens, prisoners who succeeded in escaping from the hulks would be brought to London, then smuggled on a hoy or an oyster-boat to a timber platform at the low-tide mark near Whitstable.

This platform was a mooring for the oyster-boats and fishing vessels that were prevented from reaching the true shoreline at low-tide by the two-mile wide ribbon of mud that fringes the beaches here. Mingling with fishing folk and wildfowlers, the French escapees were able to make their way back to the shore, rest up and hide for a few days, then make a clandestine departure one dark night from Swalecliffe Rock – a shingle spit close to the Herne Bay road. Relatives of the wealthier prisoners would no doubt have paid handsomely for their safe return (and the arrangement no doubt suited the smugglers) who would otherwise have had to pay for their returning.

A Cornish strategy had a landside smuggler feeding a rope down the town sewage pipes and floating it out on the tide. When it appeared at the other end, his mate attached a parcel of contraband which could then be hauled up into the main street, usually by the pub, and quickly sold and distributed. A variation on this same tale is told by the customs officer who intercepted such ropes at low tide and confiscated the booty, attaching a note saying 'The End is Nigh'.

The remoteness of some of the oyster beds made them ideal for smuggling. Orford in Suffolk was patrolled twice a week by customs and search officers from Aldeburgh. As late as 1856 one local ship's master observed that by timing his visit carefully, he could spend two days in Orford harbour unloading an incoming cargo – perhaps here wine – and loading a new one for export to the Continent. The King's Head at Orford was used as a storehouse for goods run at Hollesley Bay. Symbolically, Hollesley is now a men's open prison.

Inland oysters were being taken long distances. In Preston there was an Oyster and Parched Pea Club from 1771 to 1841. This was a small gathering originally of twelve Tories and the local schoolmaster who met for oysters, port and peas and apparently told each other ribald stories – too ribald for the *Preston Gazette* of the time, unfortunately, to deem fit for publication. Presumably such routes also allowed for the contraband to slip easily across county borders.

Curdley & Nipperkins

Wherever there are oysters, a local patois seems to emerge like a second language.

In the Thames, oystering had its own glorious, rich, onomatopoeic jargon. The talk was of *whitesick*, meaning spawning. *Hockley* meant open shell (there is still a town in Essex with that name). *Curdley* meant full of eggs. *Grandmother*, *clod* or *dumpy* all meant unwell. A *clock* was an empty shell. Predators were called *tingles* – usually whelks. *Squalders* and *gurleys* were jellyfish. *Bungalows* were clumps of limpets gathered on an oyster bed. *Chitters* and *nuns* were barnacles. *Blubber* and *pissers* were sea squirts. Sea urchins were *barrs*, *burrs*, *waterchestnuts* or *sea eggs*.

Boats had their own names. The *hoy* was a package boat that was used around the Thames, although its history seems to go back to the Dutch *heunde*, which may have been borrowed and pressed into service by the navy. In Whitstable the boats seem to have generically been called *smacks*, but these were usually of two kinds. There was the *yawl*, which was the main boat for smuggling and for oystering, which had a boomed mainsail, a topsail, foresail and jib. Even after the advent of engines, yawl skippers often preferred working the tide with just a sail. They would drift without a tiller and allow the dredge to skim the top of the oyster reef without breaking its foundations. If they went with the tide, then the catch rose up easily behind the boat, 'like taking the cream off the milk'.

Less numerous was the *borley*, distinguished from the *yawl* by her straight-cut stern like a rowing boat and her boomless upright mainsail, which let her sail closer to the shore but offered less canvas to the wind, making her less manoeuvrable. It was usually more preferred by shrimpers than oystermen. These boats were nimble and sailed square to the tide to dredge, in contrast with trawlers which employed heavier gear.

Far more confusing a language was used for weights of catch – probably deliberately. The very richness of dialect suggests the kind of sleight of hand and trading wiles that would have been employed on the harbour front. Already the parliamentary enquiry of the 1730s had discovered that a Winchester bushel was a third less than the weight of an oyster bushel, as used in Billingsgate market. At the same time, the Amsterdam pound weight was 40g more than an English pound.

Linguistically, the terminology was nothing short of genius. For the buying of spat on the Thames the measurement was a *tub*, which was the same as a *bushel*, which was 21 gallons, 1 quart and ½ a pint. Then there was a *wash*, being a quarter of a tub, which was used by oystermen selling spat to the merchant. But then a *wash* was equal to a *peck*, while a *nipperkin* was ⅟16 of a *tub* and a *bucket* was ⅓ of a *wash* or 1½ *tubs*. This was not a trade for the unwary or uninitiated: to protect their jobs, in the 1800s the Essex oystermen instituted a seven-year apprenticeship – an early form of trade union closed shop to keep the business in the family as had Kent families.

The language was different again from wholesale to retail. The merchants used a *prickle*, marked by a seal on a basket of oysters, to denote half a tub. But in Winchester, Hampshire, they had their own terms, calling two quarts a *pottle*, a more commonly used term then for fruit and vegetables, and ironic for the city that would later rule on the weight of a bushel in 1826, with the result that an American bushel and an English bushel are not the same either, even now. A *tierce* was borrowed from the wine trade, and contained 42 gallons. At Billingsgate market all fish were sold by the 'tale [sic]', except salmon which was sold by weight, and oysters and shellfish which were sold by measure.

The drinking song *The Barley Mow* celebrates such linguistic chicanery. Each verse has to change the weight of measure and add on the last one. It starts out as:

> Now here's jolly good luck to the quarter gill
> Good luck to the Barley Mow ...

And ends up, presumably after a swallow of beer at each verse, with:

> Jolly good luck to the company, good luck to the Barley Mow
> Here's good luck to the company, the daughter, the cooper,
> the brewer, the daughter, the landlady, the landlord, the full ton,
> the half ton, the barrel, the half barrel, the gallon,
> the half gallon, the quart pot, pint pot, half pint, gill pot,
> half a gill, quarter gill, nipperkin, and the brown bowl.
> Here's good luck, good luck to the Barley Mow.

Good luck to the Barley Mow, indeed. Even today there is huge scope for misunderstanding when oysters are caught and classified by the tonne or bushel; environmentalists define an oyster by inches across, while the actual oyster is sold by the price per each one.

The Literature of Oysters

The language of each era offers its own inflections and insights. From the first days of print, the oyster was at hand. Chaucer had it as a useful, if rather elastic rhyme in the *Summoner's Tale*:

For many a muscle and many an oystre,
Whan othere men han ben ful wel at eyse,
Hath been oure foode.

And in the *Monk's Tale*:

Know that a monk when he is cloister-less
Is likened to a fish that is water-less
This is to seyn, a monk out of his cloister
But thilke text held he not worth an oyster
And I seyde his opinion was good.

Shakespeare played with oyster imagery through all his plays. In *The Merry Wives of Windsor* he has Pistol saying: 'Why, then the world's mine oyster. Which I with sword will open.' In *Richard II*: 'Off goes his bonnet to an oyster wench.' In *Much Ado about Nothing* there is the intriguing 'Love may transform me to an oyster'. From *As You Like It*, Touchstone pronounces: 'Rich honesty dwells like a miser, sir, in a poor house; as your pearl in your foul oyster.' And King Lear's Fool jests: 'Canst tell how an oyster makes his shell?'

Samuel Pepys mentions oysters frequently in his diaries. He also records twice buying pearl necklaces, one for £4 10s in 1660, and another for £80 six years later. More frequently the appearances show how oysters were part of a gentleman's life. In 1660 he was at sea:

In the afternoon the Captain would by all means have me up to his cabin, and there treated me huge nobly, giving me a barrel of pickled oysters, and opened another for me, and a bottle of wine, which was a very great favour.

And then a few days later, we discover he was not such a great sailor, but oysters were a catch-all cure-all anyway:

This day, about nine o'clock in the morning, the wind grew high, and we being among the sands lay at anchor; I began to be dizzy and squeamish. Before dinner my Lord sent for me down to eat some oysters, the best my Lord said that ever he ate in his life, though I have ate as good at Bardsey.

Bardsey might have been the holy island off North Wales, or perhaps more likely it was Bawdsey in Suffolk; either way, both would have had copious resources.

The Irish satirist Jonathan Swift is usually credited with thinking up: 'It was a bold man that first ate on oyster.' Swift was not short of clever one-liners, but in this case he borrowed it from Thomas Fuller's *Worthies of England*, which was published forty years earlier in 1662 and attributed to James I: 'He was a very valiant man who first adventured on eating of oysters.'

John Gay also turned it into a more poetic growl:

> The man had a sure palate cover'd o'er
> With brass or steel, that on the rocky shore
> First broke the oozy oyster's pearly coat
> And risqu'd the living morsel down his throat.

Swift obviously overcame his own fear of oysters and went on to pen this poem, by which time he was an enthusiastic convert:

> Charming oysters I cry:
> My masters, come buy,
> So plump and so fresh,
> So sweet is their flesh,
> No Colchester oyster
> Is sweeter and moister:
> Your stomach they settle,
> And rouse up your mettle:
> They'll make you a dad
> Of a lass or a lad;
> And madam your wife
> They'll please to the life;
> Be she barren, be she old,
> Be she slut, or be she scold,
> Eat my oysters, and lie near her,
> She'll be fruitful, never fear her.

In letters Swift went as far as passing on a recipe for steaming oysters which is not dissimilar to how the Cantonese steam scallops:

> Lord Masham made me go home with him to-night to eat boiled oysters. Take oysters, wash them clean; that is, wash their shells clean; then put your oysters into an earthen pot, with their hollow sides down, then put this pot into a great kettle with water, and so let them boil. Your oysters are boiled in their own liquor, and not mixed water.

And eventually, in *Gulliver's Travels*, he has his hero gathering oysters and limpets on the shore (which he eats raw for fear of lighting a fire that might attract attention) to conserve his provisions. Bringing limpets and oysters together is curious at such an early date because the two rarely coexist. The limpet is a voracious consumer of the same planktons as the oyster and tends to destroy the latter's habitat.

Charles Dickens was an enthusiast. This, from *The Pickwick Papers*, paints what might have been a familiar Thames scene:

'Not a very nice neighbourhood this, sir,' said Sam, with a touch of the hat, which always preceded his entering into conversation with his master.

'It is not indeed, Sam,' replied Mr Pickwick, surveying the crowded and filthy street through which they were passing.

'It's a very remarkable circumstance, sir,' said Sam, 'that poverty and oysters always seems to go together.'

'I don't understand, Sam,' said Mr Pickwick.

'What I mean, sir,' said Sam, 'is that the poorer a place is, the greater call there seems to be for oysters. Look here, sir; here's an oyster stall to every half dozen houses. The street's lined with 'em. Blessed if I don't think that when a man's very poor, he rushes out of his lodgings and eats oysters in reg'lar desperation.'

In *A Christmas Carol* Dickens gives the description: 'Secret and self-contained, and solitary as an oyster.' He also wrote a short story called *Love and Oysters* which he later re-titled *The Misplaced Attachment of Mr John Dounce*, who gives up his friends and family because he is infatuated with an oyster girl, who takes his money but refuses his advances.

Henry Mayhew's chronicles of London street life in the nineteenth century, *London Labour and the London Poor*, were probably used for reference by Dickens. He said the oyster trade was one of the oldest in the city. Oysters were bought off the smacks moored at Billingsgate or further west, or else they were hawked around the streets. He mentions in 1848 the arrival at Borough market of much larger oysters, called Scuttlemouths, brought from the Sussex coast – presumably some new discovery of an ancient bed. These were highly fashionable for a time, largely because they were a cheap street food, known as coarse oysters, having very thick shells and less meat. His descriptions are precise:

The costermongers have nicknamed the long row of oyster boats moored close alongside the wharf 'Oyster Street'. On looking down the line of

tangled ropes and masts, it seems as though the little boats would sink
with the crowds of men and women thronged together on their decks. It
is as busy a scene as one can well behold. Each boat has its black signboard
and salesman in his white apron walking up and down 'his shop', and on
each deck is a bright pewter pot and tin covered plate, the remains of the
salesman's breakfast … the red cap of the man in the hold bobs up and
down as he rattles the shells about with his spade. These holds are filled with
oysters – a grey mass of shell and sand – on which is a bushel measure well
piled up in the centre.

Mayhew is also capable of daring insights into the people behind his
portraits. He describes a well-bred lady who has fallen on hard times. She
has turned to selling oysters in the street. She says:

It's not a very few times that gentlemen (I call them so because they're
mostly so civil) will stop – just as it's getting darkish, perhaps, – and look
about them, and then come to me and say very quick: 'Two penn'orth for
a whet.'
    Ah! some of 'em will look, may be, like poor parsons down upon their
luck, and swallow their oysters as if they was taking poison in a hurry.
They'll not touch the bread or butter once in twenty times, but they'll be
free with the pepper and vinegar, or, mayhap, they'll say quick and short, 'A
crust off that.'
    I many a time think that two pen-n'orth is a poor gentleman's dinner.

Mayhew estimated that 3,500 costermongers could have been involved in
the trade in London, picking up barrel loads from the boats and hawking
them around the streets, or selling them on to 'oyster rooms' or to servants
who would take them back to larger houses for elegant dinners. In some
taverns oysters were offered free on the bar to encourage drinking.

W.S. Gilbert, like Mayhew, tells us that the area around Billingsgate was
known as Oyster Street, and that Oyster Day was 4 August. 'What on
earth,' he asked, 'becomes of the shells of five hundred million oysters?'
The answer was that they went under the floorboards as insulation and
into the lime for building.

Another popular folk hero of the era was Dando, an outrageous
scoundrel. He appeared in cartoons and ballads, and even had a play
written about him. Dickens also wrote about the man who went to 'oyster
shops without a farthing' and commanded large quantities of oysters –
two dozen on some occasions – before the shopkeeper realised, 'You are

Dando!'The culprit was committed two or three times a month to prison and eventually died there, where legend has it his grave was covered with oyster shells.

Pearly Kings and Queens
London costermongers would cut oyster shell and sew it into their cords and caps as a mark of seniority and to distinguish themselves from other street traders and hawkers, or to show they were part of a particular market. Often these were not plain buttons in the modern sense, but the advent of cutting machines meant oyster shells were brought back from Ceylon and Australia to Birmingham, where they would be engraved with the heads of foxes, lions and fish. The dust and shavings from these factories was then sold on to farmers to use on their fields as an enricher.

The habit of sewing on bits of oyster shell impressed a young orphan street sweeper in Somers Town market, who admired the way the costermongers stuck together and looked after each other. Henry Croft started to collect odd buttons he swept off the streets and sewed them into his clothes so that he could draw attention to himself and raise money for other orphans, hospitals and people less well off than him. In 1875 there were no shortages of desperate and destitute souls around King's Cross. Henry Croft became the first pearly king. Many of the costermongers became pearly kings themselves. It was decided there should be twenty-eight families, one for each London borough and one each for the cities of Westminster and the City itself. It is always the king who does the designs and sewing – as an orphan Croft did not have anyone else to do it for him – and some of the outfits have thousands of smoked pearls on them and can weigh as much as 30kg. The tradition carries on today, raising money usually for churches and charities, but earlier in the last century it was to help the poor in hospitals.

Oyster Girls

The oyster girl's reputation was well entrenched. This lusty song is undated, but may originally have been Irish, pre-1800, and was a music hall classic for its voluptuous innuendoes. It is sometimes credited to London, sometimes Manchester, though the geography probably changed according to where it was being sung, usually by a comedian. It seems to have first been printed in 1794 as *The Eating of Oysters* by M. Randall of Stirling in Scotland and the lyrics have evolved along the way.

Oyster Girl

As I was walking down a London Street,
A pretty little oyster girl, I chanced for to meet.
I lifted up her basket and boldly I did peek,
Just to see if she's got any oysters.

Chorus:
'Oysters, Oysters, Oysters', said she.
'These are the finest oysters that you will ever see.
I'll sell them three-a-penny but I give 'em to you free,
'Cause I see you're a lover of oysters.'

'Landlord, Landlord, Landlord', says I.
'Have you got a little room that's empty and nearby.
Where me and the pretty little oyster girl may lie,
When we bargain for her basket of oysters.'

We hadn't been upstairs for a quarter hour more,
When that pretty little oyster girl opened up the door,
She picked my pockets and then down the stair she tore,
She left with her basket of oysters.

'Landlord, Landlord, Landlord', I cried.
'Did you see that little oyster girl drinking by my side?
She's gone and picked my pocket', but the landlord just replied,
'You shouldn't be so fond of your oysters.'

Now all you young men be advised by me,
If you meet a pretty oyster girl and you would merry be,
Sew the pockets of your trousers and throw away the key,
Or you'll never get a taste of her oysters.

In similar rollicking style, there are printed copies dating back to 1820 and examples as far apart as Aberdeen, Somerset and North Carolina, sometimes called *The Basket of Oysters*, *The Basket of Eggs* or *Eggs in her Basket* and others from the chorus. Obviously, the oyster girl's reputation as a saucy trickster was well established:

Now Jack was a sailor who roamed on the town.
And she was a damsel who walked up and down.

OYSTER GIRL.

. . . , Printer, '6, chester; sold by John. -street, Oidham Road, Man- , 176, York-street, Leeds.

As I was walking in London Street,
A pretty little Oyster Girl I chanced to meet,
And into her basket so nimbly did peep,
   To see if she had got any Oysters.

Oysters, Oysters, Oysters, said she,
If you want any Oysters come buy them of me?
They are the finest Oysters that ever you did see,
   Will you please to buy any Oysters?

O landlord, landlord, landlord, says he,
Have you got any room for a friend and me,
That we may sit down and merry, merry be,
   Till we bargain for a basket of Oysters.

We had not been above an hour in the room,
Before she picked my pocket of full fifty pounds,
And gave me the slip and out of the room crept,
   And left me with her basket of Oysters.

O landlord, landlord, landlord, says he,   [me,
Did you see the little Oyster Girl that came in with
She has picked my pocket of all my money,
   And left me with her basket of Oysters.

Its I have travelled England, Scotland, and France,
And never in my life did I meet with such a dance,
The English girl has tricked the Frenchman at last,
   And left him with her basket of Oysters.

147

IF I HAD A THOUSAND A YEAR.

Oh! if I had a thousand a year, Gaffer Green,
  But I never shall have it I fear—
What a man I should be, & what things would I
  Oh! if I had a thousand a year.   [see

The best which you can make my word, Robin Ruff
  Will not pay for your bread and your beer;
But be honest & true, & say what you would do,
  If you had a thousand a year.

I would do then—I cannot tell what Gaffer Green,
  I would go to—I hardly know where,
But I'd scatter the chink & leave others to think,
  While I liv'd on a thousand a year.

But when you're aged and grey, Robin Ruff;
  When the day of your death should drew near;
What,' midst all your pains, could you do with your
  If you then had a thousand a year?   [gains

I never can tell what your at, Gaffer Green,
  For you questions are always so queer
But as other folks die, I suppose so must I
  What! and give up your thousand a year.

There's a world that is better then this Robin Ruff,
  And I hope in my heart you'll go there
Where the poor man's as great, though he'd here no
  Ave, as if he'd a thousand a year.   (estate,

ELLEN THE FAIR,

Fair Ellen one morning from her cottage had stray'd
To the next market town tript this beautiful maid,
She look'd like a goddess, so charming and gay,
Come buy my sweet posies, cried Ellen the fair

I have cowslips, I have jessamine and air bells so
   blue,
Wild roses, and eglantine, all glisten'd with dew
The lily, the queen of the valley so fair,
Come buy my sweet posies, cried Ellen the fair.

With rapture I gaz'd on this beautiful maid,
Whilst a thousand sweet smiles on her countenance
   play'd,
And while I stood gazing, my heart, I declare
A captive was made by sweet Ellen the fair.

And if I could gain this fair one for my wife;
How gladly I would change my condition in life,
I would forsake the folks and the town, and repair
To dwell in the cottage with Ellen the fair

What need I care for the lords or the great,
My parents are dead I've a noble estate,
No lady on earth, nor princess shall share,
My hand or my fortune, but Ellen the fair

A little while after, this nobleman's son,
To marry the maid his affections had won;
While present in court the merchants did stare,
And the ladies all envied sweet Ellen the fair

147

An early sheet music of the *Oyster Girl* – the name of the city was usually changed according to where it was being sung. Compare the change of lyrics between this and the printed version.

Said the damsel to Jack as she passed him by,
'Would ye like for to purchase some quare bungle rye raddy rye?'
Fol de diddle rye raddy rye raddy rye.

Thought Jack to himself, 'Now what can this be?'
'But the finest old whiskey from High Germany.
'Smuggled up in a basket and sold on the sly,
'And the name that it goes by is quare bungle rye raddy rye.'
Fol de diddle rye raddy rye raddy rye.

Jack hands her a shilling and he thought nothing strange.
Says she, 'Here hold the basket til I run for your change.'
Jack peeks in the basket and a babe he did spy.
'Why b'damn me,' says Jack, 'this is quare bungle rye raddy rye.'
Fol de diddle rye raddy rye raddy rye.

Now to get the child christened was Jack's first intent,
So to get the child christened to the parson he went.
Says the parson to Jack, 'What's the name he'll go by?'
'Ah b'damn me,' says Jack, 'call 'im quare bungle rye raddy rye.'
Fol de diddle rye raddy rye raddy rye.

Says the parson to Jack, 'That's a mighty quare name.'
'Ah b'damn me,' says Jack, 'it's a quare way he came;
'Smuggled up in a basket and sold on the sly,
'And the name that he'll go by is Quare Bungle Rye raddy rye.'
Fol de diddle rye raddy rye raddy rye.

Now all you young sailors who roam on the town,
Be wary of damsels that walk up and down.
Take a peek in their baskets as they pass you by,
Or else they may pawn on you Quare Bungle Rye raddy rye.
Fol de diddle rye raddy rye raddy rye.

An Aphrodisiac?

Samuel Johnson's dictionary of English, written in 1755, picked up
the common implication that an oyster woman or an oyster girl was a
character of ill repute. All the early dictionaries assumed the association of
sex and the oyster – and this was perhaps apt for a bisexual creature – for
both heterosexual and homosexual circles.

In England and Scotland young girls walked the streets hawking their wares. But oysters were not a clean trade. Clothes would get dirty. Hands would be cut from the rough shells. And there was the smell too. Early photographs by Hill and Adamson of fisherwomen in the Firth of Forth around the 1840s have them wrapped in shawls and aprons, with ankle-length striped skirts, thick stockings, white wraps over their heads, scarves round their necks and striped, double linen baskets falling from their waists. For all these reasons, perhaps, oyster girls could not misbehave even should they have wanted to.

It seems strange that despite this, oysters could be the height of fashionability. They are not even a particularly polite food to eat (raw off the shell) and seem at odds with the prim ideals of Victorian mores. In American society manuals it was instructed that guests should have baskets placed on the floor on either side of them into which they could drop the empty shells, like spittoons; and they should be furnished with special thick oyster towels. In similar society advice to Midlands families in England it was suggested that oysters be eaten on the evenings when the servants had a night off, which may have been one source of gossip in itself, and that the gentlemen should feed his partner.

There is some science here found in the last decade. Oysters contain dopamine – a neurotransmitter that is administered to increase the heart rate. In 2005 George Fisher, a professor of chemistry at Barry University in Miami, Florida, revealed that oysters and other shellfish are rich in rare amino acids that trigger increased levels of the sex hormones – D-aspartic acid and NMDA, which is N-Methyl-D-Aspartic Acid. Coincidentally, the research was undertaken in Naples:

We found there might be a scientific basis for the aphrodisiac properties of these molluscs. I am amazed. For centuries, old wives' tales have said that eating raw molluscs – oysters in particular – would stimulate the libido but there has really been no scientific evidence as to why and if this occurs. We think this could be the first scientific evidence of some substance. They are not the normal amino acids that Mother Nature uses. You can't just find them in a vitamin shop.

NMDA is being used in trials for the treatment of advanced Alzheimer's disease. Tests found that these amino acids produce a chain reaction of hormones which cause males to produce more testosterone and females more progesterone. Perhaps instinct and science collide?

Boom & Doom

A government report of 1911 belatedly declared:'Oysters are more valuable than any other single product of the fisheries and in at least 25 countries are an important factor in the food supply.'World consumption was estimated at 10 billion oysters. It was said 150,000 people were employed directly in the oyster industry and half a million indirectly.

Bigger boats meant the oystermen could go further out to sea for longer. There were new discoveries in the Channel of untouched reefs. Off Jersey in 1797 more than 300 smacks from Essex, Shoreham, Emsworth and Faversham sailed for oysters carrying more than 2,000 men. By 1823 more than 80,000 bushels were brought back to Essex in seventy voyages. The harbour at Gorey, which also has Iron Age antecedents and the Megalithic remains of La Hougue Bie, the most northerly of the Armorican sites, became a boom town again. But the fishermen were greedy and within twenty years the beds had been denuded.

The Essex boats especially needed young brood stock and would go north to the Forth and west to the Solway. They were not always welcome, especially in Scotland, where they slept armed on the boats for fear of attack; but in other areas their money was good currency.

There were also oysters further out in the Channel, in the deep sea banks off the French coast, sometimes 24 fathoms deep. The Pride of Essex Sail consisted of 132 'first class' ships, able to scrape the reefs with five dredges, each with a 6ft-wide cutting edge. Another famous oyster reef was found 112 miles off Orford, where the English had massacred the Dutch traders at Terschelling. This was a notoriously treacherous and exposed area of the North Sea, where the *Lutine* was to sink later, whose bell hangs in Lloyds of London. Many Essex oystermen died trying to upload this harvest of huge oysters, known as skillingers. The boats would go out for twenty days at a time. The record set by *The Guide* in 1887 was 49,000 oysters trawled in a day.

The Coming of the Railways

Two events in the 1800s indelibly changed the English oyster industry and the way of life on the shore. Both might have seemed great technological advances to impoverished seaside communities, but were to prove pivotal from the point of view of the oyster and the communities they supported.

The railways arrived, in some cases, right up to the dockside, and oyster-gathering became industrialised. Before the railways, and roads, which only came in with tarmac around 1900, communities were disparate, individual, often poor and isolated. The local beds could sustain and replenish a small community and would naturally restock with a minimum of husbandry. Even trade with the big cities of London, Southampton, Bristol, Glasgow and Edinburgh would usually have been by boat and regulated to an extent by the oystermen themselves and their ability to delver. The railways bestowed a land-based order and organisation that destroyed the influence of the watermen and the waters forever.

Suddenly, vast quantities could be harvested and sent directly inland to emerging urban markets. In the same way that the galleons, straight roads and organised trade routes had allowed the Romans to enjoy oysters across their empire, so again here was a push and pulley mechanism to haul huge numbers of oysters and transport them swiftly to expanding cities.

The railways brought a plan for urbanisation where before there had been parochial rural agricultural markets and near-independent anarchy and smuggling on the coast. New cities were designated where others would be bypassed. In turn, the railways brought them more trade and more people. Productive fishing coves were naturally to be included in the new networks as a valued source of supply.

Swansea was chosen as a destination for the first passenger railway in 1817, which made it briefly a resort of high fashion for the gentry; Bath by the sea, it was called, although the real reason would have been for trading its oysters, its coal, copper, iron, tin and zinc, and for its shipping trade with the rest of the world. Here all the benefits associated with oysters that would have been valued back in the Neolithic could be industrialised, plundered and rationalised. The modern world began. Around the globe the city had become an important trading port and was nicknamed Copperolis. Its coal also fed its metal smelting works and it supplied a huge export industry in its own right.

In the seventeenth century oyster dredging in Swansea was still being performed with row boats, but after the railway arrived they were rigged and known as skiffs. A dredge was fitted underneath all 180 boats working the bay. Each skiff had a crew of three: two men hauling the nets while a boy steered.

It was the roaming Essex boats that showed the Welshmen how to develop their oyster beds. Special boats were built in Bristol which came to be known as Mumble Bees. At one time 600 people were employed in the Welsh oyster industry. In 1871 10 million oysters were scraped off the seabeds of Swansea Bay and the Gower.

The railway was large, rapacious and hungry, as were the city markets it supplied. It could suck millions of oysters from the sea to market in a few days. Yes, there was boom, but there would be bust too. No natural resource could meet its insatiable, uncontrolled, mechanical demands. Oysters were mined like coal. And in law there was no protection.

The numbers of people employed in oystering soared. At Whitstable in 1793, 36 people formed the original company, but by 1866 it had 408 members, of which more than 300 were working. At Colne, 73 people were registered in 1807 but over 400 in 1857. These figures were probably for boat owners because in other documents 2,500 dredge men are mentioned in Essex waters around 1836, and the Colne fisheries, in 1844, had 500 boats and employed 2,000 men, so many more worked in and around the trade.

It was a man called Outing who first discovered that if he bought oysters from Cancale and Poole and laid them on the mudflats at Southend they would flourish and fatten off quickly. He started in 1855 and soon had a tram taking 467 tons of oysters to Billingsgate; nine years later the figure was 704 tons. By 1872 the pollution was so bad that the beds were dead, although oysters were laid up at nearby Hadleigh until 1903.

Disaster, Disaster

The boom in oysters brought more people to the dockside; more people meant more housing. The waste they generated was tipped into the waters to wash away. It even seems that around the mid-1850s, town planners might have believed that such waste would enrich the oyster beds and the municipality in some cases believed that possibly the oysters would filter this waste in the same way that they filtered other impurities. Too often the oyster beds seemed to be the locations identified for the outlet of sewage pipes. The sewage works at Colchester were built next to the fish market at Hythe. Barking municipal authorities put their waste on barges and dumped it on the oyster layings off Southend.

The height of the Essex oyster industry was the years 1894–95; 2.7 million oysters were dredged one year, and 3 million the next, but already the seed of destruction had been laid.

In 1895 a public inquiry found that untreated or inadequately treated sewage pipes were pouring out effluent across some of the finest oyster-bearing creeks in the estuary. An outbreak of typhoid was linked to oysters from Brightlingsea Creek, outside the Colchester fishery, and the damage was done. The public started to question its taste for oysters.

Worse was to come from Emsworth in Hampshire. Oysters had been fished at Emsworth and Warblington near Portsmouth for centuries. There had been a major Roman villa on the site. In 1788 7,000 bushels of native Emsworth oysters were raked and dredged by a dozen master fishermen. The oyster industry flourished, as did shipbuilding.

The reputation of the Emsworth oyster brought poaching fleets from the east coast and France. When oysters became scarce the smacks would go to France and bring back spats to grow near the quay in the village. In 1901 between 300 and 400 people, out of a population of some 3,000, were directly employed in the oyster trade.

From the earliest times drains from all the homes around the harbour ran down to the water, and the waste was taken by the ebb tide. Emsworth was one of the first towns to join its drains together. Untreated sewage was emptied over the oyster beds. This story has been embellished over the years to record the death of the Dean of Westminster and the Mayor of Winchester, but in fact only four people died and none seem to have been the dean or the mayor. Emsworth oysters were served at two separate mayoral banquets on 10 November 1902 at Southampton and at Winchester. Everyone who ate the oysters fell sick and four people at the Winchester ceremony later died.

The beds were closed. The waters were consigned to their current fate to be used by hobby sailors, and the houses would eventually be sold to weekenders and retirees.

The closure of beds was a recurring theme. Local authorities no longer, it seemed, had much enthusiasm for the oyster and closure was a quick solution – and certainly a cheaper one than being sued by the oystermen for polluting their beds, or worse, run the risk of being sued by parishioners for poisoning them. So the strange anachronism of English law again meant the polluter could simply invoke public health laws and write off the problem rather than make any attempt to deal with the cause, which was the council's own sewage system. The oystermen faced an authority that was perpetrator, judge, jury and jailer. The councils locked up the oyster beds in the name of public safety; closed them and threw away the keys.

In nearby Shoreham, the beds had already been exhausted before typhoid became a concern. The railways attracted an influx of fishermen from East Anglia and brought a sudden, if short-lived, prosperity to the town – 20,000 tons of oysters were sent to London from Shoreham in 1869, hauled up by 295 boats. There was an oyster pound for underwater storage of oysters in the River Adur at Ropetackle. By the turn of the century they were all but fished out.

The beds at Exmouth were fished out by the 1880s and only used afterwards to fatten the oysters from Falmouth.

At a court case in 1909, one Lieutenant Cardale was awarded £264 in damages against the Sun Hotel, Chatham. He had fallen ill after eating oysters and was diagnosed with typhoid. His friend Lieutenant Downes had died.

Typhoid was not the oysterman's only fear. Typhoid, from an oysterman's point of view, was a small problem; the oysters could be moved to cleaner waters and would quickly free themselves of the disease.

The beds became prey to a new predator. The voracious slipper limpet had been accidentally imported from Connecticut attached to a cargo of Blue Points. The limpet does not harm the oyster directly, but it is a hungry feeder and competes for food and space. Its faeces would muddy the estuary floors. The limpet is edible, but it is so difficult to get out of its shell that the French have since developed a technique to harvest it and sell it as marine manure to farmers. There are foragers' recipes for it, some quoted as Cornish or Irish, where it is served with vinaigrette; but they are tough, hardy things if overcooked.

Restrictions on fishing during the First World War allowed the slipper limpet to overwhelm the oyster beds in the Thames to the point that sales in 1920 were less than half those of 1898, and in 1930 only a seventh. In 1920 Ministry of Agriculture and Fisheries officials removed 2,000 tons of these limpets from the mouth of the fishery.

You could argue, if you had a mind to, that other industries were more valuable; that harvesting any natural resource always runs the risk of that resource being finite; that oyster mongering is an old-fashioned, hard industry that would not create any jobs; that there is no market for oysters anymore; that attempts to reverse the trend would have no guarantee of success; that it was just bad luck that all these once-abundant estuaries, and others I may overlooked, were simply idle, haphazard victims of pollution and inevitable disease. You could argue that oysters do not matter, even if barely a century ago they were one of the biggest industries in the world; you could even argue that oysters are too dangerous a food for our times.

You could argue all that, but it would not be true.

Brython

Scotland – The Northern Axis: Vikings & Brythonics –
Pearls: the Currency of Monarchy – Holland

Scotland

Scotland's oyster history is as ancient as that of Essex. The Romans took Scottish oysters too and there are early mentions of them being eaten in Bordeaux.

In 1529 John Bellenden wrote: 'The Firth is another area where oysters are fished in abundance.' Oysters show up in rural records as rent payments for crofters, who paid anything from 40 to 500 to their landlords each month. Edinburgh's trade is documented back to the thirteenth century. Newhaven's fishing rights date back to 1510. In times of shortage the council tried to stop what must have been active export trades, especially to England but also to the Danes and others, to protect stocks. When the Essex boats came marauding they were pelted with stones.

Where today a sign reads not to eat the fish caught in the waters, in the late 1800s as many as 30 million oysters were taken a year. Charles Darwin began his experiments while still a student at Edinburgh using oyster shells he found in Newhaven, which would start him on his theory of the evolution of the species.

Loch Ryan, near Stranraer, is now the largest fishery in Scotland. It was bequeathed to the Wallace family in 1702 by William III. At its height, in 1910, more than thirty boats worked the waters taking 130 tons a year.

The oyster girl with her creel was a familiar sight, doing her rounds of the tenements. Some of this culture was caught in the following song, the oyster humbled to just two letters in the dialect as *o'u*:

> At night round the ingle sae canty are we,
> The oyster lass brings her treat frae the sea;
> Wi' music and sang, as time passes by,
> We hear in the distance the creel-lassie's cry.
>
> Caller o'u! Caller o'u! Caller o'u!
> Frae the Forth. Caller o'u! Caller o'u!

Singing was much associated with both the gathering of oysters and the selling of them in Glasgow. This song is from Newhaven and is, certainly before 1850, called *The Dredging Song*. Getting wind and kind to rhyme is almost as verbally dextrous as reducing oyster to *o'u*, unless the latter is read as o, meaning oysters, for you.

> The herring loves the merry moonlight
> The mackerel loves the wind
> But the oyster loves the dredging song
> For it comes o' the gentle kind.

Another verse of inspiration on oysters comes from Saki, the Scottish writer Hector Hugh Munro, who lived from 1870 to 1916 when they would have been easily available: 'Oysters are more beautiful than any religion ... There's nothing in Christianity or Buddhism that quite matches the sympathetic unselfishness of an oyster.'

Munro also made this wry quip: 'You needn't tell me that a man who doesn't love oysters and asparagus and good wines has got a soul, or a stomach either. He's simply got the instinct for being unhappy highly developed.'

This bawdy music hall shanty, *Oyster Nan*, is obviously also Scottish. A *fubsey* is a 'small chubby person':

> An Oyster Nan stood by her Tub,
> To shew her vicious Inclination;
> She gave her noblest Parts a Scrub,
> And sigh'd for want of Copulation:
> A Vintner of no little Fame,

Who excellent red and white can sell ye,
Beheld the dirty little Dame,
As she stood scratching of her Belly.

Come in, says he, you silly Slut,
'Tis now a rare convenient Minute,
I'll lay the Itching of your Scut,
Except some greedy devil be in it:
With that the Flat-capt Fubsey smil'd,
And would have blush'd, but that she cou'd not;
Alass! says she, we're soon beguil'd,
By Men to do these things, we shou'd not.

From Door they went behind the Bar,
As it's by common Fame reported;
And there upon a Turkey Chair,
Unseen the loving Couple sported;
But being call'd by Company,
As he was taking pains to please her;
I'm coming, coming Sir, says he,
My Dear, and so am I, says she, Sir.

Her Mole-hill Belly swell'd about,
Into a Mountain quickly after;
And when the pretty Mouse crept out,
The Creature caus'd a mighty Laughter:
And now she has learnt the pleasing Game,
Altho' much Pain and Shame it cost her;
She daily ventures at the same,
And shuts and opens like an Oyster.

It is worth just pausing a moment to consider the use of the language here. Yes, this is English, but words like fubsey, descriptions like mole-hill belly, the lilt of the rhymes suggest a different constituency, as if the very language is arriving from another place in history, like some linguistic smash of cultures. This is English of the north. It is lewd, not the effete remarks of Pepys' English or the bold grammatical drama of Shakespeare. Even now oysters are harvested along the west coast at Ardencaple, at Mull, at Skye, at Lorn, at Mar, where they are sold as Messana, meaning temperate, at Shian – names that point vividly to a different linguistic declension. The Englishness is being forced on to the language, yet they survive like so many rocks still visible at low tide.

The Northern Axis: Vikings & Brythonics

The northern axis is a fainter but traceable presence whose legacy must have been significant, especially in the Dark Ages, and quite possibly long before that. Orkney may be part of mainland Britain but it only became attached to Scotland in 1468. Before that it was ruled from Norway. Genetic research has shown that more than a third of Orcadian men have Norse heritage. In 1102 the archbishops as far away as Hamburg and York tried to assume the ecclesiastical rights over the islands, but were rebuffed by William the Old of Norway.

Orkney's history pre-dates all this by 3,000 years. The Megalithic stones and passageways at Skara Brae, the Standing Stones of Stenness, the Maeshowe passage grave and the Ring of Brodgar, stand as concrete evidence of a Neolithic community hewed out of the rocks of this northerly outpost.

Oysters are abundant across this northern coast: from Norway round Orkney, down the west coast of England, all around Ireland and down to Brittany. There is a linguistic link here too. The Welsh academic John Rhys coined the term *Brython* and *Brythonic* for the language spoken in the west – as opposed to anything deriving from Anglo-Saxon – taking the name from a Greek reference to a country called Prettanic. He followed the classical scholarly post-Roman thought line that another oyster island had become culturally and spiritually important. While the barbarian hordes swept across Europe, Ireland became a centre of learning and a haven for Christendom from the fifth century AD, keeping the embers of literacy and academia glowing until the Renaissance. The scribes and scholars built up huge libraries, which they copied into Greek, Roman and Gaelic, and sent out with their monks as missionaries of the faith. Their language, argued Rhys, was Brythonic and formed the basis of Cornish, Welsh, Breton and Cumbric, and was also found in Orkney. The archaeology, the oyster links, the evidence of pre-Roman history all rather enhance his theories by taking them thousands of years further back in time. The Romans knew of Orkney, although it is not sure if they stayed there and perhaps only traded there, giving it the name Orcades; the derivation is not Latin, but Brythonic.

In the Dark Ages the relationship between the British east coast and the Continent was manifest. Angles, Saxons, Danes, Dutch, Normans – the north men crossed the North Sea. Even today we live with the legacy of these contacts thanks to the royal family through William III. Historians enjoy dressing these contacts up in the clothes of conquest, war, pillage and invasion, but in an alternative thesis it is possible much of this activity was more passive and co-operative. For men with boats there would be a natural curiosity to sail. There were, however, attractions to the Vikings to head north, not least to avoid the European vortex of the Channel. They had the freedom of the North Atlantic. There seems even to have been an agreement with Denmark that the Danes could deal with England while the Scandinavians moved north and thereby down the west coast.

The seas may have been lawless, but a captain would not seek out hostile ports where his boat would be endangered. The last thing a prince or a general in the Dark Ages wanted was a confrontation with an equal force where he could lose more than life and limb, but dynasty, inheritance, power, even his nation. As Harold found at Hastings, you could lose everything. And Harold was more Danish than English anyway. Warfare must have been about cut and thrust, attack and withdraw, grab and run. In Britain there was hardly the idea of a state or nation to fight for, even if people could have grasped an idea of the geography. Everything was local. It was the Normans who would bring their ideas about castles, baronies and statehood.

Vikings were just the northernmost tribe in this European community jostling for influence. They knew the rich, if wild-sailing, westerly oyster route south before the Norwegians, and left their mark as clearly as a road map down as far as the Mediterranean. They knew the oyster well even if they did not seem to regard it as manly food. A warrior called Starkad criticised King Ingjald of Denmark because he 'fried and cooked his food and also ate oysters, amongst other things that were unworthy of the Viking way'.

The Vikings' reputation for raping and pillaging is vested in their raids on undefended monasteries at Lindisfarne, from AD 793, then Iona, then in Ireland. These were easy pickings of religious treasure they could haul home and melt down, but the outrage these attacks engendered was as much due to their defenceless Christian targets as their barbarity.

The Vikings may have been more important in the Dark Ages as traders and settlers – as the middlemen of post- and possibly even pre-Roman Europe. They seem to have been more mobile than other nations. Remnants of a longboat have been found made of Irish wood, so although they are credited with founding Dublin, their ideas of colonisation were almost certainly different; they were traders on the move.

Viking pre-history is being rewritten by carbon dating, and by inference so too all our northern European inheritance. On the Finnish–Swedish border, on the Torne River Valley, remains of a settlement have been uncovered that date back to 9,000 BC. In 2005 another site, nearby at Kangofors, was discovered and dated to 8,000 BC. In the 1980s Stone Age shelters were found at Voullerim and dated to 4,000 BC. And in Norway a recent find at Forsetmoen dated seven iron forges to year 0, with a concentration of artefacts around AD 400.

Oysters grow at these latitudes. Putting aside the Scandinavian Riviera thesis of climatologists, there is an easier rational explanation. While most of the waters this far north are too cold, inside the narrow, shallower fjords the summer sun can create a sun bed, reinforced by the reflection from the ice and snow on the steep sides that can create perfect conditions for spawning. The Norwegians call these bays *polls*. Stone and Bronze Age shell middens have been uncovered around the coast and oysters were common in the nineteenth century. In the seventeenth century a councillor, Anders Kock, was given a monopoly to catch oysters provided he supplied the royal household.

Alistair Moffat, in his book *Sea Kingdom*, cites compelling evidence that points to this distant, largely forgotten and ancient western community. He looks at the ruins of remote castles like Ardtornish on Morvern Bay, opposite Mull; Dunvegan Castle on Skye; and Kismuil Castle at Castlebay, Barra – each perched above protected bays and almost inaccessible by land. Such places were deliberately remote to be safe from a land attack while allowing easy access and harbourage for ships. He envisages a whole seaborne kingdom stretching from Scandinavia around Orkney, Scotland, the Isle of Man, Ireland, Cornwall, and across to Brittany, linked by such shelters.

Their language remains with us in forms of Gaelic. The Welsh word for a head is *pen*, as still witnessed by Penrith and Penarth and elsewhere up and down the coast. The prefix *aber* means a place where the river flows to the sea, or a conflux with a bigger river, as in Abertawe (Swansea) or Aberystwyth. And *ceann*, also meaning head in Gaelic, is still found in Kintyre and Kincardine. The Welsh word for England is *Lloegr*, meaning lost lands.

Pearls: the Currency of Monarchy

Vikings had a secondary agenda: a second trade route south, down to the Volga and the Caspian Sea. As Christianity took hold of Scandinavia the Vikings headed south on what came to be called, or justified, as the northern crusades. You can still find jewellers making Viking-knit bracelets and necklaces to carry their pearls. The return of the crusaders in the twelfth and thirteenth centuries had much to do with spreading the fashion for wearing pearls.

For royal houses across Europe, and for the Church, the pearl was a sign of status. It was the currency of nobility. Hardly a monarch would pose for a painting without pearl adornment. In engravings and records the Hapsburgs, the Valois, the Medicis, the Borgias, the Tudors, the Stuarts – in fact every dynasty – had their image recreated adorned with pearls. The most powerful women of the 1500s, Catherine de Medici and Queen Elizabeth I, are resplendently vain in their adornments. And it was not just women, but kings too had pearls adorning gloves, clothes, hats. Henry VIII was painted in his velvets encrusted with pearls. He wore 'a cote of greate riches, in braides of golde laied lose on russet velvet and set with traifoyles, full of pearle and stone' and 'with great butons of diamonds, rubes and orient perle'.

The prowess of the pearl was protected by local laws to stop less noble traders from competing. In France and Germany ordinary women were summarily banned from wearing the pearl. The Diet of Worms in 1495 declared that no one who was neither a knight nor a noble was allowed to wear pearls.

Even in Venice, whose fortune was made by its trade with the orient, a decree was issued as early as 1299 that only the bride should be allowed to wear pearls to her wedding, and then only one string – although from paintings it seems that successive edicts were just ignored. A common folklore persisted thereafter, and can be found even in English texts, that wearing pearls on a wedding day would lead to unhappiness.

This wealth in medieval Europe was largely furnished out of the Italian ports of Venice, Genoa and Pisa, although by this time their enthusiasm had all but exhausted the natural supplies from the ancient beds of the Persian Gulf.

Further east, the pearl was also regarded as the safest of regal investments. Eastern monarchs controlled their fisheries and horded their wealth. Some estimates claim that a third of the portable wealth of India and Persia was held in pearls. A respected old French jeweller, Tavernier, recorded his finds in his book *Voyages*, published in 1676. He considered that 'the largest and most perfect pearl ever discovered, and without the least defect' was bought by Shah Sofi, King of Persia, in 1633, for 32,000 toman, or 1.4 million livres. He also sold to Shaista Khan, uncle of the Grand Mogul, a pearl from the Island of Margarita on the Venezuelan coast, and it was, he said, the largest ever carried from Occident to the Orient.

Sir Harford Jones Brydges' description of the jewels of the Shah of
Persia at Teheran is stunning in itself. He was an agent of the East India
Company, writing around 1830:

> I was particularly struck with the king's tippet, a covering for part of his
> back, his shoulders and his arms, which is only used on the very highest
> occasions. It is a piece of pearl work of the most beautiful pattern; the pearls
> are worked on velvet, but they stand so close together that little, if any, of the
> velvet is visible. It took me a good hour to examine this single article, which
> I have no fear of saying can not be matched in the world.
>
> There was not a single pearl employed in forming this most gorgeous
> trapping less in size than the largest marrow-fat pea I ever saw raised in
> England, and many – I should suppose from 150 to 200 – the size of a wild
> plum, and throughout the whole of these pearls, it would puzzle the best
> jeweller who should examine them most critically to discover in more than
> four or five a serious fault.

The political marriage was embellished and ennobled with the pearl of
royalty. From an early point, portraits of would-be brides were traded
between families. Potential princesses could be flattered by rows of pearls.

There was a certain irony to this trade as far as the oyster was concerned.
Whereas for the ordinary people the trade was in oysters as food, for
nobility it was the pearls that travelled back and forth across the waters.
When William of Orange arrived in England in 1641, to meet his almost
infant wife-to-be Mary, he brought with him £23,000 in jewels and pearls
as a gift to the court.

Poor Mary. In her official portrait she wore huge translucent pearls
strung as necklaces around her neck and her bosom. But when she died in
1694 – of the measles or smallpox, or the bleeding that was supposed to be
a cure for either or both – Lady Stanhope took all her jewellery, linen and
plate from her bedchamber, and the Duchess of York was seen the next
week wearing the same glorious pearls.

Strangely, that same portrait illustrates another unusual closeness
between England and Holland. It was painted by Pieter van der Faes, a
Dutch portraitist who came to England and was patronised by both
Charles I and Oliver Cromwell, became court painter to Charles II and
was knighted as Sir Peter Lely. His was a conventional, historic portraitist
role, but he was, in another sense, one of the great Dutch masters of
the time who illustrated much more vividly the way people lived and
perhaps felt.

Holland

The Dutch Masters

For 1,500 years or more painters had dedicated themselves to religious iconography; then all of a sudden, in one small northern European country, they changed direction and devoted themselves to things secular. What was the trigger? The first half of the 1600s was still a period of religious passions and a formative era in Christianity. But amidst all this, one society began to accept that there were other things besides God that might be worth painting. There was an artistic emancipation which must have required a change in thinking and aspiration. What was it? Who was brave enough to commission the first non-religious painting? Or was it just an enthusiasm for setting the everyday household items alongside the riches that were suddenly being brought back from other parts of the globe? Perhaps it was simply that the Dutch, as the first to profit from empire, had suddenly become rich and secular.

The pearl transferred as a subject easily from religious painting. But the oyster itself was also a regularly invited sitter.

Johannes Vermeer's famous *Girl with a Pearl Earring* was painted in his later period, probably in the 1660s (*see plate 1*). The girl is probably his daughter, but she was no Virgin Mary – just an ordinary girl at first glance. So why the gold Turkish turban on her head? Why such a luminescent engrossed pearl? – both luxurious trappings of the new movement. How could a mere farm girl have such luxuries? She does not smile like the *Mona Lisa* but there is an engaging, knowingness to her and sophistication in how she dresses.

Intriguing is how strong a movement this outpouring of art was. Often farmers would buy up an artist's work to enjoy as investments and sold them on at local markets. And because there were regular art markets, a painter could be inspired to work without a commission.

These same Dutch collectors had, earlier in the century, developed another obsessive interest, this time in tulips, imported from Turkey and sold on and speculated over to the point that many companies went bust, until the market had to be controlled. The painting of tulips was the next best thing to owning a few bulbs, but compensatory all the same. For some the oyster swam the same tide, although in this case with less catastrophic results. Oysters would have been everyday and commonplace at the coast – Holland, Flanders, northern Germany and Belgium had oyster cultures of their own, derived from 500 miles along the Wadden Sea. Oysters still attained the status of much-treasured and ostentatious imports, and featured among the most expensive and delicious of foods. They were a valuable and much-employed symbol.

Invariably they would be displayed in paintings alongside expensive fruits or game or labour-intensive pastries, particular pieces of imported glass or pottery, or cloths from afar. Some of this was due to the new-found affluence of the middle-class beneficiaries of trade from their ports. For inland wealthy, middle-class Europeans, the oyster was seen as similarly precious and exotic. In some cases it was an artistic device to depict freshness, or even time passing. A surprising number of the great European painters of this time have a visual debt to the oyster as having helped them establish their reputation. From the early 1600s, this school of still-life painting flourished like no other before or since. There may have been a pragmatic motive here in that by painting foods, the artist might also have been fed.

The rise of still-life painting in the northern and Spanish Netherlands – mainly in the cities of Antwerp, Middelburg, Haarlem, Leiden and Utrecht – is generally put down to the increasing urbanisation of Dutch and Flemish society, which brought with it an emphasis on the home and personal possessions, commerce, trade and learning: all the aspects and diversions of everyday life. And all such products arrived at trading ports. Painters such as Abraham van Beyeren, Floris van Schooten, Frans Snyders, Jan van Kessel, Osias Beert (*see plate 6*), Pieter Claesz, Jan Davidsz de Heem (*see plate 7*), Clara Peeters (*see plate 10*) and others, all used oysters to deliberate effect. Later they would be followed by the Frenchmen Jean-Baptiste-Simeon Chardin, Édouard Manet and eventually Paul Gauguin, all of whom aggrandised the oyster in different ways.

The still-life school is categorised as one of three styles: banquet, kitchen or breakfast. There may have been symbolism in the choice of items painted, or maybe the settings were just deliberate manifestations of luxury and abundance. As women were closer to the food, some began to challenge the male trades, such as Clara Peeters.

Her tones survive, still rich, elegant and domestically formal. She, like others, used a cat as if it were about to steal the opened oysters, inviting the viewer to shoo it away. Her meticulous visual descriptions continue to impress. She painted several versions of *Still Life of Fish and Cat* (*see plate 10*), in which a reddish ceramic colander holds several fish, including an eel. You can see the textures plainly: slippery fish scales, thickly glazed clay, the cat's fur, and the contrast between the rough shell of the open oyster and the gleaming pewter dish on which it rests. There are other hints to animation here too: the small fish on which the cat has firmly planted its front paws, and some subtler details, like the two small gouges on the near edge of the wooden table, and the cat's ears are pointed back, alert to any potential interloper. Animals from cats to monkeys appear regularly in seventeenth-century Flemish still lifes, although cats were not necessarily regarded as welcome pets at that time.

Pieter Claesz liked to paint scenes in which people had apparently just left the table halfway through eating, or perhaps again this was an indolent throwaway suggestion that these people were so rich they did not need to clear all the food from the table? Or maybe the artist was only allowed in after supper? He is known as one of the most important breakfast still-life painters, but in later life he assumed a lavish enthusiasm for huge banquet still lifes. So he started his career with very simple depictions of oysters, a goblet and a half-eaten loaf of bread on a table (*see plate 9*), and ended it with the opulent banquet of *Roast Capon with Oysters* painted in 1647.

In the same discipline, known as the unpronounceable *ontbijt* (breakfast piece) was William Claesz Heda, whose *Still Life with Oysters* is more aristocratic in taste and in ingredients, usually ham, mincemeat pie and oysters. Making pies for some of these painters was an artistic activity as much as the painting itself; another indication that food was perhaps secondary payment for the artist.

Fabulous too is the work of Jan Davidz de Heem who lived from 1609 to 1684. His *Still Life with Fruit* was painted in 1652. The oysters are perched like a splash of satin to the side, hovered over by a butterfly.

Abraham van Beyeren was quite sparing in his choice of objects; an orange, a bread roll and a couple of oysters were enough for him.

A pupil of Pieter Brueghel the Younger, Frans Snyders, was admitted as a free master to the Guild of St Luke in 1602. He spent time in Italy before settling permanently in Antwerp in 1609. Business was brisk. New commissions were coming in as houses were being built, and painters made use of each other's skills to keep up. Artists like Rubens, Van Dyck, Jordaens and Cornelis de Vos all called on Snyders to produce the animal motifs in their paintings.

His painting *The Pantry* (*see plate 11*) is set in the kitchen of a vast house. A maidservant, who may have been painted by Cornelis de Vos, is carrying a tray full of quails crowned with a pheasant. She is looking at a large rectangular table spilling over with food. The painting is organised on several levels: around an outstretched white swan; around a gutted roebuck hanging by its hind leg from a hook; a lobster, a peacock and some birds are strewn around; a wicker basket spills over with fruit; a copper basin is full of quarters of meat; from a rack at the top hang two salmon steaks, birds and two hares; in the left foreground a plate of oysters is placed on a bench. A cat, again, is preparing to steal fish from a serving dish, and a dog is watching the maidservant – a provocative contrast to the dead animals.

Maybe there is symbolism beyond the abundance here in the Dutch word *vogelen*, meaning 'to bird', which can also mean to have sex. Snyders did another still life, this time with only four ingredients: a roebuck, a huge lobster, a hanging turkey that dwarfs the deer and a salver of oysters. The roebuck has been pointedly eviscerated from the groin and hung with its legs exposed almost like a pornographer. Snyders went on to paint many variations of the same set-up, all equally voluptuous displays of foods, often with oysters included.

Osias Beert was more astutely detailed. In *Oysters, Fruit and Wine*, painted around 1620, he seems to want to convey a world of abundance and beauty. Eleven opened oysters are arranged on a pewter plate, sensually realistic. Nearby, two shells emphasise the rarity of the foods in the expensive vessels arrayed on the table. Luxurious sweets decorated with gold leaf fill the Wan-li bowl in the foreground; dried raisins, figs and almonds overflow in two other Ming bowls. In the centre, candied cinnamon bark and candied almonds, coloured yellow, pink and green, fill a ceramic tazza. Quince paste is stored in simple, round wooden boxes, another delicacy enjoyed at special festivities, and both red and white wine are visible through the transparent glass of the Venetian-crafted vessels. Like many of his contemporaries, Beert minimised the overlapping of these exquisite objects by painting from a high vantage point, so his subjects look more like jewellery than food.

The kitchen still life was popularised by the French painter Jean-Baptiste-Simeon Chardin. Probably his most famous painting was also his first: *Still Life with Ray Fish* in 1728. A gutted ray is hung from the stone wall in the background; raw fish, oysters, numerous jugs, bottles and other kitchen utensils are arranged informally on a thick white tablecloth. The work won him instant acclaim and membership at the French Academy. Like in Peeters' work, off to one side, a hungry house cat eyes the impromptu feast. In other variations, also using the ray, the oysters are mysteriously missing.

Oysters, one of Manet's earliest still lifes, was reportedly painted for his fiancée and remained with them in the family home. The simple subject and thick application of paint show the direct influence from Chardin, as explained elegantly in this anonymous but admirably bracing catalogue art critique:

> The heavy yellow paint puckers in imitation of the lemons' pebbly skins, while the wet surface of the cut fruit is smooth and flat, sectioned by a few spare strokes. The oysters, plump and slick from a distance, appear upon closer inspection to be formed by a few swift undulations of a brush laden

with thick paint. This work from the early 1860s reveals Manet's developing style. Sudden transitions of colour within a limited range – not a continuous and gradual modulation of tone – give shape to his objects. Each colour, each brushstroke, stands independently on the canvas; it is in our eye that they blend to create form.

Manet also painted an enigmatic portrait of the Philosopher (beggar with oysters) in 1866, of a strolling bearded man wrapped in a blue cloak, who could be either beggar or count, but at his feet shine, almost as if in a spotlight, a small pile of oysters set on straw, symbolising perhaps the thoughts of a man who has lived too hard.

Paul Gauguin's connection to the oyster was later and more literal. He left Paris for Brittany and the farmhouses of Pont Aven, the mouth of the great oyster reserve of Belon. Here he began his essays in primitivism and post-impressionism on the fisher girls of Brittany. His *Vision after Sermon*, painted a year after going to Tahiti, shows all the latent talent that would erupt in the South Seas – and some credit him with the start of abstract art. Breton women are abstracted into visions in high lace caps, black dresses, wooden clogs; gathering oysters and seaweeds; mixing Catholic and Celt. Visits by other artists, like Paul Serusier, Emile Bernard and by association his colleague Van Gogh, to the hamlet of Le Pouldu began the Pont Aven School. Once in Tahiti, Gauguin surpassed himself with a small, carved wooden figure that is even more primitive than primitive art, but has all the sensuality of his larger paintings of native women. In the centre of the figurine's forehead is a pearl ... shiningly, dramatically, deliberately grabbing the attention.

The wealth that the Dutch painters portrayed – and others later – was to have another manifestation, where the Dutch and their oyster heritage had a role to play in different ways. Holland had discovered a small island on the east coast of North America; it was christened New Amsterdam. While the oyster was being elevated to art, other ambitions were afoot and other fates awaited it.

The Dutch Wars

The same spark that lit the genius of the Dutch masters had a darker reflection on the waters of the Channel. William III would eventually accede to the throne of both England and Holland as the reliable Protestant, but the path that led him there began more than 100 years earlier and was wrapped around the oyster histories. The 1550s had seen the Dutch colonising East Africa and Hudson Bay.

The Dutch and the English were close. They would come to Faversham in particular and buy oysters for cash for pickling. A 1630 petition of 400 women and children of Faversham protested: 'for the space of 70 years and upwards it has been usual for Flemish vessels to come into the river and with their ready money to buy oysters and transport them overseas.' The Dutch ran a privateer system. Small collectives commissioned boats to trade. They were known not just as good sailors but also for enduring hardships at sea that no other Europeans would put up with.

The Dutch boats that returned from the other side of the world excited the curiosity and greed of the English. All of a sudden, the returning cargo was no longer the familiar local trades of wine, wool and brandy. The holds were filled with spice and silks from the East Indies, tobacco from Virginia and ornaments from Turkey. And who knew what else? Their trade boats dominated the Channel.

English history books talk politely of the three Dutch wars that were fought 'purely for commercial gain'. They talk of Admiral Robert Blake's brilliance in plotting the naval broadside that would eventually lead to other great sea victories down to Trafalgar. But it was a plan hatched in defeat.

In the space of four years, English troops walked into the newly discovered colony of New Amsterdam in America and took control, changing the name to New York. In 1666 West-Terschelling was ransacked by the English fleet. They destroyed 150 fleeing Dutch merchant ships and burnt the island town to the ground. In retaliation, the Thames saw battle. The Medway shipyards were ravaged by the Dutch. Lieutenant-Admiral Michiel de Ruyter bombarded and captured Sheerness, went on to Gravesend, then up the River Medway to Chatham, where they burnt three capital ships and towed away the *Royal Charles*, flagship of the English fleet. It was the biggest naval victory in Dutch history and the worst English naval defeat. A peace was brokered but ultimately at the cost of the monarchy falling.

William of Orange invaded on 15 November 1688. He was lucky. The storm that swept him past the Thames estuary, as far as the most southerly tip of Devon at Torbay, also trapped the English fleet in harbour in the Thames. William made for Exeter. The Catholic James II was prevailed on to stand down. England was saved from Catholicism, and the nation had a king that would accede to a sovereign parliament. The modern world began.

In the intricate politics and interwoven royal households of the time there was an unseen aside to these momentous events. Forty years earlier, Charles I's wife, the curly haired and voluptuous Henrietta Maria of

France (*see plate 4*), had sailed extravagantly with her entourage from Essex to Holland. She took with her a dowry of jewels and pearls to raise money for her husband's army to prosecute the civil war. It was on her wealth and pearls that England went to war with itself. In portraits she wears her pearls not just around her neck but draped from her shoulders beneath her bust. In another concession, the Dutchman Jaon Janson Steil was licensed to export oysters from Colchester to the Prince of Orange and Charles' sister, the Queen of Bohemia. In her portraits the queen glamorously shows off her status and appreciation, her russets encircled with more pearls, her bodice framed by lace, and around her neck a necklace of more than two dozen gleaming pearls. In another portrait, by Michael Jansz van Miereveld, she wears another pearl necklace, pearl earrings, pearls in her hair and strings of more pearls embroidered into her dress down to her waist – the pearls of war, of bloodshed, of bounty on which the monarchy would collapse.

--➤ 7 ➤--

France

Cancale: Sailing against the Wind – The Caravanne – World Leader –
Gallic Love – French Gastronomy – The Enthusiastic Victor Coste

*Ostend oysters: 'small and rich, looking like little ears enfolded in shells, and melting
between the palate and the tongue like salted sweets.'*

Guy de Maupassant (1850–93), *Bel Ami*

Cancale: Sailing against the Wind

The French have phonetic masterpieces like *détroquage* (moving oysters
for the first time); *ambulance* (cages); *vagabondage* (when the spat
are swimming); a *roudoudou* (a snail drill) – words as redolent and
understandable as if they were English and barely in need of explanation.
The language suggests the closeness of oyster communities in different
countries either side of the Channel. In French there is also the expression
'stupid like an oyster'.

France, a nation that prides itself on its gastronomy, is encircled by
oysters, and in the language there is a poetic affection, even in the rhyming
of the disease *maladies des branchies*, or the tongue-twisting study of shellfish:
conchyculture. There is a sense of linguistic enjoyment.

Two old French fairy stories by La Fontaine have the oyster playing the
central role: the one that has a rat being caught in the shell of an oyster
probably has an element of truth to it; the other has two pilgrims arguing

over whom should eat the oyster they have found. They ask a passer-by who adjudicates by eating it himself: a moral for those wishing to join the French court.

An early portrait by the precociously talented American expatriate John Singer Sargent features the oyster beach at Cancale, Brittany (*see plate 13*). Four women have been abandoned with two children while their men are presumably off fishing in Newfoundland, and they have been left alone with their baskets. Sargent was as adept as the photographer Cartier Bresson a century later in capturing what Bresson called the decisive moment. Here the grandmother is overlooking the little boy pulling his trousers up above his knees. The children are barefoot, the women wearing clogs. The lighthouse provides a solitary pencil-thin solidity in a landscape of wisp and wind, a mention of danger; there is the suggestion too of a mast of a bigger ship across the bluff. Two of the younger women are gossiping, the other two are pointedly alone. Three of them have bare legs, one is wearing stockings, so maybe this woman is going to shuck rather than collect. The woman in front seems resigned, sadly beautiful, peering out to sea looking for something. Perhaps in 1878 the boats were still facing a crisis, and the forlorn resigned mood that seems to hang on the women's shoulders might be taken as one of despair that again that week there would be fewer oysters. Or wistfully and fearfully they consider that their men might not return from the icy waters of the North Atlantic.

Sargent made his name as a portrait painter and is often remembered for coining the phrase 'a portrait is a picture of a person with something wrong with their mouth'; but here none of the women are close enough to visualise their faces, the one little girl even has her head obscured by a basket. The striking thing now, though perhaps not then, is that the tide is obviously going out, but far from these women heading to a twenty-first-century-style beach picnic, they are arriving to work. The sun is shining but they wear shawls, scarves and rough aprons with ragged edges that could have been torn from sheets. A society painter is painting the working class at work. Their formation is almost circular against a soft cloud and sand background, in outline suggestively of an oyster.

In other Cancale images, women are shown a few metres down the beach. The oysters are piled high, stacked in neat, wooden low pens. The women are bent over, gathering oysters into baskets. These small parks, like paddling pools, have been fixed in the sand so the oysters can be collected at low tide ready for market.

The people of Cancale symbolise a respected grit and toughness earned in the fearful fishing journeys the men would take to Newfoundland fishing for cod, leaving the town for months and passing on the oyster cultivation to the old men, women and children. As in other parts of Brittany, the rural poverty meant coastal fishing was a crucial part of their history and survival and was tended with care. They built special flat-bottomed boats to harvest the oysters. These boats had four huge sails, sometimes with as much as 300m² of canvas to grab the wind, called *bisquines*.

Cancale's oyster shells have been uncovered in Rome; Louis XIV ordered them sent to his palace daily; Napoleon took them on the long march to Moscow.

The enormous tides – 14m – that sweep the bay below Mont St Michel, on the other side of the promontory from St Malo, give the oysters from these beds their freshness and distinction.

The pre-history of this area is among the oldest in Europe. From northern France came the Veneti and their boats; from here came France's most famous cartoon character Asterix; and here lie the oldest Megalithic stones. To here the West Country Celts fled the persecution or cruel unsociability of Anglo-Saxons before the whole peninsula was engulfed in the totality of what is now France, which in a practical sense might only have been in modern times, say 100 years ago.

The Caravanne

Cancale was known for its oysters from a very early point. It was close enough to Paris to be able to sell its oysters there, delivered either via the sea and the Seine, or overland on big-wheeled open wagons drawn by four horses. In 1545 Francis I rewarded the town with the title of 'ville' in return for the privilege of supplying the royal court with oysters – a very Roman-style bit of patronage.

The oyster might have started life in Cancale, but would almost certainly have been transferred two or three times before going to market. Courseulles, north of Caen, was the distribution point and could send oysters to Paris in seven days, three if express, or forty hours from Dieppe. Boats down the Seine took too long and oysters at Cancale that cost 3 francs for 1,000, cost 9 francs at Courseulles and 35 francs in Paris. Prices were obviously from record rigidly set down.

Before 1700 there was no shortage of oysters, even though restrictions on mussel harvesting had been brought in twenty years earlier. By the middle of the century the French navy was sent to investigate the sudden death of oysters and laid down precise regulations to be implemented by

Côte d'Émeraude
1411. - CANCALE. - Le Départ de la Caravane - G. F.

The Cancale caravanne – so many boats arrived for the opening of the oyster beds that it became a tourist attraction to see them off.

local bailiffs. The French took a very centralist approach controlled by the navy. There was to be no fishing in the summer from 1 April to 15 October. The oyster fishermen themselves were to investigate and report back each year on which beds could be fished and which ones should be left, a decision to be made by a vote of all the fishermen. The most well-known legislation decreed that all the fishermen were to fish together and would leave port at a pre-arranged time, sometimes in a spectacular 'caravanne' of boats. These caravannes, at their height, saw nearly 3,000 men manning 400 boats.

By this husbanding the oyster harvest revived, and by the next century 33 million oysters were being caught each year; by 1847 this figure had reached 56 million from Cancale alone.

World Leader

France is a world-leading producer and consumer of oysters, especially at Christmas, although in the past other saints' days have been a major excuse too. It is the fourth largest producer in the world. Britain no longer features at all on this world table and any surplus is traded out through Holland to that greatest of consuming nations, Germany.

A fourteenth-century poet, Ausone from Bordeaux, classified oysters in terms of their quality – rating those from Bordeaux chauvinistically the best, ahead of those from Marseille and Calvados, then Brittany and Scotland, and lastly from Byzantium. So perhaps these trade routes were already well known at the time and had even continued through the Dark Ages.

Normandy produces a quarter of the French oyster harvest, which comes from the bay of Vers, the oldest beds at Saint Vaast la Hougue, the open sea at Cotentin, and the newer beds at Meuvaines-Asnelles.

North Brittany's coastline of teeth-like rocks, deep ravines, deeper estuaries and exposure to the rolling Atlantic has meant that through the centuries the Bretons have fostered their oysters carefully. To the north is Cancale, nestling behind St Malo which oversees its beds in the Bay of Mont St Michel, then the Bay of St Brieuc and round to Brest, Quimper, Quiberon and Morbihan – each one more exposed than the next to the pure Atlantic plankton that feed in the protected and sheltered bays where it is stable enough for an oyster to gain ground.

Further south the oysters are tended in the shallow, warmer waters at the mouth of the Loire, at the Bay of Bougneuf, and enclosed by the peninsular of Noirmoutier. Since 1992 they have been collectively marketed as oysters of Vendée-Atlantique.

From the Charente to the Gironde is an open oyster garden in the sea; at the heart is the Marennes-Oléron, known for its greenish hue, caused by single-celled algae which forms on the bottom of the oyster parks in spring and colours the waters. There is a fable that surrounds the alleged discovery of this algae:

When the port of La Rochelle was besieged – which would date the discovery to about 1627; D'Artagnan and the Three Musketeers also fought there – some oysters were stashed away in the salt marshes for safekeeping. When they were retrieved they had turned green. With some nervousness the locals eventually tried them, to find the flavour had become like 'liquid hazelnuts'.

Although the oysters turn green, the French call it *blueing*. The science was defined by the British zoologist Ray Lankester who identified the diatom that causes the change. They have replicated the change in colour in other bays but not the taste. Further south, at Arcachon, there is a similar effect, but these beds are now mainly used as a hatchery to supply the rest of France.

In the Mediterranean there are historic waters at Thau, where the Bouzigues oysters are grown on lines suspended near the surface of the water, which allows them to fatten faster than in the sea.

Gallic Love

One unromantic source of the oyster's continued reputation as an aphrodisiac may have been a series of advertising campaigns commissioned by the Normandy growers, invoking the apparent authority of the twelfth century. Oysters were *L'Epice d'Amour* – The Spice of Love. A series of posters advertised 'an unforgettable night of love with Normandy oysters' and 'have a really big night with Normandy oysters'.

The literary lover Casanova is invariably trotted out in support of the theory. Although he was Italian he spent long periods in Paris. Some of his dalliances read more like erotica than proof positive: 'I placed the shell on the edge of her lips and after a good deal of laughing, she sucked in the oyster, which she held between her lips. I instantly recovered it by placing my lips on hers.' Casanova claimed to eat fifty oysters for breakfast each day. His mistress would bring them to his bath and he ate them off her breasts.

The French poet Alain Merat in the 1900s spoke of: 'Oh, you who make love, you who we love.'

Alexandre Dumas (the father) wrote in his *Dictionary of Cuisine* that an oyster's 'only exercise was sleeping, its only pleasure eating'. Brillat-Savarin was more generic in his advice: 'In love, you know, all crustaceans get you going.'

French Gastronomy

The oyster takes its place in the pantheon of French gastronomy, but as Graham Robb points out in his *Discovery of France*, French provincial cooking was not of any repute until the last century, or until it got to Paris and was ennobled by the huge brigades of the kitchens of the royal households and exported as the cuisine of royalty across Europe.

Escoffier, writing in 1907, only offers a dozen or so preparations – against thirty or more for lobster – and none of them derive from the French provinces. His were typically extravagant: for example puff pastry canapés filled with caviar and topped with an oyster as a garnish. Lemon shrewdly goes with both. More recently, but from the same source, the *Larousse Gastronomique* rampantly pairs oysters with the gamut of French sauces as if they were any other kind of fish and their main purpose was to glorify the cook's true art of making sauces – Americaine (shellfish); Colbert (fried); Nantua (with crayfish); Normande (with mushrooms and cream); Florentine (with spinach); Mornay (with cheese); Polonaise (with horseradish) – and as a soufflé, gratinated, on skewers, in barquettes or in pastry cases. Of course oysters could be paired like that but it does not seem to be the best use of their attributes. Spinach is the most logical and usual accompaniment because of its supportive iron, and any variation on egg, butter and cream formed into an emulsion and cooked off in the shell under the grill has become a standard, modern culinary shorthand.

The big French restaurants have all been tempted to set down their own essay on how to best treat the oyster, although there are rarely hints of ancient links to regions or styles, just the luxury of truffles or, as with the Dutch masters' paintings before them, exotic spices.

Taillevant in Paris serves four oysters parcelled up in buttered foil with two sliced scallops, truffles, sliced leeks, a splash of mineral water, the juice from the oysters and salted butter. Bake for five minutes.

At Troisgros in Roanne oysters are served warm with sorrel and cumin. At Lucas Carton in Paris – a genuine centre of creativity under Alain Senderens, both in its original luxurious incarnation and more recently in its relative value-for-money approach – large Belon oysters are roasted in their sealed shells and served with a white butter sauce with nuts, toasts and Bellota-Bellota Spanish ham, plus a glass of Manzanilla sherry. Herein at least there is some homage to the Basques from around Arcachon, where oysters are served on the shell with little crépinette sausages, bread and the local white wine Entre Deux Mers.

At Michel Guerard's Eugenie Les Bains they are served freshly opened with a zest of ginger, coriander and a Chantilly of green (unroasted) coffee.

Paul Bocuse, the avuncular totem of la cuisine Française, manages to evoke both the classicism of a vichyssoise with the local slant of adding grated Gruyère at the end but retaining the complexity of texture with fried bread. There is more than a nod here to a Marseille-style fish soup, with its Gruyère, croutons and rouille. Lyons, of course, would have been able to pick any ingredient it wanted, trading north or south along the Rhône, so this variation may genuinely be a reflection of approaches long past:

Oyster Soupe Lyonnaise

Sweat three leeks in melted butter till soft, about seven minutes. Add four peeled and cubed russet potatoes, mix well, cover with six cups of water and simmer for 20 minutes. Set aside. Fry some cubed bread for croutons. Liquidise the soup. Add a cup of cream and a grating of nutmeg and return to the pan. Add a quart of shucked oysters and their liquor and poach till they curl. Lay the soup up in warm bowls, top with croutons, a sprinkle of

Gruyère, parsley and paprika. Serve with any additional croutons, cheese, and parsley on the side.

There are other recipes, not dissimilar, where the leek, a popular pairing, and potato are used as a sauce to serve in the shell, with the oysters laid back on top and grilled, though these do not seem as well thought out as the Bocuse soup. Bocuse's greatness as a chef is his awareness and sensitivity to each ingredient. Unlike Escoffier and Larousse, it is a recipe about technique adapted to the oyster, not the oyster subjugated to an unchanging repertoire of indolent luxury.

Olivier Roellinger at Maisons de Bricourt in Brittany works closer to the water than the others and is a part of the oyster culture, but sometimes he features this daring dish on the menu using curry spices for the seasoning, embellishing a teaspoon of basic curry powder, with coriander, powdered saffron, turmeric, all spice, cinnamon, dried green mango powder – just the sort of contents that might have spilled off a spice shipment smashed on the rocks off St Malo. Roellinger does, however, conservatively use less than a teaspoon to season his stock reduction:

Oysters with Cabbage
Boil half a litre of white wine to reduce its volume, add chicken stock and 2ml of the spice mix. Infuse for 20 minutes. Separate four prime cabbage leaves, poach and then refresh in cold water and set aside. Cut two squid into strips and sear briefly in a non-stick pan. Open the oysters and put the liquor in a pan separately. Heat the cabbage leaves in the oyster juice with some butter. Reheat the wine and stock infusion, bind it with more butter. Place a cabbage leaf in a warm shallow bowl. Slip the drained oysters into the buttered infusion, which should be warm not boiling. Arrange the oysters in each cabbage leaf. Coat with the infusion enriched with the oyster juices. Garnish with the salad burnett, nori and lamb's lettuce.

At the Mirabelle in London, Marco Pierre White refined his way with oysters in the same genre. Strictly speaking he is Anglo-Italian, but he cooks in the same Michelin style. When he first made his name at Harveys in Wandsworth he served poached oysters back in their shells on a small bundle of tagliatelle, garnished with cooked cucumber and caviar and sauced with a beurre blanc. It works like this (allow one or two per serving because it is quite rich):

Make a *beurre blanc* with shallots and vinegar, reduced. Add butter and lemon and leave to infuse. Dice cucumber like tagliatelle and blanch for one minute.

Set aside. Poach the oysters for one minute and set aside. Cook enough tagliatelle to allow for a forkful for each shell. Add a forkful to the shell, top with an oyster, and garnish with the cucumber strips. Spoon over the *beurre blanc*. Garnish with caviar.

On such things are reputations built. As amazing as that dish is, White then went on to top it in a way that rationalised the oyster for restaurant purposes at the Mirabelle. It is awesomely simple and refined:

The clean shell of the oyster is lined with blanched spinach, the oysters are poached lightly in Sauterne and gelatine and then set to cool in the shell, and served garnished with crème fraiche and caviar.

It is almost the best oyster recipe in the world.

Plate Collecting

Another side phenomenon accompanied the rise of the oyster in urban dining: plates designed just for oysters. All the great French and German companies produced specialised, highly decorative plates, usually with six indentations for the oysters and a seventh for lemon or a sauce, with slight variations depending on whether the oysters were to be served on ice, in the shell or shucked. Those for ice alone are the oldest, superseded by those with indentations because they were less messy, but also the rough shells scratched the delicate patterns and so these gave way to the small shapes, which could just take a single raw oyster out of the shell. Small two- and three-pronged forks were fashioned to bring the oyster into line with the new etiquette of the table. Originally, such things were made for aristocratic chateaux, but slowly the middle classes acquired the enthusiasm to have appropriate plates and cutlery.

Naturally the plates were decorated. Some of the most vibrant and rustic examples come from the oyster region of Quimper; more supremely elegant, often floral and pale-coloured are the ones from Limoges; and more modern powerful abstracts come from Provence, as in Vallauris. Artistic fish-inspired shapes hail from the German manufacturer Waechtersbach; glass examples from Lalique, and also some individual touches from Union Porcelain Works of Greenpoint, New York, appeared in the late 1800s.

In England Doulton made two differently patterned plates with flowers around 1900; one of their former workers, George Jones, made a colourful set with large replica shells around the outside, centred on a small egg cup divot in the centre for the condiment; and the smaller, later manufacturer Samuel Lear produced a Portuguese-inspired sunflower design.

Herbert Minton first introduced his vibrant, lustrously glazed majolica at London's Crystal Palace Exhibition in 1851. This made oyster plates affordable to the Victorian middle classes, whereas before porcelain and other fine china had been the concern only of royalty and the grandest houses. Minton's oyster plate design, however, was borrowed from Sevres in France.

The oyster plate still has its loyal devotees: there is an oyster society that collects plates; there was an online museum at oysterplate.com, but this seems to have fallen by the wayside; the auction site Ebay lists daily sales – more than six pages at the last look, with 260 plates for trade. Some plates fetch prices upwards of $3,000, though most go for a fraction of that. New designs can still sell for £175. And, of course, there are essential books for enthusiasts, such as *Collecting Oyster Plates* by Jeffrey Snyder or the rival *Oyster Plates* by Jim and Vivian Karsnitz.

Predictably with oysters, even in the sedate world of plate-making controversy stalks, in this case in the validity or otherwise of reproducing old designs. Collectors are appalled.

The Enthusiastic Victor Coste

The effects of over-fishing in France were more immediate than in Britain, but while in England the crisis was met with helpless chaos, the French responded systematically and vigorously.

Their oyster beds were a precious national asset. And their laws were different. Where the freedom of the individual, which the barons had laid down in the Magna Carta, had somehow managed to impose itself, by association, on the creeks and estuaries in England, the French had no such qualms. Francis I in 1544 and then Henri III in 1584 asserted the royal prerogative to own and farm the oyster beds in the national interest and had even dismantled private fishing, which is why, in the Cancale example, it was the Admiralty that was called in to look at the state of the beds when the harvests started to decline. The Gallic presumption was that the state owned the bounty of the shorelines and would administer them as it saw fit. For the oyster, that meant for the benefit of the people; just as Colne in Essex had also supposed.

In 1840 the navy had to be called in to patrol the beds around Arcachon to protect the oysters from poachers. The French were spurred into collective action. The brilliant embryologist Victor Coste, or to give him his full name Jean Jaques Marie Cyprien Victor Coste, had seen the cultivation techniques still being used in the Bay of Naples at Lago Fusaro from the Roman times. It had been revived some 100 years before when King Ferdinand IV of Bourbon introduced a park for mussels and then oysters 'that were gathered from the pots, reeds, faggots, palisades and from the bottom of the Lake'. That was 1764.

The enthusiastic Coste asked Napoleon III for 8,000 francs to restock the Bay of St Brieuc, west of St Malo. He would import oysters into the bay, pay for a boat to guard them and then, following the Italian example, he would lay up stones, faggots and other collectors, so that when the oysters spawned, the young would have something on which to attach themselves; and the fishermen would also have something on which to lavish their attentions. A year later, in 1859, an elated Coste reported to Napoleon that the experiment had been a magnificent success. As evidence he quoted one single faggot carrying more than 20,000 spat. He recommended that the whole French coastline, and even the colonies of Corsica and Algeria, follow his lead, except where the shoreline was too muddy. Napoleon, enterprisingly, acceded.

There was a second breakthrough at about the same time, this one credited to a stonemason called M. Boeuf at the Ile de Ré, near La Rochelle. Not being a confidant of Napoleon, his first name, or names, have been lost, but his contribution might be seen as important. He noticed that in muddy waters oysters would cling to stone sea walls. He reclaimed low-tidal muddy flats by building small stone walls into small parks and laying the bottom with stones. This worked too. No longer dependent on the vagaries of the wild, the French realised they could bring in oysters from around Europe as spat and grow them in their beds and specially created parks. Soon they were importing so much spat that they had depleted nearly all the seed stock from Spain: 20 million oysters harvested in 1860 became an astonishing 350 million by 1907.

This approach was used for the nation's most famous oyster: the Belon. Again it was Coste who had the vision. The Belon comes from the Aven-Belon River, although the name is not so historic as it likes to claim and is often misused. This is not a nursery or even a growing area, but the plankton-rich waters are where oysters are taken to be finished before going to market, and will be at least three years old; some just get a quick bath and then back into the lorry, while others – *speciales* – are left for months.

Coste takes the credit for seeing that the richness of iron and the mix of sea and clear waters would make Belon an ideal environment for oyster culture, and persuaded one August Constant Solminihac to move his family from the Perigourd to plant the region in 1864, taking his first spat

1 *Girl with a Pearl Earring, c.* 1665–6 by Johannes Vermeer.

2 Henry VIII liked to show off his pearls in his hat and necklace.

3 Anne Boleyn was a fashion leader in court – the gold B pendant was draped with more pearls.

Left: 4 Henrietta Maria sold her pearls to pay for Charles I's civil war.

Below: 5 This maharajah was Subador or Arcot under the Nizam of Hyderabad, *c.* 1750.

Above: 6 *Still life with oysters, sweetmeats and roasted chestnuts* by Osias the Elder Beert, 1570–1624 (oil on panel).

Left: 7 *Still Life with a glass and oysters* by Jan Davidsz de Heem, 1640.

Opposite above:
8 *Still Life with oysters* by Francois Ykens, 1601–1693. Ykens studied under Osias Beert who married his sister. *Private Collection / Photo © Bonhams, London, UK / The Bridgeman Art Library*

Opposite below:
9 *Still life with wine goblet and oysters* by Pieter Claesz, 1630s.

13 *Fishing for oysters in Cancale* by John Singer Sargent, 1878.

14 *The Birth of Venus* by Sandro Botticelli, 1486. Botticelli was supposedly so enamoured of the married noblewoman Simonetta Vespucci, who posed for him, that he never married. Obviously the painting is not of an oyster though …

from Belgium. Later, Coste was to revive the bays at Toulon and Brest with oysters imported from England. Solminihac perceptively saw that there was no need to be a grower at all when the oysters could be spawned and grown elsewhere, and then be fattened and marketed from his river waters. His family still trade as Huitres du Chateau Belon. Four other companies now operate the concessions: Thaëron, Cadoret, Noblet and Thieblemont, and they seek to enforce strict labelling and control of the name by registering stocks and recording how long they have been kept in the Belon waters. Belon is perhaps now the most elite and coveted oyster in the world.

Coste's bureaucracy, however, was intense: inspections followed the Cancale model; summer fishing was still banned; concessions were awarded to naval conscripts; national service had been introduced as an alternative to press ganging; and an oyster concession became one of the pensions to the job. Often these were generous stipends, with grants being awarded to retired sailors in terms of free spat, free stock, free tiles and other essentials for a would-be oysterman. From Napoleon's point of view it was a deliberate exercise in social engineering. He wanted oysters to feed the poor and he wanted profitable work for his former sailors.

Coste's approach was not an immediate success but it did revive both the Quiberon and the Arcachon, the latter only after decades of the strictest enforcement policies, where in some years harvesting was only allowed by hand for one hour a year, which did not stop as many as 5,000 gatherers turning up for that single hour. But in the year of Coste's death, in 1877, these beds suddenly revived dramatically. In 1880 195 million oysters were taken. The number of concessions to ex-sailors rose from 483 to 4,239.

The Miracle of the Morlaisen

The French also had one enormous slice of luck. Small numbers of the Portuguese oyster crassostrea had been transplanted successfully from the River Tagus, which had been known as a rich source of oysters and other fish from Roman times. Then in 1868 the *Morlaisen*, carrying Portuguese oysters from Setubal bound for England, hit a tempest off Arcachon and sought shelter at Bordeaux. The oysters started to smell and the captain, Patoizeau, ordered them to be dumped near Verdon at the very tip of the Pointe du Médoc. Far from being dead, the oysters took to the waters immediately and flourished. Within a few years the whole Gironde was once again thriving as an oyster centre.

There is some argument over the precise numbers, but by 1910, when England was in serious decline, the harvest there was around 25 million oysters, compared to 500 million from the revived French beds.

Even after the abandonment of conscription and national service in 1983, the French maintained the deeply Gallic and Napoleonic philosophy of only awarding concessions to new oyster beds on strict criteria, which included: how many children an applicant might have under 16; how many years they had been in the navy or at sea; and, more recently, demanding educational diplomas for which there is now a three-year degree course. Their ingenuity and decisiveness has been needed to combat new threats besides over-fishing.

The science, however, came from the New World.

PART III

New World

*The earliest pottery yet found in the Western Hemisphere has been
excavated from a prehistoric shell midden near Santarém in the lower
Amazon, Brazil. Calibrated accelerator radiocarbon dates on charcoal, shell,
and pottery and a thermoluminescence date on pottery from the site fall
from about 8000 to 7000 years before the present. The early fishing village
is part of a long prehistoric trajectory that contradicts theories that resource
poverty limited cultural evolution in the tropics.*

Roosvely, Housey, Silveira, Maranca & Johnson, *Science Magazine*, 1991

*The prehistoric mounds in the Mississippi Valley present evidence of the
estimation in which pearls were held by a race of men who passed away
ages before America was first visited by Europeans. In some of these
mounds, erected by a long-forgotten race, pearls have been found not only
in hundreds and in thousands, but by gallons, even by bushels. Some of
these equal three quarters of an inch in diameter, and in quantity exceed the
richest collections of the present day.*

George Frederick Kunz, *The Book of the Pearl*, 1908

8

The First Americans

Admiral Columbus' Curious Lack of Curiosity – The Pearl Coasts –
A Cruel Winter in La Croix – The Island of Shells –
First contact: Durst Not Trust Them – How the Indians Sold New York –
A Pair of Stockings & Two Hoes – Shinnecocks & Blue Points –
Corn, Gruel & Biscuits – Settlement – Red Lights & Restaurants –
A Small Pearl Bonanza – Narragansetts & Lynnhavens – The First Toothpicks

There were men afoot in the Americas while the Old World was still Biblical. On Sapelo Island, Georgia, Mississippi men lived in shell fortresses around 4,000 BC. Four-metre-high walls of piled-up oyster shells survive. Radiocarbon dating has found traces of what these people ate: clams and conch mussels. Catfish and mullet must have been netted; deer, racoon, dog and possum hunted. At its widest this shell midden is 100m across. The inside has been swept clear. There have been finds of pottery, hearths and bone pins, all of which confirm domestic use. This pre-dates the building of the pyramids in Egypt. Nearby at Kenan Field are the remains of a 158-acre Indian village occupied much later, between AD 1000 and AD 1600.

The Sapelo rings provided real protection from marauding enemies wielding hand-held weapons. The walls were not just high; they would have been sharp to bare or moccasined feet, noisy for any attacker to scale and unstable to fight on.

The Timucua Indians held sway in this part of southern Georgia and into Florida when the Europeans arrived in the early sixteenth century. The French settled near Jackson, Florida, and described similar round fortifications to those built in 4,000 BC. The Sapelo rings support the idea that these were not hunter-gatherers at all, but a people who had settled and chosen a notably rich estuary which could well have supported most of their needs. They grew corn, beans, pumpkins, vegetables and hunted alligators. Meat was cooked over a wooden rack which many centuries later was called a *barbacoa*, from which the word barbecue derives.

In 1539 the Spanish conquistador Hernando de Soto ransacked a temple at Cofachiqui la Talomeco and looted wooden statues inlaid with pearls, large numbers of loose pearls, deerskins, dyed cloth and ornately worked copper artefacts. Garcilaso de la Vega, who used de Soto's own accounts, wrote later that Talomeco had about 500 houses and a funerary temple over 100 paces long and 40 wide. Its walls and high-pitched roof were covered with woven cane mats decorated with seashells and strands of pearls – the 'richest and most superb of all those that our Spaniards saw in La Florida'.

The Georgia shell middens are far from alone. The east coast of America is lined with similar ancient finds as far north as Maine. The east side of the Damariscotta River contained an enormous shell heap named Whaleback. Much of this was removed in the late 1880s to be processed into chicken feed. It is dated beyond 1,000 BC. The area is now a national park.

Early explorers in the south reported finding massive quantities of free-standing pearls by the 'bushel' and by the 'gallon'. Some of these caches amounted in a single grave to more pearls than were owned by a royal house in Europe. These were so old and damaged that they were of interest more to archaeologists than jewellers, but the quantity was notable. Along with other artefacts in these graves, sometimes the pearls were gruesomely placed inside the body, which had been skinned and reformed to house its treasure.

A well at St Augustine, between Daytona and Jacksonville on Florida's east coast, threw up another clue, implying that links between North and South America were perhaps much earlier than previously thought. In among the debris of oyster and clam shells, and other suggestions of street cafe debris, was a slender wooden stick with a carved knob on one end – a *molinillo*, an early chocolate whisk from the 1500s. It is possible it would have been brought north by a Spanish trader; equally it is a plausible link between Florida and the Mayans and Aztecs before any white man trod this way. Cacao seed was used as currency by the Indians. It came from the Amazon rainforest.

Admiral Columbus' Curious Lack of Curiosity

Entering the Gulf of Paria, between modern-day Trinidad and the east coast of Venezuela, Christopher Columbus was met by canoes of 'countless numbers wearing pieces of gold on the breasts, and some with bracelets of pearls on their arms. Seeing this I was much delighted.' And well he might have been.

Like Moses, he may have seen the Promised Land, but he never personally uncovered the extraordinary wealth that followed. He became obsessed with gold, but it was pearls he had promised his sponsors, Ferdinand and Isabella of Spain, and it was pearls that proved historically pivotal. What he had really found, though he never knew it, were the riches on which the Catholic Church and Spain was to hold sway over Europe for a century and more, and would lead to a transatlantic slave trade lasting 400 years.

Columbus had promised that he would find 'Pearls, precious stones, gold, silver, spiceries' in that order, but as Kirkpatrick Sale's brilliant account of his travels notes, he did not take with him anyone who knew the difference between 'gold and pyrite or pearl from chrysoberyl'. Or anyone to record the new botany he encountered. He even falsified his own astronomical readings of the stars, on which he prided himself, for fear of anyone else finding his route.

Kirkpatrick says the Indians Columbus met were the Taino, so named after their word for 'good', who had come up to the West Indies from further south. He was writing in 1990 and archaeology has been moving quickly since then and has linked the Taino to the Georgia tribes, and further south into the Amazon basin. The Taino also moved around in dug-out log canoes, settled in small numbers just inland and moved swiftly and easily around the coasts in what, for most of the year, would have been calm waters.

The impression from Columbus' own writings was not of brilliant discovery but of starvation, disease and a God-given right to overlord these people so he could deliver them up to his God, if necessary in chains. Slavery was not his intention but it ended up being a means of paying for his exploits. It was as if the very act of discovery exhausted or terrified him. Unlike the conquistadors that would follow him, he demonstrated neither bloodlust nor overt religious zeal, and regarded himself above amassing his own fortune. For him, his discovery was his fortune, although, as he was to find back in Spain, like many others who would follow, promises on paper are not always sacrosanct. His legacy is mythically enshrined in history but others would profit. Perhaps he was just disappointed to encounter some wild natives and not some emperor of the Indies, who might in one meeting have empowered a new era of west to east trade. If that was his mission, he barely mentions what he might have done had he met such an empire.

On his first voyage he met Indians at the Bay of Barlay, Cuba: 'The Indians said there were gold fields and pearls in the island and the Admiral saw this was a likely place for pearls since there were mussels, which are a sign of them.' In the biography written later by his illegitimate son, Hernando Colon, *Life of the Admiral*, based on Columbus' own, now lost journals, he declares: 'I tried hard to discover where they found these pearls. They told me they found them there and in the northern part of the country.' And then a few days later, with another group of Indians: 'I also asked them where they had got their pearls, and they again pointed to the west and to the north, to show that it was beyond their country.'

In exasperation he named the bay Golfo de las Perlas – he was a great namer of things, as if christening each cove would in some way be a reassurance to his patrons at home, a cartographic vision that was easier to deliver to sceptical backers. He was wide of the mark. The real treasure lay at the very western tip of the Gulf of Paria, which he sailed right past in his haste.

Colon reported much later, on the third expedition of 1498:

> On Wednesday 15th August, he left Cabo de la Conchas and Margaritas Island to the west, I do not know whether God inspired him to give the island this name on account of its nearness to that of Cubagua from which a vast quantity of pearls (or margaritas) have since been brought. For, in a similar way, after he had left Jamaica he named certain mountains in Hispaniola the Golden Range, and soon afterwards the greatest quantity of gold ever brought to Spain was discovered in them.

Columbus was aloof, unwell for long periods and amazed but seemingly uninterested by the botany he found. It was about survival. Those natives he met, he treated as chattels. He wrote in parallel of wanting to show kindness to the natives so that they might come to him and thereby to God, but by his third visit he also records how 160 Spanish had contracted syphilis – or given it to each other as well as the natives and the New World.

This passage Kirkpatrick records as the 'first account of sexual intercourse between the two cultures', from an Italian knight Cuneo at Santa Cruz:

> While I was on the boat I captured a very beautiful Carib woman whom the said Lord Admiral gave to me (!) and with whom having taken her into my cabin, she being naked according to their custom, I conceived desire

to take pleasure. I wanted to put my desire into execution but she did not want it and treated me with her finger nails in such a manner that I had never begun. But seeing that (to tell you the end of it all) I took a rope and thrashed her well, for which she raised such unheard of screams that you would not have believed your ears. Finally we came to an agreement in such a manner that I can tell you that she seemed to have been brought up in a school of harlots.

The Pearl Coasts

The dream of drifting downwards through strange waters, of plunging towards a green sea-dusk, sliding past the scaly, savage-eyed protectors of a ship's hulk that loomed ahead, a Spanish galleon ... a drowned cargo of diamonds and pearls.

Truman Capote, *In Cold Blood*, 1966

It was left to one of Columbus' pilots, Peralonso Nino, to sail back out of the most westerly port at Baiona a year later with thirty-three of Columbus' former crew in the *Santa Maria*. He uncovered the Pearl Coast along Margarita Island – Cubagua Island, Coche Island and the Peninsula de Araya. Nino traded bells, pins, bracelets, strings of crystal and rings for the pearls. In 1500 he returned to Spain with 44kg of pearls. It was the first profitable commercial venture into the New World. Nino's reward was to be accused of swindling the Spanish Crown of its share and he died destitute waiting for trial five years later.

King Ferdinand ordered a permanent settlement to be set up at Cubagua Island. For decades the New World was known only in southern Europe as a source of pearls to the European aristocracy.

The cruelty with which the Spanish strove to satisfy their masters' vanity was acute. Modern-day slavery began here; an overt European export to the New World that would set a standard of dealing with native peoples that would be repeated many times over on much larger scales in the coming centuries, to greater and lesser degrees of barbarity, especially along this coast. By all accounts these first settlers were notably indolent and lazy, so a trade where they just had to lord it over others to do their bidding suited their selfish arrogance.

The Spaniards forced the Indians to dive for oysters until they were exhausted and had to be replaced with more slaves from Venezuela and the Bahamas. The Taino from the Bahamas were considered to be the best harvesters because they already dived for queen conchs, *Strombus gigas*, one of their staple foods. When the Venezuelan Indians rebelled, the Spanish returned with 1,000 men and created the first Spanish town in South America and the New World: Nueva Cadiz. It survived barely more than a decade before it was destroyed in a hurricane. By that time, so rapaciously had the beds been harvested that it was not deemed worth rebuilding.

On paper the Spanish seemed reasonable, caring employers. There were edicts that said divers should only work in the summer when the waters were warm; that they should only dive for four hours a day; that workers should be properly fed; and that they should be allowed to sleep in hammocks off the ground, away from insects. The monk, Bartholomew de Las Casas, recorded that the divers had no such luxuries. They were forced to dive endlessly without respite, even when exhausted. They were badly fed and made to sleep on the ground. The average life expectancy of a diver working for the Spanish was less than a year.

More natural pearls were harvested in Venezuela and Colombia at this time than anywhere else over any comparable period of time, before or since. Between 1513 and 1530 they traded 118 million pearls, all of which were shipped back to Seville, where the same Garcilaso de la Vega wrote that pearls were so abundant 'they were sold in a heap in the India House … just as if they were some kind of seed'.

The Royal Treasury kept 20 per cent of the pearl harvest for itself. Ships would bring back caches weighing as much as 350kg at a time. For 100 years the ships sailing from Margarita Island were the source of the most prized treasure in the world – until the beds were finally exhausted, ruined and abandoned.

Panama was also a wealthy source of oysters and pearls, some as big as 'nutmegs' and 'like filberts'. When Cortez discovered Mexico around 1522, he found tribal chiefs living in primitive huts along the shore with quantities of pearls just lying 'carelessly' about. The natives said the fishery had been active for centuries.

Unlike the Venezuelan oysters, whose shells were too thin to have a value and were discarded, those found so abundantly in the Gulf of Panama became more valuable in time as mother-of-pearl. Some of this harvest survives and still decorates the cathedrals of Seville and Toledo.

These waters yielded much of the imperial Spanish jewellery, the most prominent of which was the Huerfana pearl. Gomara says this was secured in 1515 from the Indians at Tararequi, in the Gulf of Panama, in a large collection which weighed 880oz.

It was pear-shaped and weighed 31 carats. The merchant was so frightened of having invested so much money in a pearl that he sold it the next day to Pedrarias de Avila for his wife Donna Isabel de Bovadilla; afterward it passed to Isabella, wife of Emperor Charles V (1500–56).

In *Historia Natural y General de las Indias*, published in Toledo in 1526, Gonzalo de Oviedo wrote of having bought at Panama a pearl weighing 26 carats, for which he paid 650 times its weight in fine gold, and which he claimed was the 'greatest, fairest and roundest' ever seen in Panama. In 1620 Francois Gogibus, a native of Calais, sold a pearl from the West Indies to Philip IV of Spain. It was mounted as a button in the royal cap.

A Cruel Winter in La Croix

Explorers to the north were met with vast bays of oysters. These oysters sustained the first colonisation of north-east America and Canada and their habitats would evolve into the great eastern cities of New York, Boston, Quebec and Montreal. The cold winters posed an obstacle, however, which probably explains why the north was not attempted seriously for another century.

The American Library of Congress has a map drawn on vellum, by the French navigator Samuel de Champlain, among its most fundamental landmark references. Champlain first sailed to the West Indies in 1599 looking for a trade passage through to the east. He sailed again from Normandy, on 7 April 1604, this time landing at the mouth of the St Lawrence River. The voyage took seven weeks.

The French king, Henri IV, wanted new trading posts for the New World before the Spanish and the English. He licensed one of his courtiers, Pierre Dugua Sieur de Mons, to lead the expedition. Not just a nobleman, de Mons was a businessman looking to bring back the fashionable pelts of beavers and other furs to the courtly world of Versailles and the new Paris that Henri was busy building at home. There had been earlier fishing missions in which they stayed for the summer and left. This was a venture funded by empire, and the ambition would come later. The French had already penetrated the St Lawrence River with Jacques Cartier in 1534 and two subsequent expeditions. Cartier was a sailor from St Malo who had established a settlement – archaeology proved in 2006 – in Quebec, so the French would have known what short-term booty there was. And Cartier had certainly hit landfall at the oyster-rich Prince Edward Island, at the mouth of the St

Lawrence, which he named after the saint who was entrusted with the Holy Chalice. Cartier's false gold had become a catchword in France when he brought back minerals that he thought were gold and diamonds but proved to be quartz and pyrites – *faux comme les diamands de Canada*. But Cartier had made more meaningful contact than Columbus further south. He found an effective cure for scurvy from the Indians using the sap from the Thuja fir. He inadvertently christened Canada from the Huron-Iroquois word *Kanata*, meaning village.

Champlain's party chose to settle for the winter at St Croix Island (now Maine); a national monument, both for America and Canada, as the site of the first European settlement of the continent. They found the small island on a warm June day. It looked hospitable, safe and commanded the river on either side. They could set their cannon and defend the land from any incoming ships; they could demand rights of passage. The clement summer weather was illusory; the warm waters of the Gulf Stream veered east, bypassing St Croix, a fact they could not have known. A vicious winter was to follow.

Their food supplies froze. Ice flows cut them off from the mainland. Even though they had planned meticulously and chosen a site that was on the same latitude as their native France, the houses they had built were scant protection from the elements. Soon they had cut all the trees on the island for firewood. Then they were struck down by a disease they called land sickness. It was scurvy. They frothed at the mouth; their throats were so swollen they could hardly eat; their gums bled; their teeth fell out; and their arms and legs began to swell to the point that they could barely move about. Thirty-five of the pioneering party of seventy-nine died. Those that survived gratefully decamped across the waters to Port Royal – today Annapolis, Novia Scotia – itself a great oyster resource.

Through all this Champlain kept a log. He also drew vividly accurate maps of the areas he visited. Where the others were bound for trade, Champlain was a career explorer inspired by the great sea-faring empires of Venice, Rome and Alexandria. In his quest to uncover the New World he sailed as far south as Cape Cod, charting the coastal waters of the new America. And it is this map that resides in the Congress Library.

In 1608 Champlain marked out another bay and remarked also on the succulence of the oysters at Isle Saint Jean in the Gulf of Saint Lawrence. Today that island is known as Prince Edward Island, home of the Malpeque oyster. It was no coincidence that they should have chosen these coves, and it is very likely that the sailors themselves knew about oysters from their homes in France.

When Champlain reached the area we now know as Wellfleet, he marked it down simply and deliberately as Port Aux Huitres – Oyster Port. Unlike Columbus, he was correct in his nomenclature.

It was another forty years before other settlers returned to that bay, encouraged by the huge wealth of fish in the harbour. This time they were English, armed with a grant from the Court of New Plymouth signed by Charles I, and in total disregard of Dutch claims to the area. The fish were so plentiful they christened it Billingsgate after the London fish market. They then called their villages Truro, Falmouth, East Falmouth, North Falmouth, Sandwich, Chatham, Barnstaple and Hatches Creek. The settlers would all have been from the south and west of England so, by chance, many of them would have known about oysters. They took the name Wellfleet from the Essex oyster of the time, hoping its cachet might help build the reputation of their own fishing.

The Island of Shells

In any part of the world it is inevitable that a given food can become important for a period of time, depending on climate, geography, commerce and culture – beef in England, pickled fish in Scandinavia, chilli in Thailand, lamb in New Zealand, etc. But in a historical context these are short-lived, quite recent epochs. In and around what is now the sprawling New York metropolis and state, the oyster is American history. The original farm tracks to Queens were literally paved by oyster shells. The Manhattan skyline is cemented into the ancient oyster beds of Long Island, the very fabric of the city built with the ground-up shells of oysters as lime in that same cement.

Names like the Long Island Sound – in native Sewanahaka meaning Island of Shells – Barnstaple, Martha's Vineyard, Mountauk, Wellfleet, Falmouth and Blue Point have as much resonance with our own oyster history as they do with native Indian history. The local Sheenecock, which is also an Indian tribe, and later the Blue Point, are among the most celebrated of all oysters.

The huge mounds of shell middens, often acres wide, lie as testimony to generations of native Indians who used the oyster as food and decoration and traded them along with the clams that grew in the same coves as money or wampum. This was a skilled and laborious process for a people without metal. When the Dutch arrived in the Hudson River they quickly set up a currency using their iron drills to make wampum in factory prisons, relating it to the guilder and setting the price for fur pelts to be traded back to Europe. Within a few years they had all the local currency they needed.

The tourist guide *Touring Gotham's Archaeological Past* points out that Liberty Island, before becoming the home of the Statue of Liberty, was Oyster Island. The Dutch christened it Great Oyster Island, and Ellis Island was Little Oyster Island. When they sailed into the Hudson River there were more than 350 miles of navigable oyster beds, the greatest resource the world had ever and would ever see. New York's love affair with the oyster is vibrant and long-standing. Their stories wrap around each other like two twines of the same rope. The American Way, or the New York Way, was forged among the oystermen on Long Island. This was the first base of hard trading for boxes, for boats, for bushels. This was Wall Street at its most base. Nowhere else can say that the oyster was so fundamental to its upbringing. So much of the combustion that created this great city might be the oyster.

The squabbling for ownership of such oyster coves foretold the fate of the Native Americans across the continent. Like the immigrant and the American Indian, the oyster too has been prone to sudden, violent and fatal diseases. In some cases the oyster was totally displaced and became part of a great oyster mass elsewhere; and in the same way that Indian tribes have been redefining their history and reforming old family ties in the twenty-first century, so the oyster has begun to re-establish itself according to the quality of the waters of each new cove in which it is settled.

The oyster beds offered a safe and easy resource of food, which is why the first settlers chose those coves and displaced the Native Americans. That oysters encircled Manhattan, and the sites of the other great north-eastern conurbations, meant that new settlers who may have sailed for gold or God found that their beacon, when they arrived, was in a very practical sense the oyster.

It seems beautifully emblematic of both the city and the oyster that the shellfish itself could become as fashionable as some of the resorts that would later evolve out of its habitats; and equally wonderfully egalitarian, that at the turn of the twentieth century the oyster was both chic enough for grand hotels while at the same time sustaining the lowly street workers who built the city.

First Contact: Durst Not Trust Them

Long Island was home to thirteen different American Indian tribes, most of which lived by or near the shore. They travelled and traded by canoe;

they went inland to hunt for game; they cleared and planted the banks and meadows with corn. Each tribe seemingly knew its territory even if it was nomadic within it.

The first settlers guessed at the size of the native population by the frequent and substantial piles of oyster middens and clam shells found abandoned at coves.

A dramatic account survives of the actual discovery of New York by Henry Hudson in 1609, when he tentatively sailed in to land with a crew that was half-Dutch and half-English. His progress was blocked by a huge oyster reef. His mate, Robert Juet, kept a diary. On 3 September he records: 'At three o'clock in the afternoon, we came to three great rivers. So we stood along the northernmost, thinking to have gone into it, but we found it to have a very shoal bar [sic] before it, for we had but 10 foot water.'

The next day he wrote: 'Then our boat went on land with our net to fish, and caught ten great mullets, of a foot and a half long a piece, and a ray as great as four men could haul into the ship.'

And then, of his first encounter with American Indians: 'At night the wind blew hard at the north-west, and our anchor came home, and we drove on shore, but took no hurt, thanked be God, for the ground is soft sand and ooze. This day the people of the country came aboard of us, seeming very glad of our coming, and brought green tobacco, and gave us of it for knives and beads.'

The day after:

> Our men went on land there, and saw great store of men, women and children, who gave them tobacco at their coming on land. So they went up into the woods, and saw great store of very goodly oaks, and some currants. For one of them came aboard and brought some dried, and gave me some, which were sweet and good. This day many of the people came aboard, some in mantles of feathers, and some in skins of divers sorts of good furs. Some women also came to us with hemp. They had red copper tobacco pipes, and other things of copper they did wear about their necks. At night they went on land again, so we rode very quiet, but durst not trust them.

'Durst not trust them' sounds a fitting epitaph to the opening salvos between settler and Indian, if relationships were not fraught enough between white and brown, peasant and landed, big ship and canoe, pagan and Christian, etc. Plus the tribes themselves had their own political rivalries and agendas, so we have an American quilt made up of little patches of different coloured acrimonies.

By 1641 the English immigrants were already deeply wary of any Indian presence. Southampton settlers passed ordinance prohibiting the sale of 'guns, pistols, or any other instrument of wars' to the natives. It had taken less than thirty years to sow mistrust and fear. In that short time the first Indian nation, the Pequots, had already been decimated.

How the Indians Sold New York

The Montauk sachem of all Long Island, Chief Wyandanch, sold Gardiner's Island, Suffolk County, New York, to one Lyon Gardiner in 1639. The Gardiner family's descendants still hold that right to the land and live nearby, as do a few descendants of Wyandanch himself. The two struck up an unlikely but seemingly genuine friendship, although it was based on a bloody mutual interest and eventually the sachem would die as a result of it — poisoned by a political rival. Wyandanch was perhaps modern America's first tragic hero.

The Montauk had the respect and status of bankers to the other tribes, using the shell from the estuary to make wampum to trade. The oyster beds at Montauk were their mint.

The Pequot were known as the enforcers. The word in the shared Algonquin dialect means destroyers. They terrorised other tribes, including the Montauk. When the Dutch started trading furs around 1615, the Pequot demanded a monopoly and sent out raiding parties to steal furs and wampum and demand allegiance and ransom from the other tribes.

In a letter dated 1637, one Roger Williams wrote:

> The Pequots are scarce of provision and therefore (as usual, so now especially) they are in some numbers come down to the seaside (and to islands by name Munnawtawkit and Manattuwond especially) to take sturgeon and other fish, as also to make new fields of corn in case the English should destroy their fields at home.

A visit from the Pequots was something to be feared. There is a good feel for the realities of early life in the notes Gardiner left. When he was ordered to go to war with the Pequot Indians he wrote back:

> It is all very well for you to make war who are safe in Massachusetts Bay, but for myself and these few with me who have scarce holes to put our heads in, you will leave at the stake to be roasted. I have but twenty-four in all,

men, women and children, and not food for them for two months, unless we
save our corn field which is two miles from home, and cannot possibly be
reached if we are in war.

He kept his family and men inside the ramparts. Forays outside the walls to
get food were dangerous. Two of his men had been caught by the Pequots:
one was burned at a stake, and the other skinned alive.

Gardiner was ambushed with ten armed men and three dogs by Pequot
Indians dressed in the clothes of other murdered settlers. The group fought
'with our naked swords or else they (would have) taken us all alive'. A day
or two later, he recorded: 'I was shot with many arrows … but my buff
coat preserved me, only one hurt me.'

Gardiner was given eighty soldiers to defend the fort. He formed a
pact with the Mohegan Indians and they raided the Pequot settlements
at Mystic, slaughtering everyone by setting fire to the stockade. Gardiner
estimated that 300 died in the flames for the 'glory of God and honour of
our nation'. It became a war of attrition. The English hunted the Pequots
almost to extinction. They sold the men into slavery with other tribes
but demanded a tax on each one in return; eventually they sent the last
survivors into slavery in Bermuda. Recently, a Pequot society has been
revived and now has more than 1,000 members.

After the massacre, Gardiner had a visit from the chief, Wyandanch, who
spelt his name out in the sand as Waiandance. 'He came to know if we
were angry with all Indians. I answered "No, but only with such as had
killed Englishmen." He asked whether they that lived upon Long Island
might come to trade with us?' Gardiner said he would only trade with the
Long Island Indians, 'If you will kill all the Pequots that come to you, and
send me their heads … so he went away and did as I had said, and sent me
five heads.'

Gardiner is invariably portrayed as an enlightened man, a soldier who
was charged to set up a British fort in the area; a moderate of his time.
He used his newfound sway with the Indians to buy 31,000 acres of the
East Hamptons, spanning the present Southampton's eastern border to the
western edge of Napeague. He paid 20 coats, 24 hatchets, hoes, knives,
looking glasses and 100 muxes (a form of drill used for making wampum).
The Montauks were left with only legal rights to fish and hunt. In just
twenty-three years Wyandanch sold, bartered or had given in tribute
nearly 60,000 acres of eastern Long Island to the English settlers. When,
in 1909, their descendants petitioned the New York State courts for the
return of their lands, the judge ruled that the tribe itself was now extinct

and so there could be no rights or ownership vested in it. Survivors were just like any and every other American – they had no tenure.

Another notorious figure in the Pequot wars was John Underhill, who is sometimes credited with single-handedly destroying any friendly relations that might have existed between settlers and natives. An irreligious privateer, he had sailed from Plymouth in the 1630s and fought at Mystic, claiming to have killed not 300 Pequots but 1,000. The mopping-up operations may have gone on for months. Some New York Indians might have believed they could co-exist with the new settlers, but Underhill embarked on a series of atrocities around Long Island. The Oyster Bay historian Samuel Jones wrote of one:

> After the battle of Ft. Neck, the weather being very cold and the wind northwest, Capt. Underhill and his men collected the bodies of the Indians and threw them in a heap on the brow of the hill, and then sat down on the leeward side of the heap to eat their breakfast. When this part of the county came to be settled, the highway across the neck passed directly over the spot where, it was said, the heap of Indians lay, and the earth in that spot was remarkably different from the ground about it, being strongly tinged with a reddish cast, which the old people said was occasioned by the blood of the Indians.

Underhill eventually retired to Oyster Bay himself and has parallel reputations as both defender and desperado. For all the stories of bloodshed and barbarity, smallpox was probably the biggest killer of native Indians, and in fact most of the first settlers also died from disease and depravation.

These first settlers were desperate refugees of Europe's own poverty. They were pirates, privateers and freebooters of the sea, and mercenaries. Some were criminals, exiled from home, or were homeless, dissolute seamen, some of whom may well have been press-ganged, and were prepared to venture anything, and to commit almost any crime, to repair their broken fortunes. The next wave would hardly have been any better, being battle-hardened soldiers sent to secure the riches of the new lands. They were led by captains entrusted with grandiose ambitions of nationhood and great wealth.

The *Mayflower* and other ships, with their precious cargoes of religious and freedom-loving exiles, were doves amid such hawks and vultures of the sea. And there was no shortage of friction between the first settlers and the tribes. More British settlers arrived in the late 1640s and early 1650s. They brought with them cattle, which damaged the unfenced American Indian maize crops. The English also brought with them liquor which seemed to demoralise the tribes. And they brought more of the white man's diseases – within 100 years the Matinecock tribe, who lived in what is now Astorias (Queens) and much of south and central Long Island, would be exhausted and dissipated. The men did achieve one fleeting moment of glory as whaling harpoonists, on which industry the port of Wellfleet became prosperous a century later.

A Pair of Stockings & Two Hoes

The arrival of the white men set the coastal American Indians not with one threatening colonist, but two. The coastal Indians were being moved into what was becoming a hostile hinterland where the tribal laws were being traduced. Ownership would have been instantly as vital and as vexed as any of the land issues that would face the Native American population in the coming centuries. The white man was extremely agitated as to the precise legalities of ownership; possibly the Indians were more relaxed and regarded it is a game.

The Indian idea of land must have been different to that of the Europeans. To the Indians there was seemingly no value in land: they valued the hunting and the fishing rights, which they would reserve in most transfers of ownership. The number of claims, counterclaims, edicts and other attempts to secure sovereignty from very early on are bafflingly multifarious and complicated. Envoys were despatched back to Europe to seek permission to seize lands already taken. After this first wave came a second tranche of law-making, as small hamlets sought to ally themselves with bigger communities and eventually counties. Perhaps in some way the very act of law-making dignified a town or an area with the status of respectability. It is even strange that the tribes were paid anything at all, unless it was a token necessary for their acquiescence to be secured.

In some towns, settlement was supremely organised. Setalcott – later to be Setauket – was bought from the Indians of the same name in 1655 by five New England businessmen. Plots were allocated for a home and also for meadowland or shoreline, and settlers could, if they wanted, bid for more. Two communal plots were set aside: one for town meetings, where everything was decided, and one for a church that did not arrive until 1671.

The Indians were keen to sell more land. In 1664 the same settlers bought a vast tract from the Great South Bay to the middle of the island for a coat, a knife, a pair of stockings, two hoes, two hatchets and two shirts. The Indians were undermined in other ways. In 1671 buyers were told to 'take some likers (liquor) with them to the Indians', and charge the cost to the town.

Shinnecocks & Blue Points

The Shinnecock were a fierce and feared tribe, but their craftsmanship with shells was admired by traders and rival tribes alike. Unlike other natives, the Shinnecock did not trade everything, but retained a 300-acre reservation on their homelands of Long Island which survives as a memento of the history and lands they might have inherited. Today, Shinnecock is less remembered as the name of one of the most ancient native peoples, or as the seminal furnace of pioneer history; or even as the home of one of its most celebrated natural foods. Today it is a golf course.

The legendary Blue Point oyster takes its name from the blue haze that settles on the bay waters. The American Indians called the area Manowtassquot, meaning Land of the Basket Rush. Blue Point was sold as part of the Brookhaven patent by King Charles II in 1654 to the Winthrop family. The price was four coats and £6 10s. The oyster beds were part of a bundle of land wanted for pasture meadows to graze the cattle, which in turn would have trampled the Indians' corn. The Brookhaven community was particularly picky about who could join them and put newcomers on probation for six months before agreeing to let them in or not, 'in case they impoverish the town'.

In 1752 a Connecticut businessman, Humphrey Avery, bought the areas of Blue Point and Patchogue – which also included Montauk Point – but then found himself in so much debt that he petitioned to be allowed to hold a lottery. He split the land up into 36 plots, sold 8,000 tickets at 30s each, and made so much money he bought most of his own land back. His son Joseph's homestead was built in 1812 and is now the oldest house in the town. In 1815 Avery started planting oyster seed in the bay. The harvest turned out to be plentiful and succulent. Wellfleet waters were ideal for raising and fattening oysters on, like Belon in France.

There would be another twist about this time in the Blue Point story. While the Blue Point oysters' reputation was soaring in the metropolis, the Stillman family, devout Baptists, began performing baptisms at their bayside house overlooking the same bay. So many people turned up to be baptised that they had to build on new changing rooms around their garden and along the beach. These became bathhouses and were rented out at 25c each. Eventually, the bathing beach had 600 bathhouses and full-blown hotels, and tourism soon followed. Where oysters basked in the bay, New Yorkers basked in the sun and their religion ...

Corn, Gruel & Biscuits

The American Indians gave the settlers another food that was to forge the opening of the west and drive migration across the land – and was something the Romans also knew about: corn. The first settlers had expected to plant wheat for breads. They soon realised that the many varieties of corn the Indians grew could make a porridge to which meats or fish could be added and could sustain a community for a week. There was no need to bake; it was easily bagged, nutritious and, for the times, convenient.

An Oregon university research project turned up more than 400 recipes for oysters, which in a sense form the first chapter of American cooking. Many of them disappointingly overlap or are just European hand-me-downs, but their abundance meant oysters were used as seasoning or to extend other more precious ingredients.

Only one recipe is credited to unnamed native Indians: a gruel of cornmeal, cream and oysters. There are a number of extended variations on this, using sweetbreads as well, either in a gentle stew with celery, parsley and paprika, and slaked with a little vinegar, or slightly plainer in a pie. Oysters also appear with macaroni cooked in cream and as a bake using cornmeal, bread, eggs, parsley and butter.

Port Jefferson Scalloped Oysters are a dauphinoise of potatoes and cream filled out with as many oysters as potatoes, plus their juices and cream. To those early settlers, picking up oysters would have been as easy as digging up the potatoes. There is also a charming sense of excitement that when the first cattle were delivered by the Atlantic boats, so recipes could have milk once again. And cheese.

Wherever oysters were served there would be oyster crackers, especially if they were fried or in a stew. At first these would have just been basic flour, salt, shortening and yeast rolled out flat, turned over and rolled again and baked for twenty-five minutes. These were rudimentary biscuits sailors brought with them on the boats. An Englishman, Adam Exton, claims to have built the first cracker factory in New Jersey in 1847. A year later he had a rival when Ezekiel Pullen began baking an 'Original Trenton Cracker' in the kitchen of his home. He sold his crackers from the back of his wagon as he made his way along Trenton streets. Marion Harland's *Common Sense in the Household*, dated 1873, gives instructions to 'beat hard for half an hour', which may have contributed to its obsolescence as far as domestic cooks were concerned:

> Rub the three tablespoons of butter into a quart of flour, or, what is better, cut it up with a knife or chopper, as you do in pastry; add the salt, two cups

of sweet milk, soda, mixing well. Work into a ball, lay upon a floured board, and beat with the rolling-pin half an hour, turning and shifting the mass often. Roll into an even sheet, a quarter of an inch thick, or less, prick deeply with a fork, and bake hard in a moderate oven. Hang them up in a muslin bag in the kitchen for two days to dry.

The cracker travelled a different gastronomic route to the oyster; its pairing as dipping biscuit to an oyster and corn gruel might have formed many a sustaining dinner for the first arrivals on the continent, and something of a local triumph in achieving the means to bake at all.

Settlement

Scoops, Schooners & Slavers

Under the British New York was complicit in the slave trade, even sending its surplus of pickled oysters south to feed the plantations. By 1750 New York had as many slaves as Charleston. New Haven sustained the slave plantations in the West Indies. It shipped its food, livestock and timber to the Caribbean islands from as early as 1640, right up to the 1890s. Small sloops and two-masted schooners carried livestock on the deck and flour and vegetables in the hold. The best of the fishing catch was sent to Catholic countries in Europe, the second best was taken to respectable, middle-class Boston, and the leftovers were sent south to feed the slaves.

Oysters also offered a form of early freedom to black people in the city as a cheap way to earn a living, and many took to wheeling carts around the streets, selling oysters in the ghettoes. An area of Staten Island on the shore, which had poor soil, came to be known as the iconic Sandy Island. The sand in the loam made it fertile ground for growing strawberries. But it was the oysters that provided the subsistence and economic infrastructure for the fledgling black community. To support the oyster trade they built their own boats; they made baskets to carry the oysters; they became blacksmiths to forge the tongues and rakes to dredge the seabed. They traded oysters for bricks and built large houses. They traded their strawberry harvest down at the Washington market in Manhattan, and their quilt-making was to become famous. Sandy Ground was the oldest community established by free black slaves in North America. One of their rivals who also got a start in life supplying oysters to the Washington market was Cornelius Vanderbilt, who went on to become a shipping magnate.

Openers, Washers & Measurers

The first commercialisation of the oyster began in about the 1820s around New Haven, Connecticut. Before that people shucked oysters in their homes and sold them in their neighbourhoods or to dealers. But by 1820 dealers were packing the meats in little wooden kegs or in square tin cans for sale further away. The oyster inspector Ernest Ingersoll reported:

> There are the openers, the washers, the measurers, the fillers, the packers, etc., each of which performs only the duties pertaining to its own division … The oysters are generally taken directly from the vessel to the places occupied by the openers, who form a large number of operatives, and are composed of females and boys, who earn from $5 to $9 per week.

They would shuck by 'stabbing' – inserting a short knife into the heel of the oyster and slicing the meat free from the shell – or what was called 'cracking' or 'billing', where the front edge of the shell was knocked open with a bar, the back of a knife or a hammer to let the blade in.

By the mid to late 1800s oysters had reached the height of fashion:

> No evening of pleasure was complete without oysters; no host worthy of the name failed to serve 'the luscious bivalves,' as they were actually called, to his guests. In every town there were oyster parlors, oyster cellars, oyster saloons, and oyster bars, houses, stalls, and lunchrooms.

They were peddled from door to door. Ingersoll wrote:

> Oysters pickled, stewed, baked, roasted, fried, and scalloped; oysters made into soups, patties, and puddings; oysters with condiments and without condiments; oysters for breakfast, dinner, supper; oysters without stint or limit, fresh as the pure air, and almost as abundant, are daily offered to the palates of the Manhattanese, and appreciated with all the gratitude which such a bounty of nature ought to inspire.

There were uses aplenty for the shells too – for roads and footpaths, filling for wharfs, lowlands, fortifications, railway embankments, ballast for vessels, raw material for lime, a 'sweetener' for agricultural fields, a component in mixed fertilisers and a component of cement. By the turn of the century, oyster shells for roads cost 15c a bushel. Lime kilns of the shore towns in New England once used nothing but oyster shells. The pharmaceutical industry used ground-up oyster shell in pills to prevent osteoporosis.

Oyster shell also found its way into making paint, plastics and rubber, and was regarded as a premier source of calcium.

Red Lights & Restaurants

The first recorded salon for the sale of oysters in New York is a cellar on Broad Street dated 1763. A late-night oyster stew in one of Manhattan's all-night markets became a New York tradition, as were oyster cellars – basement bars reached by stairwells in the sidewalk marked by a red balloon and candle; the first manifestation of what we now call red-light areas.

These oyster basements were male bastions. The only women allowed were prostitutes. The men who frequented such oyster basements were no more respectable themselves, as this description of New York from 1850 by George G. Foster underlines:

> The women of course are all of one kind – but among the men you would find, if you looked curiously, reverend judges and juvenile delinquents, pious and devout hypocrites. And the undisguised libertines and debauchees. Gamblers and fancymen, high flyers and spoonies, genteel pickpockets and burglars, even sometimes mingle in the detestable orgies of these detestable caverns.

As in Rome, the oyster ingratiated itself into the one place where its reputation for salaciousness would be enhanced.

A Small Pearl Bonanza

There were small flurries of excitement from 1850 when freshwater pearls were found across America, sparking a sudden, small gold-like rush. The first was in New Jersey when a shoemaker, David Howell, cooked himself up a plate of mussels, 'in the usual grease and heat', and discovered a '499 graine' pearl in the middle, which might have been worth $25,000 if the heat of the cooking had not marred it. A few days later a carpenter, Jacob Quackenbush, unearthed another pearl nearby at Paterson and sold it to Tiffany's in New York for $1,500. No one in New York wanted to buy it, so it was sent to Paris and sold for 12,500 francs and then sold on to the Empress Eugenie where it became known as the Queen Pearl. On such stories many searched and some found, and for a while there was a great popular hysteria that carried over to other towns.

But it was in Arkansas, Ohio and the south-west of Wisconsin and along the Mississippi delta that the real find was made. In 1891 $300,000 worth of shells were taken from the waters. Even if these were not first-lustre oyster pearls, it was remarkable that so many pearls were found lying on the river bed loose, or were tilled up by farmers, long since out of their shells. And it was not unusual at this time to find a pearl in a fish or pig stomach. It seems that before this point, the value of the pearl – or perhaps even of decoration of any kind – was just simply not recognised in the Midwest.

The story of the American pearl bonanza has an unromantic end. Between Quincy and La Crosse wetlands more shell was taken than anywhere else in the world. But it was poor-quality shell. The business, therefore, found another outlet: making the buttons for shirts carved out of the mother-of-pearl, until plastics finally phased it out.

Narragansetts & Lynnhavens

By 1900, New York City had a population of 4.6 million and was eating a million oysters a day. One statistic underlines the enthusiasm of the time, where New Yorkers ate an average of 660 oysters a year; the same figure for London had dwindled to 60 and in Paris to just 26.

Estuaries had their own followings and restaurants would often list ten to fifteen different varieties. The fashionable names of the day were Malpeques, Wellfleets, Cotuits, Narragansetts, New Havens, Saddle-rocks, Blue Points, Rockaways, Perth Amboys, Raritan Bays, Shrewsburys, Absecon Salts, Cape May Salts, Maurice Coves, Lynnhavens, Chincoteagues, Assateagues, Roanokes, Tangier Sounds, Apalachicolas, Barataria Bays and Olympias.

The rounder oyster was more appreciated than the longer, and so they were graded accordingly: 'choice' was designated as not being more than one and a half times longer than wide; for 'standard' the shell could be twice as long, and 'commercial' was anything else. A fisherman would get three times more for 'choice' than 'commercial'.

New Haven spawned the wealthiest and biggest oyster firms. It was not just a producer but also a trader and a supplier. As demand grew, families imported oysters from New Jersey and then from Chesapeake Bay around 1830. From 1855–60, about eighty schooners, each with a carrying capacity of 2,000–4,500 bushels, supplied New Haven with 500,000–750,000 bushels of oysters each year. Three-quarters were shucked immediately and sold in the winter trade across the state; the rest were bedded on leases in the harbour during April and May, to be harvested in the following autumn and early winter.

Some figures have it that half a billion oysters were being harvested a year; three-quarters going to New York. The rest were shipped to London – Queen Victoria was said to be partial to Blue Points, although she found the shells rough and ordered them filed down for her – or Liverpool, or freighted to Chicago, St Louis or San Francisco.

Shuckers had to open 2,000 oysters a day to make a living. A single man working with tongues could lift 10 bushels a day, the sloops and sharpies could haul in 20–30 bushels a day, and the even more rapacious dredger would land 50 bushels in a day. Each acre of oyster bed, it was calculated, yielded 500 bushels.

A schooner would carry about 700 bushels – approximately 50,000lb in weight – through the Fire Island Inlet. The Long Island Railroad had reached Sayville in 1868 and, around 1870, some oysters were being shipped by rail. From around 1900 until the First World War, the Long Island Express Co. had four express oyster trains a day (a 75-minute ride) at 9 a.m., 11 a.m., 2 p.m. and 5 p.m. An order received in the 7.30 a.m. mail was shipped by 9.00 a.m. and delivered at Brooklyn around noon. The oysters were shipped as half-shells, 3 bushels to a barrel, or as shucked meats in gallon and 3-gallon cans.

The First Toothpicks

Restaurants made their names with oysters, especially the Blue Points which had style and swagger. Gage and Tollner's opened in 1879 on Fulton Street in Brooklyn, and was known for its thirty-six ornate gas lamps – an insurance against power failures – fine-cut glass chandeliers and mahogany tables, and only closed in 2004 when the area became hostage to discount retailers and died at night. New York's original restaurant, Delmonico's, evolved from a confectionery, serving expatriate Europeans French-style food – Lobster Newburg was invented here – and had its own oyster selection. Even in this affected and deliberate move into Frenchness, oysters might be invited as essential guests. A menu at Astor House in 1837 retained oyster pie and cod boiled with oysters. Other names were Sherry's, and Rector's on Broadway, a preferred haunt of the gourmet philanthropist railroad magnate Diamond Jim Brady, who reputedly would order four dozen Lynnhavens from Baltimore as an appetiser – Lynnhavens being

2–3 inches larger than the Blue Point. One night he supposedly went on to eat, with his girlfriend, the actress Lillian Russell, a dozen crabs, a couple of bowls of turtle soup, portions of terrapin, duck, steak, five or six lobsters, a variety of vegetables and pastries, topped off with 2lb of chocolates.

In nearby respectable Boston, the Union Oyster House opened in 1826 and remains America's longest running restaurant, originally called Attwood and Bacon's Oyster House. It was here that America developed its interest in toothpicks; hungry students were hired to demonstrate how the toothpick could be used to eat oysters politely. It was an advertising gimmick.

The new luxury hotels of the Plaza, Waldorf Astoria and the St Regis offered oysters as a mark of fashionability. And oysters were served in the plush dining cars of the railroads. The railways prided themselves on their cooking and offered as many as thirty-five entrées, with oysters served seven or eight different ways. Oysters were a way to gain prestige.

At the same time, thousands of pushcarts sold oysters on street corners, on the shell or shucked in hot dogs and sandwiches for the less well off. A New York oyster hot dog pre-dates the famous New Orleans Po'Bo. Mostly they were sold on the shell with lemon, pepper or vinegar and downed in one. Somehow the oyster managed to span the worlds of rich and poor.

Another great oyster institution, founded just after the height of this bonanza, was the Grand Central Oyster Bar & Restaurant in Manhattan. Built in 1913, not under the waves but appropriately perhaps under Grand Central Terminal, it still uses more than 283,000 oysters per year in its famous pan roasts and stews – 600 of which are made to order each day. Another 1.7 million oysters are served raw during the year; more than half are Blue Points.

An oyster stew became a traditional American Sunday night meal. Quick and easy for a skilful cook to prepare, the oysters were lightly poached in cream or milk, enriched with butter and seasoned with paprika or celery salt; the dish took just a few minutes. The American socialite M.F.K. Fisher wrote a provocative and culinarily expert short tome called *Consider the Oyster*, which was first published in 1941. She pondered why American lexicographers had never seen fit to give 'oyster stew' its own definition in the dictionary – in French it would probably translate as a ragout – and insisted on grouping it along with soups, which obviously take much longer to prepare:

Is it possible that they never knew, when they were children, the cozy pleasures of Sunday night supper in wintertime, when crackers and the biggest tureen of steaming, buttery, creamy oyster stew stood on the table, and was plenty?

Over the years, this simple broth has evolved into the definitive variation that is still found at the Grand Central Station:

Grand Central Oyster Stew

Warm the soup plates. Warm but do not boil two cups of milk and two of cream. Warm the oyster liquor from one pint oysters, add butter and poach the oysters in their juice until the edges curl. Add the milk and cream, season with paprika, pepper, celery salt. Lay up in soup plates.

9

Tales of the Chesapeake

The Mother of Waters – The Mystery of Halfman Island –
The 500-Acre Reef – The Real Pocahontas – Pirates of Turner's Point
– Squabbles, Squabbles & More Squabbles – Black Jacks –
The Bugeye, Pungy & Skipjack – Crisfield: Queen of the Honky Tonks
– The Maryland Oyster Navy – The Start of Graphic Design –
Cameron's Folly with the Dancing Molly – Shootout on Monroe Bay

The abundance of oysters is incredible. There are whole banks of them so that the ships must avoid them. They surpass those in England by far in size, indeed they are four times as large.

Francis Louis Michel, 1701

The Mother of Waters

The sun glints off the waters and turns them liquid gold; the waves, almost artificial, look like smears of oils on a canvas, eerily like a Turner painting. At another time of year the fogs descend and turn everything blue and white. The wash of the boats echo the shapes of the clouds. The flatness of the estuary gives these huge vistas, where the light can play and dazzle in the sheltered calm and where the camera can rove over cordgrass, sandbanks and gnarly old trees. Horizontal light – at dawn and dusk – is the photographer's creed and the Chesapeake is one of nature's greatest studios. The first settlers called it the noblest bay in the known world. Such reports leaching back to Europe inspired more investors, more boats, more adventurers, more edicts and more men to sail.

The Chesapeake vistas inspired early names like Mother of Waters and the Great Shellfish Bay from the Indian Algonquian – *Tschiswapeki*, or in other spellings *Chesepioc*. Algonquian itself means Country on a Great River and, like the river with its many tributaries and coves, the language itself has subdivided into many dialects among different tribes.

Conflicts and trade influenced the language, bringing lovely names like Chincoteague, meaning Beautiful Land over the Water; skipjack, originally the little fish flashing on the water's surface, became the word for the schooners sailing the waters, with their curious pyramid sails to ensure the boats did not topple over when loaded with their heavy cargo of shells. Others have transmuted, such as the emotive Pocomoke meaning Dark River, now largely a conservation park, originally a ferry station for New England fur trappers. No irony, either, that the town's business park today is home to Benelli, who make shotguns, and Beretta USA, who make handguns.

The Chesapeake Valley was created at the end of the last ice age, probably here – because ice age dates change from place to place – 12,000

A Chesapeake skipjack in full sail.

to 18,000 years ago. When the ice flows melted, the waters overran the valley and mouth of the Susquehanna River, creating a huge bay that stretches 200 miles from Cooperstown, New York, to southern Virginia, fed by 48 major rivers and 100 smaller tributaries. The confluence of the salty Atlantic tides and the fresh waters pouring in from these tributaries made it for many centuries the second most famous oyster bed in the world, after the Hudson, thanks to the complexity, scale and depth of its ecosystem. Certainly it was the most fought over and the most coveted. Its very name evokes so much that it is essential to early American history.

For the early settlers the salt levels in the estuary, which vary from 0 in the north to as much as 3.5 per cent near the ocean, were not just crucial to oysters. The ability to salt food through the winter was lifesaving and gave the southern and coastal settlers a commercial advantage over those who settled further north and inland. George Washington was to make a lucrative business salting herrings and selling them up state, and then to the plantations in the West Indies.

Chesapeake is the largest estuary in the United States. For those of us who do not live in huge countries such distances take a moment to comprehend. There are 4,000 miles of navigable shoreline, so for the early pioneers the Chesapeake would have been an unfolding story spanning many decades: 4,000 miles in a straight line spans a distance from London to Dakar, West Africa. Although it is 30 miles wide at its widest point – too far for a cannonball to fly, as the early colonists found to their chagrin – the waters are mostly shallow, rarely more than 22ft deep, which allows the heat of the sun to bless the grasslands, plankton and marine life across the estuary floor. Put a drop under a microscope and clear water springs to life with micro organisms and marine fauna.

The Chesapeake has been at the apex of events from Indian wars, piracy of the high seas, civil war, local feuding and essential trading, to the pollution and abandonment of the waters in the twentieth century. The Chesapeake, you might argue, was wilder than the west. More than 10,000 wrecks lie abandoned and disintegrating beneath the waters, lying as tombstones to the feuding between Spanish and English, Virginians and Marylanders, and others. The weekend yachting retreats of the rich stand on a bloody, bickering history.

The Mystery of Halfman Island

The map has a way of explaining the migration in its own way. The old native names survive like: Onancock, meaning Foggy Place; Nanticoke means People of the Tide Water; Poquson means Marshy Lowlands; Manassas means People at the End of the Water; Assawoman means a Rock Cove; Pungotegue means Sand Fly River. The one major cartographic concession to the Native Americans has been the rivers that have been allowed to retain their names. A glance at an early map shows quickly how the tribes here divided along its banks, sectioned off by tributaries which acted as natural borders. Mattaponi and Pamunkey are both rivers and also small reservations for Native Americans. And there is the poetically named Rappahannock River, meaning the Rapidly Rising and Falling Waters. The Potomac means the place that things are brought to, i.e. the trading river. Urbanna probably also meant a Place to Trade and was both an oyster bed and a tobacco plantation and still holds an annual oyster festival.

But other names, both of towns and counties, bring a wry sense of Englishness – Guildford, Middlesex, Deal, Stockton, Oxford, Cambridge, Richmond, Sussex, Suffolk, Somerset, Gloucester, Exmoor, Lancaster, Portsmouth – like a homesickness, each one now reads like a footnote to an epic journey, struggle or migration. Then we have defiant affirmations of loyalty to King William, King George and Cape Charles. But there is also Frenchtown, Vienna, Macedonia, Scotland, Paris and Kilmarnock. Dumfries harbour rivalled Boston and New York in importance, until it started to silt up around 1763, was overrun in the civil war and the main crop stopped being tobacco and became wheat and sugar.

The more religious elements are singled out at Temperanceville – the land was sold on the condition that no whisky was allowed – Parsonville, even perhaps the simplistic Love. Some are intriguingly literal: Woman's Bay, Dames Quarter, Cashville – probably named because it had the post office – Rogues' Island or just plain Muddy.

Others you can only speculate on – why Halfman's Island? Or Mantrap Gut?

Names changed too. Modest Town was noted in 1836 as having huge oyster beds and rich fishing. It was named after the two women who ran a boarding house for fishermen, was briefly renamed Mappsville in 1861, then back to Modest Town, and then changed again to Sunderland Hall.

Nothing is quite as literal as Bivalve, a small town on the eastern shore of the Nanticoke River just before it flows into the Chesapeake in Wicomico County, Maryland. Bivalve was originally called Waltersville after the family who owned the plantations and the port rights, but in 1887, with the opening of the post office, they needed a new name so as not to conflict with another town – or possibly with Walkersville – in Frederick

County. The postmaster, Elrick Willing, baptised it again after the town's
main pursuit. The lovelier Wicomico meant appropriately 'a place where
houses are built'. Not Native American ones though, obviously.

The 500-Acre Reef

Some say the first European to find the Chesapeake may have been the
Viking explorer Thorfinn Karlsfennias, as early as the eleventh century.
Others say the Italian Giovanni da Verrazano sailed along the coast from
the Carolinas to Maine in 1524. Another thesis puts it even later and
mentions Pedro Menendez de Aviles, the Spaniard, who later founded
St Augustine in 1566. A settlement of Spanish Jesuits at York River was
massacred by American Indians in 1572. But the early contacts were at sea
where boats from Europe came to fish in the rich waters and take back
cod – hence Cape Cod – and lurid stories of the savagery of the Indians
who 'had been flaying some alive with shells'.

The Native Americans ate the oysters raw or roasted in the fire and used
the shells for barter and decoration. The huge piles of discarded oyster shells
had been added to each year. These were not small or isolated. The largest
recorded midden was 20ft deep and covered an amazing 30 acres near Popes
Creek on the Potomac River. The town and harbour of Crisfield, Maryland,
was built on the shells of oysters used to fill in the swampy ground, a curiosity
it has enjoyed selling itself on since it was founded in 1663.

Nor were these oysters in the modern sense tidily lying unseen on the
estuary floor. When the settlers first arrived huge reefs towered out of the
waters at low tide where generations of oysters had spawned and collected
on each other. These reefs were the lungs of the estuary filtering the waters
and the plankton and purifying the waters.

A Swiss traveller, Francis Louis Michel, writing in 1701, says: 'The
abundance of oysters is incredible. There are whole banks of them, so
that the ships must avoid them. A sloop, which was to land us at King's
Creek, struck an oyster bed, where we had to wait about two hours for the
tide.' Some estimates say the reefs might have been as old as 5,000 years.
Mark Twain wrote: 'In one place, five hundred feet above the sea, the
perpendicular bank on the upper side of the road was 10 or 15 feet high,
and the cut exposed three veins of oyster shells, just as we have seen quartz
veins exposed in the cutting of a road in Nevada or Montana.'

This account of oystermen at work is from the *New York Times* in the
late 1870s:

The shoal from which the *Dennis* was loaded extended over about 500 acres, and from this shoal, on the day that she was loaded, not less than 10,000 bushels of 'plants' were taken. To do this about 250 oystermen were employed, with about 100 boats ... and yet nowhere on all this shoal would it be possible to find a spot as large as a set of tongs will cover without oysters on it. The tongs are never pushed down and pulled back without bringing with them a number of oysters. It seems as if the supply of oyster-plants in the James River could never be exhausted, yet the oystermen say they are growing less and less each year; but if they are correct in this assertion, it is difficult to conjecture in what abundance these oysters must have been when they were plenty.

The Real Pocahontas

The most famous early explorer, Captain John Smith, noted as early as 1608 that he was received with courtesy and hospitality by the American Indians who showered him with gifts. This might have been because he was a generous trader looking to buy foods to stop the first settlements from starving. He kept the company alive on a diet of sturgeon and oysters. He gives a vivid account of a first meeting with Indians:

> Entering the River of Tockwogh the savages all armed in a fleet of boats round environed us; it chanced one of them could speak the language of Powhatan who persuaded the rest to a friendly parley: but when they see us furnished with the Massawomecks' weapons, and we feigning the invention of Kecoughtan to have taken them perforce; they conducted us to their palisaded town, mantled with the barks of trees, with scaffolds like mounts, breasted about with barks very formally, their men, women, and children, with dances, songs, fruits, fish, furs, & what they had kindly entertained us, spreading mats for us to sit on, stretching their best abilities to express their loves.

And also of the Indians' reaction to Christianity:

> Our order was daily to have prayer, with a psalm, at which solemnity the poor savages much wondered: our prayers being done, they were long busied with consultation till they had contrived their business; then they began in most passionate manner to hold up their hands to the sun with a most fearful song, then embracing the Captain, they began to adore him in like manner.

The Disney film *Pocahontas* plays fast and loose with other accounts, but it does portray these first settlers as ruthless explorers looking for what they could get. In the opening song Smith is hardly portrayed as a peacemaker – 'You can't fight Indians without John Smith'– and then claims that not even 1,000 'blood thirsty savages can stand in their way'. All of which, given the true dates, is a bit premature. Also, it is fairly eyebrow-raising that Pocahontas, as the daughter of an Indian chief, could speak English at all, before John Smith had even got off the boat, although she was later to learn it. In the Disney version the American Indians are romantically portrayed as in touch with the elements and the spirit world as if they lived in some Garden of Eden, which is a bit of a non sequitur considering they were 'blood thirsty savages'.

The clash of aspirations is summed up when Smith tells Pocahontas they are looking for gold and he shows her a yellow ingot and she shows him a yellow ear of corn. In the film Smith is wounded protecting Pocahontas' father from the white man's bullet, but in other accounts he is injured in a gunpowder accident. Pocahontas did convert later to Christianity and married a religious tobacco baron, John Rolfe. She was sailed to England as part of a fundraising effort in 1616, where she briefly met with Smith again, but died of tuberculosis at Gravesend before she could return home. She became a symbol of the desire, if indeed it existed, among early settlers and Indians to trade and live together in peace, to swap Christianity and tobacco. It was retrospective propaganda but not an inaccurate tale of bigotry and greed in which the settlers are very much the bad men; a post-Vietnam essay on the morality of force and guns, and even American guilt. But then these were not Americans yet, they were still Europeans.

By comparison, the first words the sailors utter in Terence Malik's *New World* are: 'We have found oysters, as thick as your hands.' The Indians show off their piles of empty shells with pride as tokens of wealth. So short of provisions are the new settlers that their boat sails back to Europe leaving a small band isolated for the winter. Trade with the Indians is their only option for survival. In Malik's version of this first settlement of America it is the planting of crops by the settlers that offends the Indians, who see their territory encroached upon and retaliate.

We also know from accounts of the first *Mayflower* pilgrim settlements at Plymouth – where there were no oysters – that many deaths followed the immigration due to deprivation and disease.

The smaller tribes of the Chesapeake were oppressed by the larger Susquehannocks. The first settlement at St Mary's City was bequeathed to the white men because the local tribe, the Yoacomacoes, fled the area after being attacked by the Susquehannocks in March 1634. It was given to the settlers with the land cleared and ready to plant crops. The Indians even showed the settlers how to fish and gather the oysters, which would have been so plentiful their fate could hardly be in dispute. The Indians banded together to create an accord known as the Piscataways, whose tribal headquarters was just 10 miles from what is now Washington city centre. It included the tribes from southern Maryland of the Patuxents, Nanjemoys, Mattapanys, Wicomicoes, Portopacos, Mattawomans and the Chapticos. As happened in Long Island, these smaller tribes could see the advantage of befriending an armed group of settlers and soldiers to face an adversary.

The white settlers saw the oyster bays in exactly the same way as the Indians. They did not want to settle and cultivate either. They wanted to hunt and raid and sail their boats in war dances down the estuaries as shows of strength. Anything under the water had no value to these men either. They wanted only to come and take, and go too. Later they would even try to award reservation-like status to the oyster bays, but that would largely be a failure.

Pirates of Turner's Point

The Chesapeake quickly became a haven for pirates. The easterly shores provided a welcome shelter and base for re-equipping the boats for voyages south to the West Indies. Here, wild sea-hardy men seemed to find a freedom to live as they wanted between voyages and they were to find a cargo as interesting as gold – tobacco. As early as 1612, at the first settlement in Jamestown, tobacco had been seen as the new land's new crop and was being grown rapaciously to be sailed back to Europe as a cash crop. The American Indians taught the white man to smoke and they often worked together to plant and harvest. Only later were black slaves brought in, often by these same pirates, to provide a more stable workforce.

It was not really the tobacco on which Virginia was built, but the trade on its waterway – the Chesapeake – which brought it to the forefront of world affairs and brought back the buccaneers of the sea. The water was its true heritage, and it became a melting pot of Europeans, native Indians and enslaved black people.

The Chesapeake and Long Island Sound had particular advantages for pirates. The privacy of the coves allowed them places to stash their booty. The emerging new cities like New Amsterdam, renamed New York, were a lucrative market for gold dust, bars of silver, pieces of eight, rubies, diamonds, candlesticks, silks and other trinkets. Sometimes they too would plunder the homes of the new settlers looking for food or money or both, although mostly there seems to have been an uneasy truce brokered by the settlers' desire for Arabian jewels and the pirates' need to restock their ships with hams and other foodstuffs.

Captain Kidd was probably a composite figure of many pirates who plied this route at the time. He was said to have left treasure at Gardiner's Island at Wellfleet, and also at Montauk Point. There is a record of him trading a bag of sugar and a gold cloth from the trousseau of the Grand Mogul's daughter, taken from a Moorish ship he ransacked off Madagascar. While Kidd had the freedom of New York City, he made the mistake of sailing into respectable Boston, where he was arrested, deported to England and hung.

There is a fanciful but intriguing tale of the shipyard of Thomas Skillington. It was said it was positioned at the remote Turner's Point so that Skillington could count on good custom from the pirates of the coast. Supposedly, his son Percy continued the trade until around 1730, suspiciously ending business around the same time that good pirate lads like Stede Bonnet, Blackbeard Teach and Captain Kidd had either died in battle or gone to the gallows. Well into the 1750s gold pieces of eight, chequins and pistoles were found among subscriptions to the Talbot County free school, so perhaps there is truth in the story.

Piracy flourished on the high seas. The tobacco boats were lucrative targets, as were slave ships. The eastern seaboard of the Americas was 'so full of pirates that it is impossible for any ships to go home safely', wrote the Governor of Virginia. And any captain of a ship could find himself taken for a pirate depending on the political whim of the moment in Europe. Many did turn to plundering and raiding the settlers, laying up in canoes in the reed grasses until night and then striking silently, demanding food and valuables, and disappearing as quickly as they had arrived. Others used the Chesapeake as a base to raid as far as Africa and Asia.

Squabbles, Squabbles & More Squabbles

In many of these fragments of history there is a sub-theme. Rather than declaring their great vision at the momentous discovery of a continent, the insight is how petty and bad-tempered everyone was. Perhaps these people felt lost in a vacuum, trapped in a dangerous new land, marooned from their history. One does not read any great sense of joy or hope; one does read a lot of small-minded nit-picking. Possibly that was the stuff of letters, and the everyday enjoyment of life was not considered a necessary subject for putting down on paper. In the Chesapeake they enjoyed one of man's greatest natural citadels, and yet the two sides of the water – Virginia and Maryland – were straight at each other's throats, and the petty feuding would last fractiously until 1962 when President Kennedy finally intervened and took governance away from both parties.

Virginia had exacted a toll from Marylanders seeking access to the sea. Maryland, on the other hand, owned the entire Potomac River. It retaliated by forbidding Virginia to fish there. Their history is littered with tit-for-tat expeditions.

In 1644 the American Indians watched the naval battle of Blanck Point as the would-be colonisers rehearsed the civil war at home between roundheads and cavaliers. The Indians, under Chief Opechancanough, took their chance and massacred 500 settlers in a bid to oust the newcomers. It took an Act of Parliament in England to provide the equipment and arms for an expedition to put down the uprising.

There followed some outrageous acts of sheer bullying, strange idealism and thorough bad temper. Richard Ingle was authorised by the English Admiralty to seize any ships 'hostile to Parliament, or having traded with any of the inhabitants of such a place since their desertion of King and Parliament', which left him with a pretty broad brief, open to any kind of interpretation he chose, as to what qualified a ship as a legal prize. His armed ship, the *Reformation*, arrived in Maryland waters and decided to 'plunder the Papists'. Over the next two years more than £2,000 worth of Catholic property was seized or destroyed, as was thousands of pounds' worth of tobacco, and Ingle required all colonists to take an oath against King Charles. Those that refused were plundered.

The population of Maryland dropped from 400 to 100. Many fled to Virginia, and most of the first official records were destroyed. Ingle reapportioned much of the confiscated property to Protestants, keeping their valuables for himself but giving the locals the animals and food supplies. Having brought this havoc with him, in April 1645 he simply sailed back to England, leaving the Marylanders alone again. Such were the times. This hardly seems like imperialism, colonialism or empire building, just plain thuggery of which this is just one example.

Black Jacks

For many black people, working the boats represented a freedom and a step up in the world, however tough the conditions. It also gave them a respect in their own community because they brought news from other parts of the world. In 1796 the federal government issued Seamen's Protection Certificates, which defined these black merchant mariners as 'citizens' – they were America's first black citizens. Black Jacks they were called.

Other legislation was more openly racist and vindictive. In 1836 a Maryland bill forbade black people from captaining any vessel large enough to require being registered. Any owner breaking the law would have his boat confiscated and sold. Half of the proceeds went to the informer who reported the offence.

But oystering was a natural pursuit for black people, as it was for others without better means. With little capital outlay required, and a high demand for seafood, anyone could make a modest living alongside larger companies that were operating for much bigger stakes. Gathering oysters was one of the highest paid jobs for black men.

Wielding the traditional tongs was hard work, the more so in bad weather through the winter, and particularly back-breaking in deeper waters. These tongs were from 7–24ft long, like two garden rakes together, but with teeth to clip the oysters off the reef and drop them into a basket. It was slow, demanding, awkward work that required a lot of skill to do at any speed, but for a great many black people, especially after the civil war, the oyster trade offered a chance of self-employment, however hard it might be.

Before the civil war, out-of-state poachers solicited the slaves to help in raiding the beds. The citizens of Gloucester and Mathews County petitioned the Virginia authorities to crack down and save their beds. This is dated 1843 and accuses the poachers of corrupting the slaves in order to find the location of the oyster beds:

> The acts of Assembly at present in force prohibit the catching and taking of oysters by citizens of other states, but not their purchase and removal. Claiming the provision of this feature of the law, vessels from other states frequent our river in great numbers, but not with the view of trafficking lawfully with our citizens; but availing themselves of the night time, when the white inhabitants are asleep, they carry on a most ruinous and demoralizing trade with our slaves who are seduced by the promise of gain and the liberal supply of ardent spirits to expose themselves at all times of night to most inclement weather. The result of which is that oysters are taken in such quantities as to tend to their utter destruction, and the additional, and greater evil is superinduced, of rendering our slaves corrupt, and worthless, which will eventually lead to their elopement, as the most ample facilities are afforded by the foreign craft.

By 1890 more than 32,000 people, over half of them freed black slaves, were working in the oyster trade in Maryland alone.

The families who subsisted on oysters lived typically in two-room log huts on the shore. They had become a community apart, looked down on by the high-standing Anglican nabobs and lawyers who had already made their money out of tobacco, fruit or other trade. On the water it was another world: rough, tough, liquor-drinking, one-pot cooking, existing on salted meat, bread and, of course, oysters. The oppression bred a sense of community and the watermen preferred alternative forms of Christianity like Quakerism and Presbyterianism, if they cared for religion at all. Life was cheap. Winters were icy and harsh, women were exhausted from childbirth at 25 and the men grizzled. Summer brought malaria-ridden mosquitoes, spiders, hornets, wasps and the occasional but destructive hurricane.

Those dependent on the waters were poor. In the new cities seemingly people prospered, and in between were the emergently powerful farming communities. The defiant watermen and their families wore trademark striped jackets, pants rolled up to the knee and little round hats with pride. In summer they used their boats to ferry watermelons, salted fish and sweet potatoes to the cities. They were hard and rebellious and a nation among themselves. In the civil war they declared for the Union and ran guns for the Confederates. They were individuals who then, and also much later, lived on the margins of the emerging society, a fact that made them, and the oyster beds they relied upon, politically weak compared to other vested interests that wanted to use the bay, like chemical companies, real estate developers and even sports fishing groups through the twentieth century.

Their skill on the water was their bonding. This incredulous account is from the mid-1800s:

To see the oystermen balancing themselves in one of their canoes, and working with so much energy at the same time, was quite a novelty. Many of these canoes are so narrow that should a novice step into one it would almost probably be overturned; yet the oystermen work in them all day long in smooth weather, and sometimes in pretty stormy weather, and apparently keep them properly balanced without any effort. To propel them through the water they use a long paddle, and, balancing it over the stem (the canoes, of course, are sharp at both ends, having no row-locks and no indentation to aid them in keeping their paddle in place), they move them swiftly.

The Bugeye, Pungy & Skipjack

Shipbuilding was as important to the Chesapeake as it was characterful and essential. The first boats that brought the Europeans, the *Susan Constant*, *Godspeed* and *Discovery*, were much admired by the American Indians who met them in their canoes and who had not developed the art of sailing, possibly because in the relative calm of the estuary and its tributaries there was no real need. The canoe was sturdy enough to cut through the choppy bay waters. They were usually made of loblolly pine or tulip poplar trees; the log was slowly burned and the ashes were scraped out of the inside. The English settlers added sails to the canoes. The canoe was cheap to build and easy to replace. Some evolved to three and five logs wide, which in shallow waters of only 10–15ft worked well enough. In the summer they would hold canoe races, which are still a feature today.

The oyster business, and especially the rapacious demands for dredging the oyster beds, gave rise to three types of boat on the Chesapeake. The colourful, twin-masted, strangely named pungy was painted pink and bottle-green, and was a direct descendant of the fast Virginian schooners that ferried larger cargoes, mail and passengers around the bay. They were graceful, quick and had enough heavy draft to let the oystermen dredge the bottom in deep waters, but they were expensive to build and less workable in the shallow waters.

The pungy was replaced by the cheaper, easier to handle and similarly oddly christened flat-bottomed bugeye, which some claimed was so called because it could turn on a bug's eye; although just as believable was that it came from the Scottish immigrants working in the shipyards and derived from the scotch *buckie*, meaning oyster shell. They were rigged with triangular, narrow-headed Bermuda or leg-of-mutton sails, pointed at the top to minimise the weight aloft, and the low cut would also save the boats from tilting when loaded with their heavy cargo.

The skipjack, nostalgically regarded by old sailors and marine architects as harking back to a time of greater oyster abundance, was really a product of the start of the resource's collapse. Named after the bluefish that could be seen flicking the surface of the bay waters, the skipjack was a simple boat that could just about be handled by a lone sailor.

With the advent of steam, the bugeyes were cannibalised and rigged down and turned into 'buy boats', serving as wholesale merchants and collectors of oysters dredged by smaller boats. The buy boat captains set prices based on the market as they saw it, with a mark-up sufficient to pay their freight and assure a profit when the catch was carried to shucking houses ashore.

To police this fleet, the *Governor McLane* was commissioned in 1884 for service in the Maryland fight against the poaching of the oyster beds. She was built of iron in Philadelphia, was 114ft long, 21ft in beam and had a draft of 9.2ft; she was screw-propelled and could steam at 13 knots, outrunning almost all of the bay's brigand vessels. She was armed with a 12-pound howitzer on her foredeck that saw substantial service during her patrols and combat missions. The *McLane* led Maryland's little navy until 1932.

Crisfield: Queen of the Honky Tonks

At the start of the oyster boom, Crisfield in the east became as notorious as San Francisco in the west. Crisfield was originally called Somers Cove, after Benjamin Somers who had been awarded 300 acres around Annemessex. Versions vary, but around 1866 a prosperous lawyer from Somerset County, John Woodland Crisfield, saw the wealth of the fishing in the town. He planned to bring the railway right up to the harbour so the fishermen could send their catch directly to Boston. Some say that the town rewarded him for his vision. Others say that he was a fat and ungainly man, and on a site inspection of the harbour one of the boards gave way, ducking him in the icy waters of the Annemessex River. The only way the town could placate him was to rename itself after him.

Either way, the dock front teemed with sailors and the saloons were full. There was gambling, wenching, drinking, and then more gambling and more drinking – the oysterman's main vices. Crisfield was the Las Vegas of the time. It had as many ships registered as Baltimore and many of these made a basic living plying oysters up and down the Chesapeake.

After the civil war, and newly ennobled commercially by the railway, Crisfield became a get-rich-quick, rickety city built on stilts and surrounded by moored boats. Here modern boxing was born, with rings set up in restaurants and bars, recreating the slugfests between Virginians and Marylanders that happened for real on the water and brought back to land to create an organised spectacle. These were lawless times. Harvey Johnson was a well-known saloon keeper and justice of the peace, who opened his court proceedings with the reminder: 'Gentlemen, the court is now in session, but I call your attention to the fact that business is still going on at the bar.'

Passengers on the *City of Norfolk* were startled by what they found on their day trips. John R. Wenersteen explains in his seminal book *The Oyster Wars of Chesapeake Bay*: 'To their surprise they saw a shanty town built on stilts, a town of poles and myriads of boats of all sizes and descriptions. A

town of oysters, built on oyster shells, such was Crisfield, the queen of the
honky tonks and mistress of the oyster empire of Tangier Sound.'

It became a mecca for the poor, for the newly arrived, for disenfranchised
slaves – many shuckers were black and much prized if they could open an
oyster, as many could, in a deft slice of five seconds and then pass it over to
a 'skimmer' to wash off. They were paid by the gallon shucked; $3.50 was a
good wage of sorts.

But this new workforce was not welcomed by all the townspeople. The
respectable communities of strict non-drinking Anglicans and Methodists
resented the influx of homeless men and black people. Public whipping posts
and pillories were still prominent features of villages as the community sought
to protect itself from this arrival of lawlessness and supposed unrighteousness.

The oyster boats carried cannon. Pitch battles were fought at night. In
this world probably everyone was a pirate of some sorts. It was not the
cowboys of the Wild West with their cattle; here it was the boatmen with
their oysters to pillage or protect.

Paid Off by the Boom
Crisfield became notorious for shanghaiing sailors – usually young,
innocent, newly arrived, often German immigrants who spoke no English
– who would be press-ganged into service. Black ex-slaves had long
since refused to work on the boats and the only people who would work
the dredgers were the unknowing, usually lured from the slums of the
northern cities on false promises of work and money. No local waterman
would sail with them, which created another social division.

The new immigrants were forced to work long hours on low pay, or had
usurious charges levied against their so-called wages for being advanced
for board and ragamuffin clothing, and so were kept in debt and servitude
so they would work through the winter's worst conditions.

At a voyage's end many were 'paid off with the boom' – swept overboard
by an intentional swing of the jib which brought the mainsail and its
heavy spar across the deck like a scimitar. Once in the cold water, with the
skipjack sailing away, men were simply left to drown.

The oyster boat captains were cruel, exploitative and ruthless, until
eventually their antics had to be curtailed by the federal government. But
before that law came into force in 1907, they meted out terrible hardships
and punishments to their crews.

Shipping agents recruited immigrants straight off the boats at Ellis
Island, usually they were Irish, Italian or German, but they came to be
known collectively as Paddies. They were brought by rail at night and

packed immediately on to boats and distributed among the dredgers in the middle of the bay. They were made to work from five in the morning, slept without bedding and were locked in the hold to stop them escaping. The work was harsh, especially in winter, and caused 'oyster hand' – a violently painful inflammation that took months to heal. The men were needed to crank the handles on the windlass and haul in the catch. The captains carried guns and beat anyone who would not work or shot anyone who became mutinous. At sea there was no law to protect these innocents and the captains were never prosecuted; often enough they might even be the magistrates. Some Paddies were kept in ghetto compounds on shore as a free labour pool for any passing captain.

It was these white slaves at the mast that hauled in the oysters at the height of the Chesapeake boom. One man fought against it, a young self-made immigrant marine lawyer, Louis Hennighausen. He heard of the murder of a young German immigrant called Otto Mayher who had had the temerity to complain of seasickness; he was beaten by the captain with a rope, a marlin spike and then strung up by his thumbs, and eventually, when he tried to crawl away at the dockside, had his neck broken.

The captain, one John Williams, was a well-known and apparently respected member of the Somerset County community, and as such was also invited to sit on the coroner's jury. It recorded a verdict of accidental death. Hennighausen was so outraged by this story that he persuaded the German Society to employ a private detective and made a case against Williams, eventually securing his imprisonment for eighteen years, to the outrage of other Somerset dignitaries.

It was not legislation or the courts that stopped this vicious exploitation, but the technology that brought in the petrol engine, which meant four men could do the work that had required eight before – but that was not until the turn of the century.

The Maryland Oyster Navy

In 1869 563 vessels were licensed in Maryland; the dredges employed 2,107 white men and 14,530 black men. Another 3,000 or so worked smaller boats and perhaps 10,000 people worked the trade on land. Orders were coming in from dealers in Colorado to feed the miners, and San Francisco to supply the gold rush. It was boom time.

Along with the boom came disputes, wrangling, fighting and open warfare: the tonguers resented the dredgers; the watermen resented the interlopers from the city; the Marylanders resented the Virginians and vice versa; the Chesapeake oystermen resented the boats from Long Island that came south; the gentry resented the watermen; the pious resented the drinker. Each morning the Chesapeake produced a new harvest of corpses murdered in the night.

In 1868 the Maryland General Assembly commissioned a state Oyster Navy, and gave it a cadre of fifty men to keep the peace. All the time the reefs were being plundered by everyone, or in the jargon of the day, the dredges were the 'tongues licking the reefs'.

The Oyster Navy was weak. Politicians were anxious to canvas the watermen for their votes and patronage was rife. They would solicit votes by handing out whisky and cigars. There was too much money to be plundered from the oyster beds for anyone to take law-making too seriously. Even when poachers were apprehended, the courts often threw the charges out. In one famous case a miscreant was hauled before the judge: 'Son', asked the judge. 'Were you not in my Sunday class when you was a boy?' 'Yes sir', said the man. 'That's what I thought. A boy like you couldn't possibly be guilty of anything serious. Case dismissed.'

Other moves were more spiteful political manoeuvring. Virginians refused to sell oyster seed to Maryland so the beds were not restocked. In turn the Marylanders refused to sell the Virginians the shells back to provide the essential clutch on which the larvae might grow. Just as inland buffalo were hunted to extinction, so the bounty beneath the sea was raped and defiled.

The Start of Graphic Design

Graphic design came out of Baltimore and from it the idea that foods could be harvested and transported across huge distances, wrapped, sterilised and encased in dynamic typography, primary colours and iconic logos. In winter it was oysters; in summer it was Florida fruits.

Early attempts at preserving foods involved glass bottles, but glass broke on the wagons going west and proved too fragile. In 1819 Thomas Kensett and Ezra Dagget canned the first oysters in New York, and within twenty years Baltimore was the centre of canning. Tins were hand-cut and rolled around a cylindrical mould and soldered together. The tops and bottoms were also hand-cut and soldered. A hole was left in the top to drop the oysters through and this was then sealed by solder again. A deft craftsman could make sixty tins a day.

Kensett's son was one pioneer of the new industry and Baltimore became a centre not just for the tins, but for labelling and shipping networks. Oysters were the main business and fruits became important to fill in the down times of the year in the summer. To underline just how far ahead Baltimore was, canning did not get started in Florida until 1884, Biloxi in 1916 and Puget Sound, Washington, only in 1931. Crabmeat was not tinned until the 1930s.

The first examples were elemental and direct. Companies took obvious brand names like Chef, Epicure, Sun, Full Moon, or were geographically inspired like with Pride of the Chesapeake, or by an idea, Reliable Oysters – 'Reliable is our name and our motto'. As examples of a medium that was instantly understood, the tins were direct, to the point and effective, sometimes even graphically or at least typographically brilliant. Those that survive still hold a cachet among collectors and can sell for upwards of $2,000, although more often it is closer to $20. You can still find tins with oysters in them.

Cameron's Folly with the Dancing Molly

The Chesapeake oyster wars were a public pantomime played out to both the amusement and horror of the new nation. The police of the 1880s had neither enough men, acumen, guns nor courts behind them to be effective in the face of a giant seascape littered with boats that could vanish in a wisp of mist, or who had no qualms of firing back or even ramming would-be law enforcers. Police were politically appointed and had little interest in risking their lives, or their secure sinecures, to do their job. The grandiose language used on shore held little sway on the water.

In a series of episodes, the flamboyant Virginia governor William E. Cameron set out on a personal crusade to stop the dredging of Virginia waters by night-time marauders. He armed two steamers and set sail on 17 February 1882 to catch poachers on the Rappahannock.

They found seven schooners at work. He arrested them and turned the men over to the sheriff of Mathews County who, escorted by fifty deputies, marched the prisoners 5 miles to the county jail. Unfortunately for Cameron, only one of the schooners turned out to be foreign: the *Mary Tauline* was out of New York, but the other six were Virginia boats; worse for Cameron, they were out of Onancock in Accomac County, on which he had relied for his political support. The Peninsular Enterprise declared wryly:

Half, at least, of the men captured by the expedition were … those upon
whose votes the Coalition-Republican-Readjuster party relies for its
majorities, and without whom … not one of them could be elected to
office. The Democrats of Accomac will not forget this attempt to stigmatise
so foully, for so unworthy a reason, men who … have hitherto borne
unblemished characters.

Cameron was forced to climb down and pardon the men. Worse still was to
pass when the Court of Appeal forced the county to pay the captains back
$8,600, in compensation for the boats which Cameron had auctioned off
after the raids. Undaunted a year later, Cameron planned a second surprise
raid on 27 February.

He summoned two companies of militia without notice and marched
them fully equipped from their armouries to the Boston wharf, where
they embarked on the steamers *Pamlico* and *Peed*. Their mission was to trap
poachers at Smith's Point near the mouth of the Potomac River. Cameron
announced that he was 'determined to enforce the law, and that he
would see that on this occasion there was no escape should he succeed in
capturing any of those now engaged in violating the laws'. Grand words,
but as the steamers left harbour at around midnight, Cameron was about
to regret inviting the press and local dignitaries aboard with him.

The first calamity of the night was when the steamers hit bad weather.
Around 3 a.m. the ship, which carried no ballast, began to pitch violently.
According to the *Norfolk Virginian* of 1 March 1883, the main cabin was
in turmoil, where 'colonels, generals, privates, civilians, swords, chairs,
bayonets, blankets, spittoons, coal scuttles, &c., were tumbled about and
mixed together fearfully'. The aft cabin fared worse when 'a violent lurch
of the vessel overturned a red hot coal stove and scattered the burning
coals everywhere'. The captain of the ship was burned throwing the
stove overboard and half the crew were seasick. Things would get worse.
Reports had cited more than fifty schooners illegally fishing in the bay, but
when Cameron arrived in the morning there were only eight boats to be
seen. Cameron opened fire. The boats scattered and all but one made its
escape safely.

The one boat Cameron did capture was from Maryland, but even then
the captain and half the crew escaped in a row boat. Cameron arrested the
remaining seven men on board. But more indignity followed as Cameron
bore down on the *Dancing Molly*, which seemed to have been abandoned.
The crew had fled but the captain's wife and two daughters had stayed
on board. When they saw Cameron's steamer approaching they called for

help, but when none came the girls unfurled the sails themselves and set off for the sea. The *Norfolk Virginian* reporter recorded:

> The women were equal to the emergency. All three were skilled in handling the sails and were determined not to be taken. Despite solid shot flying past them, the three women continued on their way and reaching the open waters of the Bay, easily escaped into Maryland waters with a stiff breeze behind them.

Spectators had somehow been alerted to the not so secretive raid and had lined the banks, applauding the women's escape. 'Though opposed to dredging ... everyone really wished for the safety of the tiny craft when they saw it was simply manned by three women, and when the *Dancing Molly* got safely out, the group of Virginians chivalrously gave three cheers for the pirate's wife and daughters.' Cameron became the butt of every newspaper jibe, his career was finished and his deeds immortalised in song by James F. Duncan:

'Twas off the Rappahannock's mouth,
About the break of day,
We saw with sails all gleaming white,
The Pirate Dredgers lay.

With steamers 'Peed' and 'Pamlico,'
About four knots an hour,
With rifled guns and jugs of rum,
The seas we'd come to scour.

Oh! It was glorious fun
To see the rascals run
From the City Guard and Norfolk Blues
And five big jugs of room [sic].

Poaching on the Chesapeake carried on unabated. As the oysters were plundered and the market for their harvest dwindled, the watermen were given a lifeline in the form of Prohibition. To a whisky-drinking culture, such laws were an invitation to smuggle. They helped bootleggers unload their boats at night and get their precious cargo to Washington. Briefly the Oyster Police became the Rum Police. To an area that had become accustomed to hard times, even the start of the Depression represented no large-scale change of circumstances; not as much as the four-day hurricane that hit on 19 August 1933 and devastated the beds of Tangier Sound, dumping it with fresh water, churning the beds to silt and killing the once fertile grounds.

The Second World War ushered in a new era of technology – the outboard motor. The watermen turned it to their advantage. So did the poachers. Poaching remained rife through the 1940s and 1950s, especially along a 25-mile stretch south of the Route 301 Harry Nice Bridge. A so-called Mosquito Fleet of fast, inboard boats armed with 'poaching dredges' outran police and worked at night without lights, retreating into ports on the Virginia side, just outside the reach of Maryland law.

As post-Second World War outboard motor technology caught the fancy of boaters, high-powered Mercury or Johnson motors continued to outpace the enforcers. It was a colourful time, even though men were shot and killed, and the oyster resource continued its inexorable decline. *The Washington Post* on 4 November 1947 reported:

> Already the sound of rifle fire has echoed across the Potomac River. Only fifty miles from Washington men are shooting at one another. The night is quiet until suddenly shots snap through the air. Possibly a man is dead, perhaps a boat is taken, but the oyster war will go on the next night and the next.

The price of oysters in peacetime had started to rise again and there was a living to be made poaching the Chesapeake waters again.

Shootout on Monroe Bay

It was the death of Berkley Muse that finally brought the oyster wars to an end, and saw Maryland and Virginia stop their political squabbling. Muse was a well-liked, well-moneyed man from Colonial Beach who farmed, played at real estate and, like everyone else, sometimes tongued for oysters, legally or otherwise. He was married with three children and was a successful businessman, but he still hankered after his hell-raising youth. On 7 April 1959 he was playing pool when some friends invited him to go oyster dredging.

By 4.30 a.m. the men had pulled 7 bushels of oysters from near the mouth of Monroe Bay when they found themselves in the middle of a police stake-out. Four hundred feet from the beach at Reno Pier the police boat opened fire. The men made to get away with a pair of 70hp engines but they ran into a second police launch, which also opened fire. Muse died in the hail of bullets.

Muse's death shocked the town. It led to a shake-up in the Maryland Oyster Police and alarmed the legislators in both Virginia and Maryland into action to stop the bloodshed on the bay. President John F. Kennedy signed the Potomac River Fisheries Commission Bill into law on 5 December 1962, handing control of marine research and inspection over to the new body and ending 300 years and more of colourful pirating and feuding.

10

The South

The Prowess of the Karankawa – The Coming of Ice – Biloxi –
New Orleans Cuisine & the Origins of Jambalaya –
Kitty West & the Emergence of Burlesque – Mexico –
The First Submarine

*This coast is the Kingdom of oysters, as the great Bank of Newfoundland, and the
gulf and the river St Lawrence are that of the cod-fish. All these low lands, which we
coasted as near as possible, are bordered with trees, to which are fastened a prodigious
quantity of little oysters, of an exquisite taste: others, much larger and less dainty, are
found in the sea in such numbers that they form banks in it, which we take at first for
rocks on a level with the surface of the water.*

Pierre de la Charlevoix, 1690s

*The sizzle of gumbo. Oysters the size of a baby's fist. The head of a crawfish oozing
in the sun. A pelican alighting on a black metal balcony, gulping at the hornets as they
vex it. A widower, a Creole, was her client that afternoon.*

Joseph O'Connor, *Redemption Falls*, 2007

Although the south was the first part of America to be discovered,
settlement came much later – some of the French colonisers were second-
generation re-settlers from Canada. From further east, creek American
Indians from Georgia and Alabama migrated south in the 1700s and settled.

Apalachicola means the People on the Other Side. Round the bays there is the same evidence of huge early middens of the first Indian civilisations.

William Bartram, a naturalist writing in 1792, found mammoth oysters jutting out from a cliff along the Savannah River. They were '15 to 20 inches in length with hollows sufficient to receive an ordinary man's foot'. Geologists have dated them to 50 million years BC. The chalky white Shell Bluff at Burke County survives and looms 100ft high, the oyster shells still perfectly intact although surrounded by debris and mud from some prehistoric disaster. At some point this was probably the coastline.

Oysters are found around the Gulf of Mexico from Lower Laguna Madre and Aransas Bay in the west, through the French settled bayous of Caillou Lake and Terrebone Bay, round the Mississippi Sound to Mobile Bay and the Apalachicola Bay in the east. Some of the reefs are so big they appear on early maps as hazards to navigation.

The oyster industry lagged behind the east coast by as much as 100 years, until the railway arrived to open up trading between the Gulf of Mexico and the new cities of New Orleans, Lafayette and Baton Rouge.

A sense of the change that was about to engulf the area is found in the language. The city of Mobile, Alabama, pronounced Mo-beel, takes its name from a Native American dialect, a trading lingua franca used around the coast which itself belonged originally to the native Mobile Indians of the central Gulf Coast. It was used from Florida westward, as far as Texas, to facilitate trade between tribes and various settlers all speaking different languages. The dictionary calls it a pidginised form of Choctaw and Chickasaw that also contains elements of Algonquian and colonial languages, including English, Spanish and French. It has a simplified syllable and sound structure and elementary grammar compared to its primary parent language Choctaw, the language of the Mississippi Indians. Enthusiasts and Native Americans still preserve this language as part of their culture. It was even used as a secret code during the First World War.

A Texas tale tells how a group of rangers trapped a party of renegade Indians at a cove between the bluff and the waters near Corpus Christi. The lawmen made camp and waited overnight to attack. In the morning the beach was empty; the Indians had vanished. All that was left was a trail of hoof prints leading into seemingly impassable waters.

The Indians had taken the Reef Road, an invisible bridge made by a series of interconnecting oyster beds beneath the surface, which linked up to the bay at Neuces and could at low tide support the weight of wagons and horses and had allowed the renegades to escape. At high tide the submerged road was invisible.

These Indians may have been lucky. The indigenous coastal tribe, the Karankawa, were wiped out long before the civil war, mostly, it seems, by disease.

The Prowess of the Karankawa

The Karankawa, or Carancahueses, were nomadic along the coastal prairie grasslands from Galveston down to Corpus Christi. They were tall – more than 6ft – well-built, muscular men, stark naked when the first settlers met them, with pierced lower lips and nipples. They smeared their bodies with alligator grease to protect themselves against the mosquitoes.

The Spanish explorer Cabeza de Vaca was taken in by them when he was shipwrecked in 1528, and recorded their huge physical prowess: 'They go naked in the most burning sun ... in winter they go out in early dawn to take a bath ... breaking the ice with their body.' He said they could shoot an arrow right through a bear and it would carry on for another 40m. Even at distances of nearly 200m, he said, the arrow would sink into the soil up to the feather shaft. They had a reputation as fierce warriors and also for cannibalism, although this seems to be more to do with the ceremonial eating of the souls of their enemy rather than a dietary preference. De Vaca also admitted there had been cannibalism aboard his ship, which apparently horrified them.

The Karankawa had dug out canoes which they used to fish for oysters, clams, scallops, other molluscs, turtles, fish, porpoises, alligators and underwater plants from the shallow waters. They would gorge on foods in season, oysters notably in early spring. Their first contact with Europeans was typically disastrous. The first white men after de Vaca were Spanish slave traders who took the men and left the women with white man's diseases. Then came the French who plundered their settlements.

Their language has all but died out with them, but it is thought the name means 'dog rearers' because they hunted with coyote-like hounds. Those that survived disease probably died in the Texas-Mexico wars. Their name does survive in a legend, which if true can be dated to 1816 and was the cause of gossip right into the last century.

Around 1820, a band of settlers set up homestead in Texas near the Karankawa settlement. They had argued for months with the Mexican authorities before finally agreeing on a site near St Bernard, which is still a choice spot for oysters. Their concern was the cannibalistic reputation of the Karankawa.

One evening, a naked Karankawa warrior strode into their camp and started speaking to them in semi-fluent English. He said he had learned English from a mad white hermit. The man, he said, had been shipwrecked. It was an American Indian taboo to harm a mad man, so he was left to himself as a recluse, but this Indian had befriended him and learned how to speak English. Around his neck the Indian wore a European locket and inside was the image of a young, white woman. The name Theodosia was engraved on it.

A great storm, he said, had given him his 'white wife', but she had died and all he had of hers was this locket, and she had begged him to find white people and tell her story: There had been a huge storm. The Indians had strapped themselves to cedar trees to survive. When it subsided he went down to the beach where he found a galleon wrecked on the reefs at the mouth of the river. The crew were all dead. He went aboard to see what he could find and heard a cry for help. Down in the galley he found a naked white woman chained to the bulkhead. He prised her loose and carried her back to shore. He gave her water. In his arms, she explained that the storm had been as bad at sea as it had been on land.

She told him she had been on another ship that was attacked. It was set on fire and she had been taken prisoner and kept on this second galleon. Everyone else on the first ship was killed. She had been kept in the galley, chained for three years and used as a slave.

She gave him the locket. She asked him to pass it on with her story to any white people he might meet. She said her father was an important white chief, misunderstood by his people, and that her husband was also a chief, but not as important as her father. She died in his arms and he buried her on the shoreline. Karankawa Indians, he explained, usually only buried someone from their family, so he considered her to be his 'white wife'.

This might just be taken for a bit of fancy storytelling by the camp fire, except for a number of facts that have leached out over the years and give it some credibility. A storm and tidal wave was recorded as engulfing Galveston in 1816. Archaeologists have since found the wrecks of old ships in what might have been the mouth of St Bernard (now landlocked), but probably the same storm changed its course at the time.

So who was Theodosia? Records showed that a coasting-barge named the *Patriot* had left Charleston harbour on 25 December 1813, bound for New York. Conditions were good; the sea was calm. But the *Patriot* vanished without trace. On board was the wife of South Carolina's governor, Mrs Joseph Allston. There was no obvious connection because although she was known as an independent and spirited woman, she had travelled under her husband's name.

But she was no stranger to politics. She was Theodosia, and her maiden name was Burr. She was the daughter, and only legitimate child, of former vice-president Aaron Burr – who had been waiting for her at the time in New York. She never arrived.

So even in those times, pirates could capture a vice-president's daughter and a governor's wife and use her as their slave without being held to account or captured, or even discovered, except by pure chance on a beach by a passing Indian, who is said to still haunt that place.

The Coming of Ice

The Apalachicola Bay encompasses the waters of St George Sound and St Vincent Sound, a 210-square-mile estuary, wide and shallow, averaging between 6 and 9ft deep at low tide. The tonguers sailed small wooden boats, 20–23ft long, raking up the oysters from the shallow waters. The oysters were sorted on board and then packed in coarse, woven burlap bags and shaded until they reached the shore. On shore, the seafood houses employed 'housemen' who sorted the oysters and packaged them for sale either in bags or boxes, or sent them to be shucked, washed and sold in pints or gallons.

Dr John Gorrie, a local physician, had invented an ice-making machine in 1851 that changed the area, so much so that they built a museum in his name where the original machine still stands. But it was not to be ice-cream that would make the area's fortune. The Apalachicola businessmen were quick to spot that the new invention of artificial ice had other applications; and they foresaw the arrival of pasteurisation which would allow them to send oysters across the continent. Before the turn of the century, more than fifty cities were being fed on the newly preserved oysters, freshly packed in ice.

John G. Ruge was born in Apalachicola in 1854, the son of Herman Ruge, who had migrated from Hanover, Germany, in the early 1840s. John and his brother George worked for their father in his machine shop and hardware store until they changed the name of the firm from Herman Ruge and Sons to the Ruge Brothers Canning Company in 1885. They had studied the work of Louis Pasteur in Europe on bacteria and adapted the process of pasteurisation and sold it out under the Alligator brand.

The Apalachicola Northern Railroad arrived in 1907 and ran an Oyster Special to Atlanta, with oysters packed in ice. By 1915, some 400 men manned 117 oyster boats under sail, 250 shuckers worked in various oyster houses, and a number of other workers were employed in two canneries. Fifty thousand cans of oysters were being sent out daily.

Biloxi

Another important oyster town was Biloxi which has an unusual story of its own.

Biloxi is the oldest French settlement in the Mississippi Valley. Since its discovery, it has changed hands many times and served under eight different flags: France, England, Spain, West Florida Republic, Mississippi Magnolia, Confederate States, Mississippi State and finally the United States. The name Biloxi means First People and was settled by the French looking for the mouth of the Mississippi River.

As early as the 1850s Biloxi was a fashionable resort. Elegant hotels graced the waterfront, steamers from New Orleans, Louisiana and Mobile made regular stops in Biloxi, and fresh seafood was always available. The cool Gulf breezes and sandy beaches lured tourists and summer residents, but it was oysters and other shellfish, especially shrimp and also sponges, that would make it famous.

There had been some early trade with sailors from Dubrovnik (in what was later to become Yugoslavia). They seem to have developed a special relationship with the area as early as 1700. Unlike other American cities, the port attracted a different mix of people who found they could make a living from the oyster business or tourism and stayed. Descendants of early French settlers still live in Biloxi. The coast abounds with family names such as Ladner, Moran and Necaise. They developed the Biloxi boatbuilding tradition and later passed this knowledge on to Slovakian arrivals.

The railway arrived in 1869. The first cannery, Lopez, Elmer & Company, opened in 1881. It was owned jointly by two local men, a Spanish immigrant, who had made money in Cuba, an Englishman from Hull and a northerner from Fredericksburg, Indiana.

Setting up new factories required more labour; camps with their own stores and shotgun housing were set up around the factories, like the paternalistic English mill towns, self-contained, self-sufficient communities. Cheap rent and a company store that carried basic supplies kept the workforce concentrated in the area around the factories. For the workers, they had the advantage of being able to live among family and friends, and retain some of their culture that might otherwise have been lost or more roundly Americanised as it was elsewhere.

The city's population had reached 3,234 by 1890. By the turn of the century, Biloxi had five canneries, nine oyster dealers and five Bohemian camps for the Slovaks. Nearby Barataria employed 500 people, half in the factory and half on the boats. Lopez and Elmer had a fleet of sixty vessels.

The greatest immigration occurred in the first years of the twentieth century. The men would work on the boats, the women in the canneries. The failure of the sugar cane crop in the 1920s put many Cajuns out of work. Where the African American moved north to Chicago to the other big cities, these Cajuns moved south towards their French and Spanish roots.

Life was no easier ashore than at sea. Each factory had a whistle with its own distinctive sound, which signalled the arrival of the catch and summoned people to work. The factories were always cold, especially in the winter during oyster season. Women wore heavy stockings and wrapped their legs in newspaper to keep warm. Their hands grew cold after working with the icy shrimp, hour after hour. One woman recalls how her mother would bring bowls of hot water from home for her children to warm their hands.

Oyster shucking was piecemeal work. Women equipped with an oyster knife, a glove and finger stars – small pieces of cloth to cover the thumb and forefinger of the hand holding the knife – stood eight to a cart, four

Children help out with the shucking at Baton Rouge around 1910.

on each side, shucking oysters and placing them in a cup. The oyster cup attached to the side of the cart and held about a gallon of oysters. A series of railroad tracks ran from the loading docks into and throughout the factory. The men unloaded the oysters into the carts. Four or five carts at a time rolled into the steam boxes to steam open the oysters, and from the steam room, a line of about nine carts travelled on one of the tracks to the shucking room. The eight women who worked at each cart usually worked together all the time. In a sense, they were a team. They tended to be friends or relatives, sometimes all Slovaks or all Cajuns.

To support the huge demand for oysters, boatbuilding became an important ancillary industry. They designed boats specifically suited to their needs and the Gulf waters. Flat-bottomed, double-sail boats, called cats, had been the most common boats used in the earliest days, but as demand grew they struggled to carry the kind of loads the factories wanted. Schooners, because of their size and sail power, replaced catboats as the vessel of choice.

A hurricane in 1893 destroyed a large portion of the fleet. The boatbuilders replaced their losses with a new type of boat known as the Biloxi schooner. Similar to the Chesapeake and Baltimore schooner, the Biloxi had a broad beam for large crews, a shallow draft suited to inland bodies of water, and sail power enough to drag the oyster dredges and shrimp nets. Builders used cypress from the Louisiana swamps for the frames and planking, and Mississippi long leaf yellow pine for the keel, masts and spars. They ranged in size from 50–60ft. The largest ever built, the *Mary Margaret*, could carry 500 barrels of oysters.

Schooners also acted as freight boats carrying lumber, charcoal and fruit between New Orleans and Mobile. Although they were good work boats and heavy haulers, they earned the nickname White Winged Queens because of their grace and beauty under sail. They survived until the mid-1930s, when most owners simply converted their schooners to power boats by cutting off the masts and installing engines.

Boatbuilders later designed a power boat known as the Biloxi lugger. On this boat the cabin rests astern and the foredeck is clear for unloading and culling the catch. In 1933 the Mississippi Seafood Conservation laws approved power boat dredging, and the Biloxi schooner was obsolete.

The men stayed on the boats to protect the beds from poachers. Whatever state edicts were passed the lawlessness on the waters remained unabated. Here, it was in 1870 that the taking of oysters during the summer months was outlawed. Thereafter there have been successive waves of legislation trying to impose good practice on the water, much of which has been largely ignored. Even today, oyster rustlers face fines of $750 and 120 days in prison.

The arrival of the Vietnamese in Biloxi in the 1980s was almost a carbon copy of how the Slovaks and Poles arrived a century or more before – their skills on the water and desire to be together lured them to the oyster business. Before Katrina, more than 2,000 Vietnamese, that's 51 per cent of Mississippi's entire Vietnamese population, lived in Biloxi.

The Vietnamese settled in Biloxi with their own shops and cafes. The bonanza was no longer oysters, but gambling, legalised in 1992 and attracting 60,000 people a night to the old dockside.

New Orleans Cuisine & the Origins of Jambalaya

The melting pot of people and cultures around New Orleans produced a cuisine that was as innovative as it was inspired and deserves its own consideration.

With or without an engine, life on the boats was tough and unrelenting. Men lived and slept on the boats; their only respite was mealtimes. The Biloxi schooners had a charcoal stove with room for one pot. The cook, an appointed crew member, prepared everything in that one pot, slumgullion style – one ingredient over another.

The principles for a proper or an original jambalaya are set down by how it is cooked. The onions are sweated down in the pot, as many as can be packed in, and then slow-cooked for at least an hour to form a base. Then comes the seasoning – celery, garlic, Worcestershire sauce, ketchup, cayenne pepper, Tabasco, some water, and it is left to cook for another thirty minutes or more. At this stage it is almost a variation on a French onion soup, but on to this base goes rice, parsley, onion tops, mushrooms, oysters, oyster juice and salt, and this is poached in the onions for at least another hour.

This variation on jambalaya takes it down almost to abstracts and seems like a true cook's visionary early recipe that was making use of the small things around to produce an interesting and sustaining supper. It is almost a risotto, but at the same time it has that essential jambalaya friction that something has arrived here from Spain, from France, as well as Italy, or perhaps grabbed from Indian cornmeal gruels:

Onions and garlic are sweated in a pot. A pint of oysters and their liquid added. Then half a cup of water and rice. Then chicken livers and/or gizzards. Cook until the rice is done and leave to stand for 5 minutes to let the flavours come through.

The Biloxi bakeries made a special bread for the fishermen called Boat Bread which sold for a nickel a loaf. Boat bread or hard tack accompanied every meal. While every boat prided itself on the variety of its cuisine, drinks were always the same: coffee, Barq's root beer brewed in Biloxi or sweet wine with water.

The south had its own sense of hospitality and restaurants which have also produced iconic dishes that have travelled the world, not least of which is Oysters Rockefeller, credited to Jules Alciatore of Antoine's in New Orleans in 1899. It was a twist on a dish they had been doing with snails, but snails were becoming expensive. It was named for John D. Rockefeller, who had seemingly little connection to the area, but the oil magnate was the richest man in America, as well as a philanthropist, so the christening was in the spirit of richness and giving; or perhaps Jules was hoping to attract him as a customer. Even today the menu pointedly notes this dish as 'our creation':

Oysters Rockefeller

Shuck the oysters, keeping the juices, wash out the shells and lay back in the cleaned shell and set on a tray. Dice rocket, spring onion, watercress, garlic, parsley and sweat in butter for two minutes. Mix in the breadcrumbs and oyster juices. Cover each oyster shell generously with the mix. Grill at the hottest heat possible for 30 seconds or until the top starts to colour. Serve with lemon wedges.

Some recipes suggest spinach or celery; some, more dubiously, cheese. Although there are many recipes pairing cheese and oysters, few of them are totally convincing. There is a lazy version which is just a hollandaise flamed under the grill. Many variations go for Tabasco, which comes from New Orleans anyway, and Pernod, of which New Orleans has its own version, Herbsaint. Anchovies and Worcestershire sauce sometimes appear, but the real crux on which this recipe should stand is the garlic and the parsley; even the fennel/absinthe/Pernod route is probably an inessential distraction. Alciatore's admission that the dish was designed as a replacement for snails proves that beyond parsley and garlic anything else is an add-on. He is said to have sworn everyone in the restaurant to secrecy as to the precise quantity of ingredients.

And that was not his only oyster dish. He also claimed: Huitres Thermidor (with tomatoes and bacon); Huitres a la Ellis (with mushrooms and sherry); Huitres a la Foch (fried and crumbed oysters set on foie gras on toast); and Canapé Balthazar (breaded and buttered). The restaurant also claims Oysters Bienville, the oysters grilled in a sherry-laced béchamel, dated to the 1930s and christened after Jean-Baptiste Le Moyne, Sieur de Bienville, the second colonial governor of Louisiana.

The French influence at Antoine's is rigid, but in other parts of the city the mix of Spanish, Indian, Caribbean, Cajun and Creole all meet.

Creole fried oysters varied the classic French egg, breadcrumb and flour batter with its own twist. The oysters were marinated for an hour in a mix of egg, ketchup, Tabasco and Worcestershire sauce, and pepper, before being rolled in cornmeal and then shallow fried.

However, the oyster sandwich, or the Po'Bo, is a hand-me-down from northern European culture, which New Orleans has adopted, although it does make guest appearances in club sandwiches in other parts of America and is obviously a descendant of the middle-class, well-to-do oyster loaf. Aficionados say the bread – a style of French loaf split open – is critical to the Po'Bo and should come only from certain New Orleans bakeries. The dressings are optional – add lettuce, mayonnaise, tomato and bacon, or not as you choose. The fried oyster filling stands alongside the shrimp and the beef with gravy as one of the flags of the region's cooking. For the New Orleans oyster festival in April the local chefs get together and vie to create the longest Po'Bo in the world down Bourbon Street – the record is currently 34ft of sandwich.

Tabasco sauce itself comes from nearby New Iberia and has since travelled the world with the oyster. It has been made by the McIlhenny family since the end of the civil war. Avery Island is an old salt flat, 7 miles south of New Iberia. The American Indians traded the salt as far away as Ohio. Edmund McIlhenny was no crofter, but a New Orleans banker who was given some dried peppers by a soldier returning from the Mexican wars. His wife planted them in their garden.

When civil war erupted they fled, as Union and Confederates fought bitterly over the salt flats. Twenty years later the family returned to a wasted Avery Island where the only thing still surviving was the capsicum plants. Edmund determined to start up in business and in 1868 produced his sauce using the local salt and the chopped peppers; he bottled the first batch in perfume bottles. He sent a sample to the federal governor, General Hazard, whose brother had one of the biggest wholesale grocery businesses in America. On that order he was on his way. Tabasco means 'place of coral or oyster shell'.

The other locally brewed flavour is Herbsaint, an obviously French derivation of absinthe that slakes through the cooking, even in the mayonnaise, to go with what is effectively an oyster variation of the Scotch egg, making a crust of andouille sausage and breadcrumbs in which the oysters are egged and wrapped before deep frying.

Kitty West & the Emergence of Burlesque

New Orleans also gave rise to the modern burlesque shows, the forerunners of striptease and lap dancing, and sure enough one of the first was the *Oyster Girl* starring Kitty West. Burlesque was a floor show with a simple story, erotic dancing and huge sets that started in the 1940s on Bourbon Street. About midnight the doors would shut, the stage would fill with smoke and a voice would announce: 'In the swamps of Louisiana at midnight the big oyster shell opens up …' And out would pop Kitty West.

Kitty's colourful story was not untypical of many poor farm girls. She was Abbie Jewel Slawson from a poor Mississippi family of six who learned to dance in the cotton fields. Her mother claimed to be a cousin of Elvis Presley, who later came to admire her performance. At 14 her father ran off leaving them destitute and Kitty and a friend found their way to New Orleans. She was instantly captivated by the showgirls and billboards. 'They looked like royalty to me,' she wrote later.

She got her break at Gasper Gulotta's club when the star, Miss Hurricane, suffered an epileptic fit. Gulotta had seen Abbie dance and persuaded her to step in. Quickly they dressed her in false eyelashes and high heels. The master of ceremonies went out on stage and introduced her as Kitty Dare.

> I walked out on stage and I just stood there for a minute. I was dumbfounded! The lights – I stood there. All I could see at that particular minute was my grandfather. Like he was looking right at me saying 'What are you doing?' 'Cause I felt so guilty, like I was really committing an unforgivable sin! Then all of a sudden the people were screaming 'Dance! Dance!' And they started dancing and clapping their hands. And the band started … I really didn't know all of her routine but I more or less made up my own as I went along. And then I would take the veils off one by one and then I would put them over my eyes. But I made a big mistake; I was giving the veils away. The guys were hollering, 'Give me a veil!'

Kitty's dancing was the talk of Bourbon Street and she transferred to the Casino Royale with her own show *Angeline: The Oyster Girl*, which in vaudeville circles is still around in various forms today. In a sense she was the original oyster girl, glamorous but typical of so many other country girls who left the farms for the city and were not as fortunate as her. But she was 16 in a world of Italian-dominated machismo, and she had her share of exploitation:

> What happened to me, I hope no one has to live through it. And some things that happened to me on Bourbon Street were quite bad. Things that, even in that time, people say, 'Well, those things – that doesn't happen.' But they did.

Kitty was to go on dancing across the Midwest, putting on shows that were the forerunners of today's Las Vegas extravaganzas. She was no shrinking violet and shot to national fame when a rival act was billed ahead of her one night. Divena had perfected an underwater striptease performed inside a giant tank. Not to be upstaged, Kitty marched out on stage halfway through the first act wielding a pickaxe: 'I just wanted to break the tank in a million pieces, and I did. I went out there and I just started pounding away at the bottom. I didn't want to hurt her, but I was just in such a rage that I didn't want her to take all the spotlight.'

Water rushed out of the tank and Divena sunk to the bottom, dumbfounded. The audience ran for the doors as 300 gallons of water flooded the tables. Fortunately, Kitty had had the foresight to pre-warn a *Life* magazine photographer of her plan. As the police hauled her off to jail, she obligingly posed half naked with the arresting officer in front of the jail bars. The next week the story made headlines as it went out over the AP wire. Kitty did not spend one night in jail, and was fined $10. The reputation of the Bourbon Street burlesque queens was assured. Her reputation and succession intact, Kitty romanced singer Mel Tormé and then married the jockey Jerry West, eventually licensing other girls to fill the role.

George Schmidt, a jazzman and painter, caught a rather less romanticised and probably truer version of New Orleans high life in one of his paintings of a front parlour. Centre stage is a voluptuous red-headed stripper, naked except for her earrings, in the middle of a packed, respectable New Orleans gathering, about to pass a salver of opened oysters around. She is coyly holding one hand over her pubic hair, in the other she has an opened oyster. The *joie de vivre* disappears as you realise the decadence unfolding. Something has been organised, but it is not clear what. It is only a snapshot, frozen on a moment. In the foreground one smiling, cheering, leering male face is holding up an oyster as if to say, 'Look what I got!'

It is one of New Orleans' great paintings, and catches the depraved nuances of boom time in oyster towns: the respectability and the sleaze all at the same time; as ever the oyster inhabits more than one world simultaneously.

Mexico

Chilli, Ceviche & Beans

The Mexican oyster trade is still one of the largest in the world. In the ruins of the Mayan temples here oysters have been found in the walls. Most of the oysters stay in Mexico because there is a long-standing tradition among men to eat them usually as cocktails in bars. Classically this will be with tomato, onion, chilli and oil; or with lemon, salt, ketchup, hot pepper and onion; or on the half-shell. Oysters feature in some pillars of Mexican cuisine, notably in a hot sauce with onions and tomatoes; in a soup with blue crabs, shrimp and clams; and, of course, breaded in cornmeal and fried. Demand is highest during Lent. The lagoons mix oystering with catching shrimp and other fish, but economically the oyster is the most important.

The approach to cooking changes as you go west and Tex Mex starts to mingle in. This so-called Texas caviar is suggested for serving with smoked oysters, which originally might have just meant laid over the barbeque. Obviously in the beginning these would all have been cooked down together:

Sweat chopped red onion, jalapeno pepper, carrot, red and yellow pepper, oregano and shallot in good olive oil until they are soft, about 5 minutes. Then add a can of cooked black-eyed peas, a splash of red wine vinegar, oyster liquor, sugar, parsley and Tabasco. Take off the heat and leave to marinate in an airtight jar. They will keep two weeks in the fridge. Eat in a tortilla wrap with fresh, roast or smoked oysters.

Similarly, there are Mexican recipes for cold oyster ceviche which are transparently very old and date to the times before refrigeration. They are simple to follow but exotic and fiery in their flavours, as you might expect:

Sauté a base of onions and garlic in a pan until soft. Add chopped and blanched carrot, cauliflower, bay, marjoram, oregano, pepper, lime juice, wine vinegar and the oysters with their juices and strips of jalapenos. Cook until the oysters start to curl, then macerate overnight.

The oysters are still hand-harvested by wading and wearing tough gloves, and in some cases still dived for in Mandinga lagoon where the waters can be as much as 4m deep. Wearing a face mask, a diver can usually bring back twenty-five to thirty oysters in a single drop. They work in four-hour shifts.

The Mexican government insists there are always two men in a boat – one to catch and one to shuck and throw back the shells. Only 20 per cent of oysters are allowed to be sold on the shell to ensure that the shells stay in the coastal area and can be replanted, due to a law first passed in 1976.

The First Submarine

There is one other innovation that belongs to the North American story of this era. A young immigrant engineer from what is now Lithuania, Julius Kroehl, became fascinated with how diving bells were being used to build the bridges around Manhattan in the 1850s. He filed a patent for the Improvement of Iron-Bending Machines. In the civil war he tried to sell his idea of a moving underwater ship to the navy who ignored him. Undaunted, he became chief engineer and a partner in the Pacific Pearl Company.

The *New York Times* of 30 May 1866 reported on the first dive of the Sub Marine Explorer. Kroehl, with three friends, dove to the bottom of the harbour at North Third Street. Bystanders waited anxiously for an hour and a half before the steel monster reappeared and the hatch slowly opened. Kroehl, in the best of spirits, was puffing away at his Meerschaum pipe and holding up a bucket of mud, freshly collected from the bottom of the harbour.

The news caused a sensation. The Explorer was dismantled, shipped to Panama's east coast and then taken overland by train through the jungle to Panama City on the Pacific. Panama at the time was a wild shanty town, a trading post between east and west, the link from New York to San Francisco, a town of hotels and gambling, a continent in transit. The arrival of the submarine was greeted as an important event.

As far back as the days of the conquistadors, divers had been digging up treasures from the depths of the Archipelago de las Perlas, just 30 miles off the coast. One of the islands, Contadora, had been a stop-off for the Spanish where they counted their booty in secret. The name means Book keeper.

One of the most famous pearls of all time, La Peregrina, probably came through Contadora. Garcilasso de la Vega said it was found at Panama in 1560 by a black man who was rewarded with his liberty, and his owner with the office of mayor of Panama. It appears as a brooch in two portraits of Queen Margarita of Spain by Velasquez, dated 1634, and is often linked to the same brooch worn by film star Elizabeth Taylor in the 1960s. The

Pacific Pearl Company knew what this new invention was about, and where it was going. The *Mercantile Chronicle*, a Panama paper, described how the revolutionary machine-boat worked:

> Before submersion, enough air is filled into the compressed air chamber using a pump with the power of 30 horses mounted on another boat until the air in the chamber reaches a density of more than 60 pounds.
>
> The men enter the machine through the tower on the upper side and as soon as the water is permitted to fill the ballast chambers, the machine sinks directly down to the ocean floor where a sufficient amount of compressed air is promptly fed into the working chamber until it possesses sufficient volume and power to resist the enormous pressure of the water, so that the men can open the hatches in the floor of the machine and begin recovering oysters.

Kroehl was anxious to get started. He ordered trials to begin immediately. He was on a mission and in a hurry to work deep underwater. In his haste he could not have known about what we now call the 'bends'. Rising too quickly in his submarine from a great depth, the nitrogen in his blood expanded, literally causing his blood to foam. His invention killed him on its first day at work. The local doctors announced his death on 9 September 1867, reportedly from 'fever', but that was not the case.

Two years later the *New York Times* reported another story, about a pearl-diving expedition to an island it referred to as St Elmo. The Explorer had remained submerged for four hours and finally surfaced with 1,800 oysters on board. The process was repeated on each of the next eleven days, until the crew had collected 10.5 tons of oysters and pearls worth $2,000. The paper then recorded, 'all divers succumbed to fever'.

All too had died of the bends. The world's first submarine was publicly damned as a vessel of misfortune, madness and disease.

Nothing more was heard of the Explorer for 137 years; then in precisely this same bay, off San Telmo, it was discovered by chance in 2001 by Jim Delgado, the director of the Vancouver Maritime Museum. It had been languishing, abandoned for more than a century. Locals had just presumed it was a piece of wreckage from the Second World War.

Proper working submarines were not really invented until after the First World War. Kroehl had so nearly succeeded sixty years earlier. Technically, perhaps, he had, but he was driven by the lure of the pearl, not war, although pearling was hardly a less demanding occupation than being a soldier. From the earliest accounts slaves had stones wrapped to their legs to make them sink further and faster. Ironically, it was the salvaging of the boats sunk in the First World War that presented the commercial spur to build the first working submarines. Diving helmets pre-dated all this cast and were invented in England by Smeaton to repair bridges in Northumberland. But for divers looking for pearls, who needed mobility and to be able to work in different places, such cumbersome early headgear was useless until rubber was discovered in 1839, and it would take many decades and lost lives before it found its way to the remote pearl islands.

II

The West & Canada

San Francisco & the Hangtown Fry – An Awful Silence –
Of Cabbages & Kings – Land of the Beausoleil & the Malagash –
The Caraquet & the Acadians

San Francisco & the Hangtown Fry

*And the winds of adventure blew the oyster pirate sloops up and down San
Francisco Bay, from raided oyster-beds and fights at night on shoal and flat, to
markets in the morning against city wharves, where peddlers and saloon-keepers
came down to buy.*

Jack London, *John Barleycorn*

The California oyster was so abundant that their crushed, wind-riven shells
produced a 'white glistening beach that extends from San Mateo for a
dozen or more miles southward', reported one settler as late as 1893. Some
of these have been dated back to 4,000 BC. Shellfish figured prominently
not just in tribal diets but also in their spiritual beliefs. The shells were
given trading and talismanic qualities.

In San Francisco the native oysters were plundered as quickly as the gold.
There were barely 600 people registered as living in San Francisco in 1848,
the year before General John Sutter struck gold. It was still a naked, mud
city, with very few women and only illegal gambling for diversion, when
it was suddenly overrun by a desperate influx of people. Forty thousand

arrived within a year, and more the year after. They came overland; they came round the horn from the east; they crossed by land at Panama; they came from South America. They came in their thousands and created an almost instant combustion for a trading city.

The zenith of the oyster trade was 1899 when 2.5 million pounds of them were sold in a year, but by 1908 the growing urban sprawl had polluted the waters to the point where production was half that, and by 1921 the beds were dead.

The gold rush is commemorated in one of America's most famous oyster recipes, the Hangtown Fry, which is often credited as the first recipe of Californian cuisine. One variation of the story has it that a condemned man in San Francisco was asked what he wanted to eat for his last meal, so he ordered the two most expensive ingredients in town. Other versions are richer, more detailed and maybe not so believable. It is often credited to the Cary House Hotel, the first brick-built building in the state. But the hotel, which is still standing, makes no mention of it on its website. The recipe is usually dated to 1849 but as the hotel was not built until 1857, that seems suspect. More likely, perhaps, that the year 1849 is just synonymous with the 49ers striking it rich, so it is a convenient storytelling date, but anything much earlier is not that plausible because there were few settlers before then.

Hangtown is now known as Placerville. It was a supply base for the gold panning on the South Fork. It got its old name from the day that three (or some stories say five) desperadoes were hung from the same giant white oak tree, the stump of which is said to still survive in the cellar of one of the high-street bars.

The local version of the story has the recipe originating in the saloon of the El Dorado Hotel, now the site of the Cary House Hotel. The hotel sat across the street from the Hangman's Tree and was where the lucky miners who struck it rich would go to celebrate. The El Dorado burned down and legend has it that there was enough gold found in the ashes to pay for the building of the new Cary House.

According to the story, a prospector – who is sometimes even named as Shirt-tail Bend – rushed into the saloon of the El Dorado Hotel, announcing that he had just struck it rich in the creek near the town and was looking to celebrate. He untied his belt and spilled the gold nuggets on the bar for everyone to see. He turned to the barman and said: 'I want you to cook me up the finest and most expensive meal in the house. I'm a rich man and I'm going to celebrate my good luck.'

The chef said all he had were eggs, which had been carefully packed to make the journey over the dust and rock roads; bacon, which had been shipped from Boston; and fresh oysters which were brought on ice daily from San Francisco. 'Take your pick,' he said. 'I can cook anything you want.'

The prospector replied: 'Scramble me up a whole mess of eggs and oysters, throw in some bacon, and serve 'em up. I'm starving. I've been living on nothing much more than canned beans since I got to California, and at last I can afford a real meal.'

A less romantic version by George Leonard Herter and Berthe E. Herter, in *Bull Cook and Authentic Historical Recipes and Practices*, attributes the dish to San Francisco:

> In 1853, a man named Parker opened a saloon called Parker's Bank Exchange in the Montgomery Block, a famous building built by General Halleck. Parker invented and served a dish called Hangtown Fry. Its fame spread all over San Francisco and the surrounding areas. A few drinks and a Hangtown Fry was and is considered a gentleman's evening.

Whatever the true origins, the dish became a feature of the gold-mining camps of the late 1800s. Hangtown Fry was a one-skillet meal for hungry miners who had plenty of gold money to spend. It cost as much as $6 a time, which was indeed a fortune then. Ordering a Hangtown Fry was a mark of prosperity, the status symbol of the day. The recipe swept the entire Northwest Territory, from California to Seattle.

The Herters rather cryptically and tantalisingly suggest that the dish is actually a long, slow cook which modern restaurants cannot be bothered with. They are probably alluding to whether you mix it throughout like scrambled egg, or just fold it over at the end like an omelette; the latter seems more believable because effectively it can be a Spanish omelette using oysters and bacon in place of potatoes. The Spanish influence is quite plausible too, in a culinary sense, because many of the Californians were pre-gold rush and still Catholic and Mexican enclaves.

It would also seem logical that the affectation of egg and crumbing the oysters and frying them separately may be a later embellishment. Since its origination, different versions proliferate either by adding milk, cream, Parmesan, cognac or brandy, or sometimes lazily just throwing the bacon on as garnish. The cartoonist A.I. Vermeer stressed: 'Fry very slowly. If the business is done too dry, you will immediately be banished from California.'

This credible version of the recipe is attributed to the now defunct Blue Bell Cafe on Main Street, Placerville:

Fry two slices of bacon in another skillet until just before it becomes crisp.
Beat two eggs lightly. Place the bacon like railroad tracks off-centre in a frying
pan, pour a bit of the egg over the bacon. Place the oysters on the bacon and
pour the remaining eggs over. Cook and then fold the omelette over.

In other versions the oysters are breaded and fried and everything is
cooked together. It can also have peppers, onions, even garlic thrown in
to sauté, first with the bacon, then the oysters and lastly the egg, which all
seems more of a pragmatic cook in one-skillet dish. An easier way to cook
it today would be to lay everything in a low-sided dish in the oven.

The bacon aside, there is another famous early American recipe known
as Williamsburg Oysters, which was popular in Long Island and on the
Chesapeake, which pre-dates the Hangtown Fry by as much as fifty years
or more:

Put 24 oysters into a pan and add two slices of crumbled bread, onion, parsley,
celery, walnut ketchup, butter, lemon juice and rind, salt, pepper and a pinch
of cayenne pepper. Cook for 15 minutes over a low heat, stirring constantly.
Then add two beaten eggs, mixing them in thoroughly. Fill the reserved oyster
shells with this mixture. Sprinkle with the breadcrumbs and brown in a hot
preheated oven for about 10 minutes. Garnish with lemon slices.

Fried oysters were an American thing. Again pre-dating the Hangtown Fry,
this simpler version is from *Young Housekeeper's Friend*, published in 1846:

Make a batter of two eggs, three gills of milk, two spoonfuls of flour, and some
fine breadcrumbs. Beat it well. Dip each oyster into the batter, and fry in lard.

Take away the eggs and the skillet altogether and you almost have Oysters
Casino, credited to a casino in Hampton, New York, but is so obvious it
is really just an elegant urban evolution. The difference is the oysters are
cooked in the shell, spread with a mix of finely chopped shallots, green
peppers, parsley and butter, and seasoned with salt, pepper and lemon. It is
then topped with strips of bacon and grilled until the bacon is crisp.

An Awful Silence

The west coast story differs from that of the east and south. Francis Drake
sailed its length in 1579, followed by the Spaniard Juan de Fuca in 1592, but

it was another 200 years before white men's ships started to be seen again, especially in the northern waters. Settlements were barely established before the 1860s. This was wild country. And hostile American Indians, hard winters, violent seas, majestic, untamed wilderness inland and sheer isolation made the north coast one of the last areas to see settlement.

George Vancouver sailed into Hood Canal in the spring of 1792 and wrote about the fjord's 'pristine stillness', and how nature's 'awful silence was only now and then interrupted by the croaking of a raven, the breathing of a seal, or the scream of an eagle'.

The Hood Canal is a glacial fjord between Puget Sound and the Olympic Peninsula. Five major rivers run into it from the east, each one creating prime oyster beds: the Dosewallips, Duckabush, Hama Hama, Skokomish and Big Quilcene. The latter is now the largest oyster hatchery in the world. These rivers are fed by numerous smaller streams and creeks that flow west from the Kitsap Peninsula. The Squaxin Indians used huge cedarwood canoes to navigate and trade the length of the waters.

The remoteness of the territories further north came to be a safer depository for the oyster. Washington State was known for its oysters. The native west coast oyster takes its name from the state capital Olympia. But oysters were also found and cultivated as far south as Manuela Lagoon, Enseñada, Mexico, and in the north by the remote Tlingit community that live on the Alexander Archipelago in Alaska. Oregon provides its own lexicon of oyster names: Yaquina, Tillamook, Winchester and Coos bays.

Many of these businesses are still in the same family or have connections back to early settlers – or maybe these people were better termed 'pioneers'. Jack Brenner was from Wisconsin searching for gold. He sold his horse to the Indians in Puget Sound in return for some trays to start gathering oysters. He walked twelve hours to work and back each day. That was 1893.

The Olympia Oyster Company was set up on the now famous Totten Inlet in 1878. Almost next door, the neighbouring inlet was first cultivated by Jeremiah Lynch, who left County Cork, Ireland, in 1849 to seek his fortune in the California gold fields, but finally found it thirty-five years later when he settled on the Washington Territory's Little Skookum Inlet. The Taylor family, who still farm oysters in the inlet, claim their grandfather, Justin, ranched with Wyatt Earp in Arizona before heading up to Washington.

In 1907 the Wachsmuth family opened Dan and Louie's Oyster Bar in Portland, which is still there. They also founded Oregon Oyster Farms. To ensure the continued stock, they still take the old oyster shells from the restaurant and store them for a year, before recycling them back into the

Yaquina Bay for the young spat to clutch on to. Meinert Wachsmuth was a German sailor, stranded when his schooner, *Anna G. Doyle*, was wrecked off shore.

By 1850, schooners would drop anchor in Willapa Bay, known then as Shoal-Water Bay, and later Puget Sound, and gather up huge quantities of oysters to sell further south to gold prospectors and entrepreneurs in northern California, who were already busy exhausting their own oyster stocks. Oysters were being sold for a dollar each in the city, but were 50c a bushel in Washington. For a time, Oysterville, or Shoal Water, was the wealthiest town in Washington, earning it the nickname the Baltimore of the West.

One of those early boats was the schooner *Juliet*. In 1852 it was forced ashore off Oregon by a storm. The crew was stranded for two months in the Willamette Valley. The captain reported that the Yaquina River was abundant with oysters, clams and fish of all kinds. By 1863 two businesses had been set up and the Indian agent demanded a levy of 15c for each bushel of oysters to be paid to the tribes.

One of these businesses was founded by James Winant, a New Yorker. He owned a fleet of schooners which he plied along the west coast, whaling and hunting walrus in the northern Alaskan waters, or trading in the booty he found on shipwrecks to the San Francisco markets. Oysters were his ballast on the return trip.

An 1864 description by a visiting soldier describes the scene at this early settlement:

> Oysterville is built on the steep side of a very high bluff; indeed it seems clinging to the mountainside. A very narrow trail leads from house to house. The shore is lined with floats and boats, and these boats are crowded with squaws, busy 'culling' for which they obtain 12 and a half cents per bucket (one bushel). An industrious squaw will easily make $1.25 per day. The schooners *Cornelia Terry* and *Anna G. Doyle*, and the sloop *Fanny* are at anchor in the sound opposite town.

There was no road until two years later. These first settlements were exclusively populated from the ships, which would then carry their trade to the cities in the south. The communities were mostly seamen from far-flung islands, some from Russia, Scandinavia and the Orkneys. They often married local Indian girls.

These would have been a different kind of settler, lured by the prospect of trade in furs, timber and fish rather than colonisation, secure perhaps in their contacts with the captains of the ships, who were their lifeline to the outside world. These settlers would have been tempted too by a life that did not run either the perils of storms and pirates at sea, or the confines of a ship.

If the boats missed a delivery of supplies, the settlers subsisted on the fish and killing bears, elks and some wild cattle, which were thought to have been left to go feral from an older Spanish landing.

The Native Americans here were summarily dispossessed of their rights. Their culture of living from the sea and rivers was alien to these new people, who were firstly missionaries then traders, and then farmers more interested in land than water.

Of Cabbages & Kings

One of the greatest poems of the nineteenth century brings together the colonial spirit of the walrus – a powerful deep-sea predator – and the carpenter – with its Christian overtones – and casts the oyster in a totally different light. The curious thing is when and where it was written: 1871 in England. Perhaps Lewis Carroll was alluding to the settlements in the north-west of Canada, the religious and moral battleground that was San Francisco and the desolation of the Puget Sound and southern Alaska, where walruses may have shared the waters with oysters. Historically speaking, it was a long distance for someone writing a continent away, but perhaps stories had stolen back to him. You could read it as an allegory of emigrating to the new America.

Carroll was familiar with oysters, more so than we are. The old ones are wily: 'The eldest Oyster looked at him, but never a word he said.' The young ones are innocent and gullible: 'But four young Oysters hurried up, all eager for the treat.' And Carroll has them 'All hopping through the frothy waves, and scrambling to the shore' – which you could even infer as a reference back to Aphrodite in her frothing waves.

Multiplicity is everywhere: the old oyster that cannot protect its young and colludes in their death by sprucing them up for the walk; the young oysters are both friends and dinner, a naked yet apt reflection of their interaction with humans. Walruses are usually found in more northerly waters than oysters, but they are divers after shellfish, especially clams. They will use their tusks to rip open larger shells and will squirt water into the mud to discover any crustaceans hidden on the ocean floor.

The verses are so stark, the imagery so clean and so literal, that there is an invitation to think on more than one level, like with an abstract painting.

The nagging interaction between absurd and obvious tempts speculation. Carroll plays with the ridiculous:

> Their coats were brushed, their faces washed,
> Their shoes were clean and neat –
> And this was odd, because, you know,
> They hadn't any feet.

And yet also odd that oysters should walk at all: '"O Oysters, come and walk with us!" the Walrus did beseech.' Or talk: 'A pleasant walk, a pleasant talk, along the briny beach.'

Carroll strays playfully into other areas, as if making the point that where oysters are concerned there will be other elements – the sun is out when it should not be, the moon is sulking, there is the surreal chatter about whether seven maids with seven mops could sweep the sand. And then comes the famous nonsensical conversation:

> 'The time has come,' the Walrus said,
> 'To talk of many things:
> Of shoes – and ships – and sealing wax –
> Of cabbages – and kings –
> And why the sea is boiling hot –
> And whether pigs have wings.'

All of this is helping to make a case for such imagery to be the language of settlers – shoes, ships, wax, cabbages, kings – they could all have been everyday conversation in the new territories, or even washed ashore from a shipwreck, as might have been an empirical discussion as to whether the beach could be swept clean and reclaimed.

At other moments the poem is stunningly, deliberately and abstractly primitive: 'The sea was wet … the sands were dry', and the forebodingly prophetic: 'No birds were flying overhead – there were no birds to fly.'

Primitivism is backed by the very simplistic rhyming of certain words – so/low/row and chat/fat/that and need/indeed/feed, and so on, which seems in Biblical terms to point to the fundamentals of the world from the very beginning, set up by each of the opening verses, the first for the sun, the second for the moon, the third for the sea and the fourth for the creatures living on the shore. There is also an allusion to some unseen paternalism: the oysters stand in a row; they have been scrubbed up. The walrus is the protagonist and the gastronome:

'A loaf of bread,' the Walrus said,
'Is what we chiefly need:
Pepper and vinegar besides are very good indeed –
Now, if you're ready, Oysters dear, we can begin to feed.'

Another touch suggests the New World, possibly even the Connecticut Blue Point:

'But not on us!' the oysters cried, turning a little blue.

As we reach the end there is a character change. The carpenter gets tetchy:

The Carpenter said nothing but 'Cut us another slice.
I wish you were not quite so deaf – I've had to ask you twice!'

And the walrus becomes conciliator:

'It seems a shame,' the Walrus said,
'To play them such a trick.
After we've brought them out so far,
and made them trot so quick!'
The Carpenter said nothing but 'The butter's spread too thick!'

Is this just a woolly fairytale rendition about our relationship with the things we eat? 'After such kindness, that would be a dismal thing to do!' declare the oysters. To which the Walrus replies:

'The night is fine,' the Walrus said.
'Do you admire the view?'

What else can an oyster do?

The characters fit neatly into the roles of exploiting politicians. The walrus is fat and well fed – the friendly, jovial type who cajoles the oysters. The carpenter portrays a politician's promise to rebuild and improve society, when in fact he and the walrus are really colluding to eat the oysters up. The pair are dreaming grandiose and impossible ambitions and intrigues, and how grand it would be to sweep such quantities of sand.

Carroll's subtext might have been social villainy – the exodus of the starving Irish peasantry to the slums of New York perhaps. Regardless, it is an extraordinarily beautiful linguistic masterpiece.

Nearly all writers enjoin in Carroll's sense of fun. Here is Ogden Nash, dated 1931:

> The oyster's a confusing suitor
> It's masc., and fem., and even neuter.
> But whether husband, pal or wife
> It leads a painless sort of life.
> I'd like to be an oyster, say,
> In August, June, July or May.

Nash also coined the lyrical line: 'While the oyster broods in inedible moods.'

Comics too have had some fun with oysters. Roy Blount said: 'I prefer my oysters fried; that way I know my oysters died.' Woody Allen said: 'I will not eat oysters. I want my food dead. Not sick, not wounded, dead.' And only a bit part here, albeit essential, from S.J. Perelman: 'The waiter's eyes sparkled and their pencils flew as she proceeded to eviscerate my wallet – pate, Whitstable oysters, a sole, filet mignon, and a favorite salad of the Nizam of Hyderabad made of shredded five-pound notes.'

The dancer Isadora Duncan reflects a different era of social mores from around her birth in 1878:

> Before I was born my mother was in great agony of spirit and in a tragic situation. She could take no food except iced oysters and champagne. If people ask me when I began to dance, I reply, 'In my mother's womb, probably as a result of the oysters and champagne – the food of Aphrodite.'

Songwriters have used the oyster as a lens on the human condition. Music teacher Stephen Walker, from Oyster Bay, found more than 100 songs with oysters in for his fundraising book *What Kind of a Noise Annoys an Oyster?* Most enduring, Cole Porter sings in *Let's Do It (Let's Fall in Love)* the lines which he actually composed on the dock at Oyster Bay itself:

> Romantic sponges, they say, do it,
> Oysters down in Oyster Bay do it,
> Let's do it, let's fall in love.

Porter wrote a second, lesser-known song which has a wry twist at the end. It is the ballad of a lonesome oyster who wanted to see the world; he makes it to the table in a fine restaurant:

Hearing the wives of millionaires discuss their marriages and their love affairs
Thrilled little oyster!
See that bivalve social climber
feeding the rich Mrs Hoggenheimer.
Think of his joy as he gaily glides
down to the middle of her gilded insides.
Proud little oyster!

Later, Mrs Hoggenheimer feels unwell on her yacht and the little oyster
'Finds that it's time he should quit his cloister and up comes the oyster!'
The idea of an oyster escaping the beds and joining high society is not
uncommon. In *Gay Old Oyster*, Charles Bingham recounts: 'For a gay old
oyster full of fun am I and a jolly sport the girls will love you see ...' But
not so: 'And the girl who loved him most ate him served up hot on toast.'

You're Not the Only Oyster in the Stew was popularised by Fats Waller,
written in 1934 by Johnny Burke and Harold Spina. Earlier titles include:
The Ballad of the Oysterman (1849); *Champagne and Oysters* (1878); *Oysters
and Wine at 2 a.m.* (1873); and *Oysters and Clams, The Rag-Time Oyster
Man* (1904).

This is a favourite, sadly anonymous lyric published in the *Detroit Free
Press* in 1889. The rhymes are very Cockney music hall so maybe there is
an English influence in there somewhere:

Let us royster with the oyster – in shorter days and moister
That are brought by brown September, with its roguish final R
For breakfast or for supper, on the under shell or upper
Of dishes, he's the daisy, and of shellfish he's the star.

We try him as they fry him, and even as they pie him
We're partial to him luscious in a roast.
We boil him and broil him, we vinegar-and-oil him
And O he is delicious stewed on toast.

We eat him with tomatoes, and the salad with potatoes
Nor look him o'er with horror when he follows the coldslaw.
And neither does he fret us, if he marches after lettuce
And abreast of cayenne pepper when his majesty is raw.

So welcome with September to the knife and glowing ember
Juicy darling of our dainties, dispossessor of the clam!

To the oyster, then a hoister, with him a royal royster
We shall whoop it through the land of heathen jam.

Wherever people gathered around a piano, there was no shortage of oyster songs. One from New York, *How Do you like Your Oysters*, has the rousing chorus:

How do you like your oysters?
Raw, raw, raw.
What will I bring you next Bill?
More, more, more.

Some Saddlebacks or Blue Points
The best you ever saw.
But how do you like your oysters?
Raw, raw, raw.

Next is an older country idea of how people regarded the oyster and the problems it might bring, by Oliver Wendell Holmes:

It was the pensive oysterman that saw a lovely maid,
Upon a moonlight evening, a sitting in the shade ...

And he has leaped into the waves, and crossed the shining stream,
And he has clambered up the bank, all in the moonlight gleam;

O there were kisses sweet as dew, and words as soft as rain –
But they have heard her father's step, and in he leaps again!

And the father harpoons the young lad. His daughter swoons:

But Fate has metamorphosed them, in pity of their woe,
And now they keep an oyster-shop for mermaids down below.

Land of the Beausoleil & the Malagash

Canada might easily claim to have the most evocative oyster vocabularies. Place names are road accidents of native Indian Micmac, poetic French and efforts by the English speakers to keep up. The fiercely French town of Caraquet, off Chaleur Bay in New Brunswick, in Micmac Indian means the Meeting of Two Rivers, although its more recent history is deeply Gallic and it was the arrival point of French refugees between 1755 and 1763. French is still the first language. In other towns the French parentage of Beausoleil and Malpeque is plain, with names like Savage Harbour or Sea Cow Head, both on Prince Edward Island. And others are obviously native – the lyrical Tatamagouche and Malagash are both in Nova Scotia, and Malaspina is on the other coast in British Columbia.

Sometimes there is a mix of two or more cultures, like Bedeque Bay oysters at Salutation Cove. The linguistics are not lost on the catalogue writers either. Pickle Points are said to have 'ivory lips, slender skins with muted chestnut crowns, these are raked from [Prince Edward Island]'s icy sole. When winter hits the hardest, they are cut from the ice until the saws can reach no more.'

The Maritime Provinces of Canada have two world-famous oysters in the Malpeque and the smaller more delicate Caraquet, but these owe their fame to a long time ago and the proximity of the New York markets, where today the oyster canon reverberates equally to other names. The reputation of the Bedeque Bay oyster seems to have been known from quite an early time, certainly pre-1850. The railway brought the Malpeque to nearby New York and established the currency of the Canadian oyster in restaurant terms. Then in 1900, the Burleigh brothers entered some oysters from the Peter Creek bed in a world oyster competition at the Paris Exhibition. Despite the long sea voyage, the Malpeque won and its reputation was assured.

The Caraquet & the Acadians

When John Cabot sailed from Bristol under the flag of Henry VII, he landed most probably at Cape Breton, Nova Scotia, and claimed the land for England and the Catholic Church in 1497.

Nearly 400 years later, an 1861 audit said:

> The rivers abound with excellent trout, eels, flounders, mackerel, oysters, lobsters, and salmon; the coast with cod and herring. The oysters of this island are very superior, and large quantities of them are exported annually. The halibut and sturgeons that are caught on the coast are usually very large. In former times, the walrus was wont to frequent the shores in large numbers, and it was a source of considerable profit. The harbour seals and harp seals float on the ice towards the north shore in large numbers.

There is no evidence of shell middens north of the Canadian border, but there were people here. Archaeologists have found potteries from eight different tribes, some dating back to 3,000 BC. It was a tough climate. Certainly there are records of First Nations people gathering and selling oysters to settlers around Lake Victoria, north of Seattle, then a remote fur-trading post.

The first French fishermen decamped before the cold winter set in to migrate back to France. They had no ambition to settle. A dangerous Atlantic crossing was still preferable to a Canadian winter. Nicolas Denys' first account of the settlement in Acadia (in the Canadian Maritime Provinces) dated to 1672 and said all the fishermen could do in winter was chop down trees. He also noted that the local chief, Rechibouctou, at Miramichi was a 'conceited and vicious Indian'.

The original fifty families of Acadian émigrés moved from their first home to the relatively fertile fishing and farming of Port Royal on the Bay of Fundy, Nova Scotia – another oyster cove. As others joined them they spread around the whole bay, from 1630 to 1714. Most were from the Loire Valley round to La Rochelle, so would have been familiar with oyster culture. They stayed neutral, caught between the English on one side and the Indians on the other, and were diligent dyke-builders, reclaiming the land and creating new marsh. For dykes read oyster work, because even where oysters are not directly mentioned, the obvious conclusion – as happened on the west coast – was that these dykes were for cultivation and early aquaculture.

These oyster beds hold a dark secret of colonial war and the hatred between French and English, although the Acadians were no agents of the French Crown. The English rounded up the Acadian settlers and burnt their homes. They stole the harvests of 1755, adopted the children to make them Protestant and raped the women. The men mostly – more than 8,000 – were deported by rickety boats to two other oyster strongholds – Maryland, where they were prohibited from landing, and finally to New Orleans and Louisiana.

The American poet Henry Wadsworth Longfellow wrote *Angeline*, about an Acadian girl separated from her love who searches America to find him. As an old lady, working in Philadelphia as a nun, she finds him among the destitute and he dies in her arms. It did much to highlight the awful plight of the Acadians.

When the colonial war broke out twenty-five years later, the Louisiana militia – which included the Acadian people – was said to be the most ardent of all patriots as they took Baton Rouge. The Acadians became a part of the great Cajun mix. The English ceded the valuable fishing industry to the infant USA. Slowly, many Acadians have returned, often to the very places where their families first settled, in what is now Nova Scotia and New Brunswick. The oyster for them, as in France, and the Caraquet in particular, is a potent symbol of their ancestry, but for different reasons to elsewhere on the continent. There is a certain irony for them today that the pure clean northern waters survive whereas colonial waters were polluted and the oyster has now died out.

12

South Seas

Polynesia – Australasia – Oyster Sauce – Japan

To be of the first water, though, they must be perfectly spherical, or symmetrically
pear-shaped, like a tear without a point, and skin and orient must satisfy: that is their
texture must be delicate and flawless, of an almost translucent white, and their sheen
must be subdued and yet iridescent.

M.F.K. Fisher, *Consider the Oyster*, 1941

Polynesia

The Black-Lipped Pinctada

The Spanish missed the pearl cultures of the South Seas. Álvaro de
Mendaña first sighted the remote corals and rolling surf of Pukapuka,
part of the Cook Islands, in 1595. Pedro Fernandez de Quiros discovered
Rakahanga in 1606. These islands may have been populated on and off
for 1,500 or more years. Mendaña's voyage was reported as a failure. They
admired the people and the vegetation but 'found no specimens of spices,
nor of gold and silver, nor of merchandise, nor of any other source of
profit, and all the people are naked savages'.

The islanders were far from savages. And Mendaña missed a source
of pearls that would rival the beauty of anything taken from Persia or
Venezuela – those taken from the black-lipped pinctada margaritifera
would adorn the crowns of Europe's nobility. The pinctada can live up to
thirty years, grow to 30cm in diameter and weigh up to 5kg. They produce

the largest and finest pearls when they are 3 to 7 years old. Even today these oysters are remarkable. The calcium they secrete is aragonite which is orthorhombic, meaning it has three triangular sides which act as tiny prisms. These prisms create the effect that jewellers and gemmologists refer to as orient.

The black-lipped pinctada can secrete three or four layers of aragonite each day. Over a two-year life cycle, some 2,000 layers may be washed around the shell, each one micron (0.001mm) thick. The bigger the shell, the more aragonite, the bigger the pearl, and the more light it refracts.

It may be that Mendaña and Quiros came at the wrong time of year. The atoll around the Tuamotu Islands was only harvested for a few weeks of the year or on solitary trips.

The use of pearls was part of Polynesian society; they were traded as tithes and taxes, and worn as jewellery by noble families. The flesh was eaten, but not prized. They used the pearl as decoration and as a payment.

American historian Douglas L. Oliver explains in the three volumes of *Ancient Tahitian Society*: 'With some tribal work projects, many members made their contributions in the form of objects in lieu of services ... and delivery – on "standing order" – to tribal chiefs of such luxuries as turtles, pearls, and ... other objects.'

The first discoverers here seem to have been of a different cut to Columbus and the conquistadors, or even those pilgrims to North America. They were wary of the Indians. Their boats were often attacked. Even much later, in 1820, the Russian oceanographer Fabian Gottlieb von Bellingshausen recorded: 'The inhabitants (of Rakahanga) came out in canoes and challenged us to fight by throwing stones and spears at the ship.' Perhaps by then they had good reason to throw sticks at visiting Europeans.

They came with religion. The first Protestants tried to set up missionaries, but these were not empire-builders, more likely they were traders plying the horseshoes of oyster towns around South America, New Zealand, Polynesia and up past Korea, Vietnam, China and Japan. They were adventurers. When they found the South Sea islands, their priority was food, shelter, drink and women, usually in that order. Many stayed and married into the local community but there was no sense of colonisation or treasure to be plundered, perhaps because it was so remote, or perhaps ideas had changed in Europe and moved on to trading.

The archaeology suggests the natives may have left South-east Asia 3,000 to 4,000 years ago and began to arrive in present-day French Polynesia around AD 300. The archipelago was ruled by chieftains who commanded fleets of rugged outrigger canoes. These canoes – in this case double-hulled, on which a platform could be bound with rope and be strong enough to carry two dozen families and their goods from island to island – and their ability to move around the South Pacific are a constant theme in all early accounts. Hawaiians claim to have explored the oceans before the Vikings.

Some have tried to make the case that these people could have come from the Americas, but this theory has big flaws in it. The writer Thor Heyerdahl led a famous 1947 expedition across the Pacific, from South America to the Polynesian Islands, named after the Inca sun god Viracocha, for whom Kon-Tiki was said to be an old name. It became a bestselling book and film. The 101-day journey proved it was possible. But the discovery of Lapita pottery across the region throughout the twentieth century points the other way due to its obvious similarities to styles found in China and Taiwan. The pottery shows that people were already in Fiji, Toga and Samoa between 2,500 and 3,000 BC. The pottery evidence also indicates that it probably took them no more than a few hundred years to move from island to island through Melanesia, some 2,000 miles east of their starting point, probably off New Guinea. There is other evidence too – the linguistic trail points east and the only South American food found in the diet is sweet potato.

A burial mound in Vanuatu, discovered in 2003, found thirty-six bodies in twenty-five graves. Each had been beheaded, after death, and the necks surrounded by shells. Further north, in Luzon, Cagayan province in the Philippines, shell middens have been dated back to 3,000 BC.

Paradise on Earth

The first European visitors to the Cook Islands were Samuel Wallis in 1767, the Frenchman Louis-Antoine de Bougainville in 1768 and James Cook in 1769. They returned with stories of a paradise on earth inhabited by 'noble savages' and Venus-like women, whose sexual favours were freely offered to the visitors. Their tales lured writers like Herman Melville and Robert Louis Stevenson and the painter Paul Gauguin.

This was the setting for *Mutiny on the Bounty*. It was on Tahiti and the Austral island of Tubuai that Fletcher Christen and his mutineers sought refuge after setting William Bligh and his faithful crew members adrift in a tiny open boat near the Tongan.

The Polynesians often spent several weeks, even months, at sea, covering huge distances in their large voyaging canoes, heading into the trade winds. The sheer expanse of territory may go some way to explain the culture in the South Seas. There are seventy-seven atolls and one upraised island in the Tuamotu Archipelago. They can be just specks of land out in the heart of the trade wind, lost in the enormity of the blue Pacific. They straddle an area 1,500km long and 300km wide, the most extreme and remote of coral islets that form just 885km² of sparsely populated land. An idyll for sure, but wild and unkempt with a necessary interdependence.

While some fishermen went about stocking up fresh fish, others did the cooking on a fire kept alight permanently in a container of sand. Some canoes even had large ovens capable of cooking several pigs. Fresh water was kept in calabashes and coconut milk was used to quench their thirst. Their canoe culture was distinctly advanced.

The first accounts of a South Sea pearl trade start in 1802. The lagoon reefs were so rich with oyster shells that men had only to wade into the water up to their waist to collect hundreds of kilos a day, according to one written account. Thirty divers would spread out across a lagoon with three dinghies ready to take their catch. A diver would grab three or four oysters at a time from a depth of what was recorded as between 5 and 13 strokes from the bottom. They wore no protection and risked deafness, paralysis and even insanity from going too deep. The white traders paid them in muskets, powder, clothes and knives, and always with alcohol. Here there seems to have been a mutual respect between trader and diver, even admiration:

Pearl divers in the Tuamotu Archipelago had truly exceptional skill, frequently reaching depths of 30.5–39.6 metres, remaining under water for as long as three minutes. Unlike divers in India and Ceylon, Tuamotu divers did not use stones to weigh themselves down. Instead, they prepared for a dive by hyperventilating, sometimes accompanied by singing. Once in the water, they used only the strength of their arms to pull themselves down.

The Polynesians developed a different relationship to these early adventurers than has been seen in other parts of the globe. By 1825 they had imposed a tax and ordained that no oysters should be taken without royal permission. They remained in control. No armies were sent to overthrow them.

There was a duality in their relationship. The trading boats brought items to barter and stayed short periods before moving on to the next port. The trading arc might have spanned from Shanghai and beyond. They were well armed and could defend themselves. The pearl trade grew quickly and Pomare Vahine, regent in Tahiti, exercised a political acumen in controlling the region. In Tahiti the pearl was used as decoration and for barter, but they had no pearls of their own. Anyone collecting pearls without the regent's permission was liable to have their boats seized.

The value of a pearl to the Europeans depended disproportionately on whether a society could drill a hole through it and therefore make necklaces and earrings. Tahiti had grasped this technology, possibly from an earlier contact with white men, but the remote Tuamotu had no metals. Pearls were often ruined by clumsy attempts to bore through them with a shark's tooth. This was another reason why the Polynesians often attacked European boats: to sink them and claim the booty. Nails were much prized.

The piercing took time to learn. Captain Wallis noted on his first trip that the two dozen pearls he traded for were chipped by piercing attempts. Wallis, like all the other first European navigators to visit Tahiti, says 'feathers, shells and pearls were part of the ornaments and finery'.

James Cook made a similar observation when visiting Raiatea. The pearls, he said, had a good colour and form, but were ruined by the piercing efforts. Máximo Rodriguez noted on 30 March 1775 that he was being greeted by members of the Tahitian royal family, one of whom wore two pearls, each as big as a chickpea. But both were crudely pierced. Bougainville commented: 'I know of only one rich article of trade here; they are the very beautiful pearls.'

The best pearls arrived in Europe very quickly. The Duchess of Portland's personal collection in 1786 included two ear ornaments made up of six pearls coming via Tahiti. The Cambridge Museum had a pendant dating back to Cook's first or second voyage to Tahiti. Catherine the Great of Russia had a necklace of thirty black pearls, the largest weighing 3.9g, when she died in 1796. The Austrian crown of the same era was also set with thirty black pearls. The French Empress Eugénie, consort of Napoleon III, had a necklace of black pearls, and the Russian Crown jewels included a necklace with a black pearl centrepiece that was called the Azra.

Australasia

Eruption at Wahanga
The question of whether the world was inhabited from west to east or east to west has always been a source of continental rivalry and pride. In one sense the oyster provided explosive scientific proof.

On the night of 9 June 1886 the township of Rotorua, on the southern shore of the lake of the same name on New Zealand's north island, trembled to a series of convulsive, consecutive earthquakes, culminating in a huge eruption. Mount Wahanga was split asunder by a volcano, and the blast blew the top off the mountain. A pall of black cloud rose like a shawl, darkening the dawn across the north of the island from the Bay of Plenty to Hawke Bay, lit by shards of lightning and the tremulous din of rolling thunder. Shortly afterwards, there were two other eruptions. Mount Tarawera and its twin cone Ruawahia detonated, and spewed lava and rock into the dawn sky.

Molten debris was launched 10,000ft high; the rift ran 12 miles long. The basin of Lake Rotomahana detonated at the same time sending hot rocks and mud raining down over an area of 6,000 miles². The explosion lasted the whole night and was heard as far away as Auckland, Napier, Wellington and even Blenheim, in the south island. The nearby town of Wairoa was covered 10ft thick with ash, clay, mud and stone. More than 150 people died.

The Pink and White Terraces of Rotomahana were the eighth wonder of the natural world – New Zealand's most famous tourist attraction. Visitors travelled by steamship, then horse and cart, a two-hour canoe journey and finally on foot to see the glistening pink and white terraces of silica, formed by the hydrothermal volcanic heat rising beneath the crust of the earth. The crystals that form quartz, sand, flint, agate, and are used to make glass and concrete, flowed from the earth's heart like water in temperatures that must have peaked at 1,300°F.

The white terraces, Te Tarata, the Tattooed Rock, covered 7 acres and were 30m high, while the pink terraces of Otukapuarangi, Fountain of the Clouded Sky, were smaller and lower. At the foot of the steps were pools of clear, blue, hot waters. The explosion blasted them to pieces.

Who knows whether it was on this occasion – New Zealand's greatest natural tragedy – or if it was during another episode in the long history of the north island's rogue and untamed volcanoes demonstrating the awesome power that lies beneath the ground, but in one such incident the blast was so enormous that the oysters at the foot of the volcano were yanked out of their beds at a phenomenal velocity and catapulted into the night sky and projected all the way to Chile. The distance between Auckland and Santiago is about 10,000km.

Perhaps it was not the whole oyster that survived, but just tiny spat clinging for their lives on to a shell; or perhaps just fragments of fragments hurtling through space until they plummeted seaward into the coastal waters of the southern Americas. A big bang indeed.

The stunning and amazing result is that the oysters survived this transfer from one continent to another. Not only did they survive, but they took hold and colonised in the waters of Chile. We can deduce this because for many years Chilean and New Zealand scientists argued over which of their oysters came first. In New Zealand the oyster was called Bluff, Dredge or Foveaux Strait oyster. The Chilean oyster was known technically as Tiostrea Chilensis.

It was assumed at first that the Chilean oysters had probably rafted the open ocean on the Antarctic circumpolar and Humboldt currents, but molecular analysis revealed that pumice from the New Zealand volcanoes was the more likely medium. The New Zealand flat oyster had arrived in Chile in some huge cataclysmic shower of volcanic oyster debris. The science was categorical – these New Zealand oysters breed differently to other species; they are ostreas not crassostreas.

As amazing as the oysters being hurled between continents and surviving is that those that remained seem to have survived the molten heat and disruptions. Wairoa is still a centre of cultivation. For a creature that is apparently so sensitive to light, salt, noise, slight adjustments of temperature and small adjustments in the food supply, neither volcanic eruption nor being shot across continents proved fatal.

Captain Cook takes his Bearings

Captain Cook landed at Cooks Beach in the *Endeavour* in November 1769 to watch the passage of the planet Mercury across the sun, and literally 'put New Zealand on the map' by establishing its accurate longitude. He planted the English flag on the beach and declared New Zealand for King George III. He stayed for eleven days making astronomical observations while the ship took on fresh provisions. The abundance of oysters and shellfish in a local stream impressed him and he quickly named it Oyster River; only later did it revert to its original name Purangi.

> On the sand and mud beds are oysters, mussels, cockles etc which I believe are the chief support of the inhabitants who go into the shoald waters with their little canoes and pick them out of the sand and mud with their hands and sometimes roast and eat them in the canoe, having often a fire for that purpose, for I know no other it can be for.

By the 1930s the New Zealand oyster was a mainstay of the economy. More than 60 million were taken from the Foveaux Strait and some estimates put the stock at 20 billion. Scientists commented how the white shells reflected the sunshine back from below the water creating 'a great carpet of white shells'.

Ostrea Commercialis

The precise provenance of the Australian oyster was argued as fiercely as that of the New Zealand. Originally it was the rock oyster, the crassostrea *commercialis*, now called the Sydney rock oyster. Scientifically it has changed its name from *saxostrea commercialis* to *glomerata* to *cucullata* to *commercialis* – *glomerata* is the current vogue. It was found densely clustered on the eastern, southern and south-western coasts, sometimes as far as 50ft out to sea, and also attached to mangroves in muddy swamps. Their ability to survive low tides and long exposure to the sun is credited with giving them their distinction and longevity to the market.

There is an argument that Australia may have been populated before Europe. Three early sites have been discovered in Penrith, dated about 47,000 BC; in Western Australia, dated at 40,000 years old; and at Lake Mungo, New South Wales, dated at 35,000 years old. Before ice ages changed the landscape Australia may not have been so remote, and could, as in the South Seas, have been reached by a sophisticated canoe-travelling clan. The Aborigines were used for gathering oysters, and they used the shells to sink lines for fishing. Some of the shell deposits in aboriginal kitchen middens are substantial, up to 400m long and 4m high. Middens in northern New South Wales and southern Queensland are made up largely of Sydney rock oysters, although as you travel south the native, now rare, flat oyster appears more and more.

The first settlers were not shy in gathering the oysters in, and so by 1870 laws were being issued to protect the reefs and the ancient middens, which were being burned to create lime. In the gold rush, police stations were usually made of lime to ensure strong prisons. From 1860 there was extensive flat oyster fishing in South Australia. About thirty sailing vessels and some eighty fishermen harvested the oysters with dredges at 5–20m until they were fished out by 1885. Similar oyster dredging existed in Victoria and Tasmania around the same time. In Tasmania alone, nearly 2 million dozen (sic) oysters were landed annually between 1860 and 1870.

Bobbing Up & Down

Exploration by imperialist powers might have been seen as a deliberate attempt to uncover new wealth. The commerce had changed. Investors wanted plantations and a long-term return. Anything as hit and miss as pearl fishing was left to chance. The oyster trade grew off the opening of shipping lines and was often as haphazard as beachcombing. Farmers complained they had to teach the Aborigines to swim. The first pearlers were sheep farmers, and they forced their aboriginal workers to go 'bobbing down'.

Henry Taunton describes the early days:

> The work was far from easy. It was exhausting and perilous for the divers, and full of privation, exposure and danger for the white man. Only the hope of a prosperous season reconciled one to the life. When shells were plentiful and the weather fine, the work was exciting and interesting ...
>
> As may be imagined when three or four white men had to control and compel some thirty or forty to carry on work which they detested, a very strict discipline had to be maintained. It was a rule that no talking was allowed among the divers.

He also mentions in passing: 'It is not infrequent for divers to go down and not come up at all.'

Broome Town

The dangers did not seem to deter the Japanese, Malay and other Asians from taking the sheep boats to Cossack, Broome and Onslow – all towns that suffered and enjoyed first sheep, then gold and then pearl booms, and were 'no Sunday school when the fishermen are in'.

Broome was a shipping port, and the boats spread the word. South Sea pearls of all kinds came to be known as Broome Pearls. Within three years of the original discovery, Australia was supplying 75 per cent of the world's mother-of-pearl, although much of it went unglamorously, as in the Mississippi, into making shirt buttons.

The difficulty with getting labour quickly resulted in the first diving suits around 1879. These were welcome not least because of the dangers from sharks, rays and other predators. A diver with only a minute or so of air in his lungs could be snatched to his death trying to make for the surface. A man in a protected suit could bide his time until danger passed, or even startle a predator by releasing air bubbles from out of his sleeve. The first suits were especially used by the Japanese, who could work underwater for as long as two hours gathering shells.

Broome is now a tourist town famous for its Cable Beach, but there is still a cemetery for the Japanese. There are more than 900 graves there. For those who survived, the average working life was five years. Four out of five deaths were attributed to semi-paralysis.

A better known homage to the oyster is the Sydney Opera House itself, begun in 1957. Architect Jørn Utzon admitted to using the oyster as his inspiration, a white bleach symbol both of modernity and national identity, but also as an acknowledgement that Bennelong Point, on which the opera house stands, would have been a source of food for native Australians.

Australasian Cooking

The footprints of the many different travellers who found their way to Australia can be seen in the cooking of the region. Asian cooking casts many accents on the Australian kitchen. The first colonisers in Australia may have arrived with their Anglo-Saxon ideas, but in the warmer climates of Sydney they soon adapted.

The Sydney rock oyster has its place in the Australian pantheon of barbecue culture, roasted over white-hot coals until they open, and are then served with melted butter or a simple DIY relish of horseradish, ketchup, Worcestershire and Tabasco sauce – an almost complete hand-me-down of empire flavours. The exotic Asian influences soon hurry along to gatecrash the party. So quickly we see sprightly fresh flavours like mixes of coriander, chives, soy, lime and sugar for dressing an oyster, or rice vinegar, grated ginger, lemon and spring onion. Suddenly the oyster came to be paired with bean curd, with chilli, with garlic.

Rather than the English oyster sausages, stuffing and loaves of northern cooking, there was an easy and logical assimilation into the Chinese canon, so the oyster could become part of a spring roll minced with spring onion, water chestnuts, ginger, soy and sesame oil, and then wrapped up in wun tun pastry and briefly deep fried until crisp.

As you move around Asia the batters change from rice to potato flour, with or without eggs, with subtle variations. In Fujian Province the oyster cake is as large as a hand, the crust burnished with peanuts, the filling a mix of oysters, leeks, scallions and a bit of minced pork. Variations become more luxurious only with the use of more oysters and more pork and can be found in hawker markets from Singapore to downtown Brooklyn. The fried oyster cake has its own status which is parallel to the basic fried oysters found in the cooking across Asia, culminating in the Japanese tempura with its showy crisp, hot exterior, and when properly cooked the oyster is just barely warmed through inside and is still tender and juicy. Here the batter is usually corn flour, no egg, perhaps impregnated with sesame seeds, and the combustion comes from the cold and fizzy liquid into the hot oil – the condiments are the hot, green Japanese horseradish wasabi or wasabi mixed with rice, wine, mirin and soy. Most elegantly, the oyster can be wrapped first in little squares of nori seaweed, seasoned with the basil-like shizo leaf, before being battered and fried.

Oyster Sauce

The myth is that oyster sauce was 'invented' by Lee Kum Sheung in his little cafe in Nanshui, Zuhai, in Guangdong Province in 1888. Like Alfred the Great and his cakes, he supposedly left his oyster broth on the stove too long but was amazed to find that far from being ruined, the broth had caramelised and thickened into an aromatic brew. Sheung was certainly the first to bottle his sauce – and it is still available under the Lee Kum Kee label based now in Hong Kong – but it stretches the credulity to think other cooks had not reached the same conclusion earlier; otherwise how could it have been assimilated so quickly as one of the planks of southern Cantonese cooking? Here was a true cook's interpretation that managed to harmonise many traditional oyster pairings into what we might take for granted today as Chinese restaurant classics, with stir-fried beef, in a chow mein, with green vegetables. You could make a case that oyster sauce is the most versatile bottled ingredient any cook might need. Although many brands use additives like MSG and colourants, there is no real need (except to extend the shelf life) as the original is simply oysters simmered in stock or water until reduced to a sticky viscosity and starting to turn dark brown as it caramelises. By comparison, recipes for carpetbagger steak (the oyster slit in the meat), or an old-fashioned steak and oyster pie, this Thai variation is quick and efficient and draws the key elements together:

Stir Fry of Beef Fillet with Oyster Sauce
Slice the beef thinly and marinate in soy, oyster sauce, sugar, pepper. Warm groundnut oil in a wok and add the garlic and chilli to season. Throw in some spinach and stir fry until it wilts. Lay up the spinach on a plate and add the beef to the hot wok and fry for two to three minutes. Lay over the spinach. Wash out of the wok with rice wine (or sherry) and pour over the beef.

Or this for chicken, where the cooking is longer and more pronounced:

Chicken Wings Baked with Oyster Sauce
Sweeten the oyster sauce with garlic, sugar, chilli. Use half to marinade the chicken wings for two hours or more. Warm the oven or the grill and cook

the wings for 30 minutes gently, then baste again with the remaining sauce and flip over. Serve with coriander, green onions and lime and a cold beer.

Thai cooking rivals Japanese in its vivacity and imagination, but it is less restrictively disciplined. As a nation that uses a lot of fish, often their recipes seem the most far-sighted of all. So oysters might find themselves in a salad with banana blossoms (in the west you could substitute chicory), lightly poached in coconut cream, seasoned with palm sugar, fish sauce and garnished with fried shallots. Or they might be served on their own with Asian celery, lemongrass, shallot, mint and coriander, and dressed with their juices, chilli, lime, white sugar and fish sauce. Or maybe as a salad with cured pork, shredded ginger, red shallots, mint, coriander and deep-fried peanuts served with a dressing made of pounded coriander root, salt, garlic, dragon's eye chilli, sugar, lime and fish sauce.

If oysters are expensive or scarce they might just take a supporting role in adding their juices and meat to the dressings for other salads. One obviously Thai take on oyster soup explodes with flavours and textures – a cross between a soup and a rice dish, bursting with all the fragrance of the Thai markets, and, for once, a Thai recipe without chilli:

Oyster Soup with Coriander and Galingale
Fry minced pork with large amounts of pounded garlic. Add three cups of Jasmine rice, 24 oysters along with eggs, galingale, coriander, spring onions and pepper. Stir fry for two to three minutes. Add coconut milk.

Japan

Japan was not fully settled until the third century BC but there is evidence of habitation going back perhaps to 30,000 BC. Japan would probably not have been an island then but connected to the Korean peninsula. Flint tools have been found and dated back that far. By 10,000 BC, a new culture had arisen known as Jomon, after the pottery which shows that the making of pots probably preceded agriculture. It is thought to be among the earliest examples of pottery in the world and was marked by a distinct cord pattern. The Jomon lived by the coast, around Tokyo Bay near Hiroshima, and surrounded their villages with enormous horseshoe-shaped middens of discarded oyster shells. Perhaps these were not simply waste dumps, but possibly sites for trading, where the oysters might have been pickled for sale inland in exchange for stone tools.

The oldest and most valuable pearl on record, which comes from Japan, is credited to 5,500 BC. To put the dates in context, rice was not harvested or cultivated in Japan until 100 BC.

Seafood and seaweeds had religious meaning and were offered up at Shinto shrines. In AD 764 the poet Yakamochi Ohotomo transplanted a species of unspecified bivalve from Kishyu, on the Pacific coast of Honshu island, to Ecchyu in the Sea of Japan. This is one of the oldest surviving records of attempts at aquaculture. Another mention occurs in 1081, when a seaweed was transplanted from Kouzushima, an island in the Izu Archipelago, to the Izu Peninsula.

The nori and oyster culture started in the 1670s, from which sushi evolved. The development of both seems to have gone hand in hand. At first spawning lakes and fattening grounds were separated, and bamboo was used to collect the young oysters. Rafts and hanging baskets did not come in until the mid-1920s for oysters, and similar approaches were adopted for the cultivation of nori seaweed ten years later.

The Amazing Mr Mikimoto

With the opening of trade routes to the west, the Japanese pearl was immediately prized and the beds quickly exhausted. At this point one of the most extraordinary figures in oyster history, and also fashion, was to emerge. Kokichi Mikimoto observed this plundering of the beds and embarked on a succession of experiments to try and raise an artificially cultured pearl at Ise-Shima. On 11 July 1893 he raised one of the bamboo oyster baskets out of the water to show his wife Ume. They opened one of the oysters, and there, inside the shell, a shining pearl had been cultured. This was perhaps the first time in the modern era that man had cultivated a pearl.

Mikimoto was no simple oysterman. He was born and raised in a noodle shop in the 1850s. But in time he was to prove himself as a businessman, a designer and a scientist. He founded the world's first store specialising in pearl jewellery in Tokyo's Ginza area, and in 1906 he moved the store to a new building in Ginza 4-chome, where it still stands – an art décor, glittering, beach-like skyscraper. This was ten years before Jacques Cartier opened his first shop in New York.

Mikimoto's shop was no backstreet curiosity. He commissioned jewellery designers to set off his pearls beside the most lavish of gems, and he held monthly art-style shows. He even dressed his young staff in designer three-piece suits. To an extent this was high-street fashion before fashion, and Japan's first international brand. He opened a store in London in 1913, and later in Paris, New York, San Francisco and other US cities, as well as Bombay and Shanghai. There is a statue to him in Shoba, by the pearl farm, and a museum.

In 1914 he opened a culturing site for black-lipped pearl oysters on Ishigaki Island in Okinawa. He also sent a team of researchers to the South Pacific island of Palau, which remains a thriving industry. In business terms, Mikimoto bought out his rival developers and for a while held a complete monopoly.

The ancient skill of inserting a statue or sand grain into an oyster or mussel produced a blistered pearl. The innovation was to produce a pearl that grew inside the oyster so it was unblemished by the shell. In scientific terms, the freshwater pearl is cultured using mantle-tissue nucleation; the South Sea pearl is cultured using bead-nucleation. Bead-nucleation is used to define the size of the pearl – the bigger the bead, the bigger the pearl.

The bead is made from a freshwater mussel shell and inserted into the oyster. Only one pearl is grown at a time. If the oyster produces a marketable pearl, the oyster may be implanted again. The subsequent nucleus must be slightly larger; so the second-generation pearl is larger.

The oyster is returned to the waters for eighteen months to three years, but as an oyster ages the quality of the pearls it produces diminishes. Lustre is highest in the first generation.

The English Connection

Two years before Mikimoto, William Saville-Kent, an English scientist, undertook similar experiments on Thursday Island in the Torres Strait, Queensland, Australia. Saville-Kent gave evidence of his cultured blister pearls in 1891. After much trial and error Mikimoto lodged a patent for his pearl cultivation in 1908, but a year previously a carpenter, Tatsuhei Mise, and a government biologist, Tokichi Nishikawa, also published independent patents for pearl production, which were much more practical. The procedure was thus named the Mise-Nishikawa method. The suspicious thing was that neither of them seemed to have done much research. It was also suspect that it was the same year that Saville-Kent died. The rumour was that they had just borrowed Saville-Kent's work. Mikimoto stopped any debate and bought them out.

Mikimoto had been concentrating on trying to raise the pearls on the edge of the mantle of the akoya oyster. In the Mise-Nishikawa method a starter bead from mother-of-pearl wrapped in the flesh of an oyster is inserted into the sex glands. The tissue from the donor oyster stops the pearl from blistering. These beads now mostly come from three kinds of mussels: pig-toe shell, the three-ridge shell and the washboard shell, which are harvested mainly in the Mississippi and Tennessee rivers. Because of the mussel bead at its heart, quite large pearls are grown. The largest, most perfect, Tahitian-cultured pearl in the world is known as the Robert Wan Pearl. It measures 20.92mm in diameter and weighs 12.5g. It was harvested in May 1996 at Nengo Nengo atoll in the Tuamotu Archipelago.

The same technique can be applied without the bead, just using a piece of oyster tissue, but this is largely now confined to what are called freshwater pearls, usually raised in rivers using mussels. They will not grow as large, although the Chinese, where 90 per cent of freshwater pearls now come from, claim they can rival the saltwater akoya pearl.

Before he died in 1954, Mikimoto revealed that he had made more money in the financial year at the end of the war than at any time previously. He had made $200,000 selling pearls to the occupying US troops. This was, he said, 'a significant milestone in my post-war rehabilitation'.

PART IV

Modern Times

As I ate the oysters with their strong taste of the sea and their faint metallic taste that the cold wine washed away, leaving only the sea taste and the succulent texture I lost the empty feeling and began to be happy and to make plans.

Ernest Hemingway, *A Moveable Feast*, 1958

He is not saying anything. Like a big oyster on the bottom of the sea shore. He has burrowed inside himself and locked the door, and he's doing some serious thinking.

Haruki Murakami, *The Wind-up Bird Chronicle*, 1994

13

The Science

Arrival of the Pacific – Genetics & Washing Lines –
Epidemic at Wesleyan – Parasitic Protozoans: Dermo & MSX –
Deadly Vibrio – Cancelled Due to Lack of Funds – News of the World –
The Politics – Some Economics: The Sherbet Lemon Argument

Arrival of the Pacific

The science evolved from the pioneering spirit of the American west coast. The pickings were not so easy; the native beds were quickly plundered by the gold rushers. As early as 1895, the Washington legislature passed the Bush and the Callow acts which allowed the tidelands to pass into private ownership. That simple act of taking ownership probably made the north-west coast pivotal in leading the way into aquaculture.

The west coast oystermen developed their own ways of raising oysters. Tides in the Puget Sound swell from 3ft below sea level to more than 16ft above. The receding waters leave vast exposed flats. Out of water, the oysters died from the heat in summer and cold in winter. The oystermen covered the estuary floor with dykes of cement and wood and levelled them with shell and gravel so that each held 2 to 3 inches of protective seawater at low tide. In some places there were as many as five levels so oysters could be moved as they grew – all of which was done by hand and by scow.

It was by no means a quick success. The oyster's mercurial stubbornness defeated them time and again. Oyster farming, they found, was unlike agriculture. On a farm, one field can be put over to wheat, and another and another. Or to grass, and sheep and cattle graze happily. The oyster was not so malleable. It thrived in one creek and not another, seemingly without explanation. A century of trial and error has shown that the Olympic oyster likes Oakland Bay, Oyster Bay, Mud Bay, Little Skookum and most of the southerly Puget Sound. But only a few miles away, even transplanted under scientific supervision, the same oyster refused to settle in Hoods Canal. Other attempts to move Olympics from Ladysmith, British Columbia, and Oyster Bay to northern Puget Sound, near Bellingham, also failed.

They tried to transplant the eastern oyster to the Pacific. They brought them across America by the carload, literally, and planted them in San Francisco Bay, and later in Willapa Bay and Puget Sound waters. The spat died. They brought over fully grown oysters to fatten off in the cool waters, but again, too many did not survive either the journey or the strange water. They tried to import the Chilean oyster. That died too. And those that did survive in the colder, cleaner, northern waters would only spawn in warmer summers, so there was no time for the native beds to recover after a harvest.

In 1899 the United States Fish Commission opened talks with the Imperial University in Tokyo about importing the larger, faster-growing Japanese oyster. The beds at Akkeshi Hokkaido on the northern island were thought to have the best chance to migrate. The first shipments came in 1902, from Hiroshima to Bellingham. The oysters all died en route. For nearly twenty years oysters were taken across the Pacific. Each shipment failed.

Then, in April 1919 another disaster turned to triumph. Four hundred cases of oysters from the Miyagi prefecture, near Sendai, were shipped from Yokohama on board the *President McKinley*. The voyage took sixteen days. The oysters were watered each day to keep them cool, but when they were unpacked at Samish Bay they all appeared to be dead and so were dumped overboard. A few months later, to much surprise and relief, the waters came alive with young oysters that must have attached themselves as spat to the shells of their dead parents.

The consignment was commissioned by two young Japanese men, Emy Tsukimato and Joe Miyagi, who worked as students on the beds at Oyster Bay near Olympia. They noticed that the native Olympia oyster took four to five years to grow to a marketable size, and even then it was still smaller than its Asian counterpart. It took 2,500 oysters to make a gallon of oyster meat. But with the larger Japanese oyster (the Pacific) they knew it would take only two to three years to reach maturity. They calculated that only 120 Japanese oysters would yield a gallon of meat.

They tested Quilcene Bay and Willapa Harbour, but eventually picked a defunct bed at Samish Bay, near Blanchard, Washington, 16 miles south of Bellingham, for their business. They got backing from a local fishmonger and a few others, and bought 600 acres of underseabed from the Pearl Oyster Company. The earlier experiments had shown them that older oysters died in transit; to survive the oysters needed to have had one winter in which to harden up and they needed to be moved in the spring.

The Issei & Kumamato

Their enterprise was rewarded by an epic sideswipe of xenophobic legislation. Anti-Japanese feeling had been running high on the west coast for more than fifty years. In 1921 Washington passed the anti-alien laws. Foreigners were prohibited from owning or even leasing land in the state.

Racism against Asians on the west coast is overshadowed by more fashionable black causes. In 1882 the Chinese Immigration Act prohibited all Chinese immigration. Of the women who came in the thirty years or so before that, more than half were brought or forced into prostitution. The men were only allowed to do 'dirty' jobs, which was one reason why so many became cooks and introduced Asian food to America.

The Japanese were imported as cheap contract labour to work on the farms, which antagonised the unions and made relations worse. Where the black man's rights had been recognised after the civil war, no such amnesty was extended to Asians. They were banned from becoming citizens. A Japanese man was forbidden to bring his wife in case he started a family. A white woman marrying an Asian could lose her citizenship, which strangely did not stop the trade in picture brides of young Asian peasant girls being sent across the Pacific to meet some unknown settler or pioneer. More than 150,000 Japanese defied the obstacles and still emigrated during that time. They are still known as the Issei.

As had happened with the Native Americans, the enterprising young Japanese people's efforts, in bringing over the first intercontinental consignment of oysters, were simply dismissed. Their company was bought by Barnes and Earl Newell Steele, who became the founders of what would be a pioneering west coast industry. The first thing they did was change the name from Japanese Oyster to the Rock Point Oyster Company.

Their first customer was Don Ehle, owner of Don's Seafood and Don's Oyster House in Seattle. He put these bigger oysters on his menu as a daily special. The new oyster came up against another form of resistance: a reluctance by customers to try a new oyster; in addition these oysters had a darker rim. Steele, a natural marketeer, addressed the issue with an advertising slogan, making the most of adversity: 'Look for the oyster with the velvet rim. It assures you that it is grown in the pure waters of Puget Sound, and that it is fresh. It has a velvet rim the same as the Olympia Oysters.'

He gave away free samples, fried and served in a cracker sandwich. In the first year, 1923, they sold 46,975 oysters in the shell at 3.5c each, and 303½ gallons of opened oysters at an average price of $4 per gallon.

The Rock Point Oyster Company was not the only visionary to see the potential of the cool waters of Puget Sound. Other imports followed and the market became saturated. Between 1929 and 1932, 4 million seed oysters were imported; the price plummeted. Growers and packers formed a trade association to speak up for the infant business. One of the association's first actions was to rename the Japanese oyster. They voted on four names: Pacific oysters, Cascade, Western and Chinook. By a show of hands Pacific won the day.

World war brought the trade to a halt, but it is revealing to see how quickly the Americans were ready to exploit post-war Japan's resources, and how important the Pacific aquaculture must have been deemed at the time.

The first edict of Supreme Commander Douglas MacArthur's occupation was to save this industry. He sent an order to Fusao Ohta, head of Kumamoto village, after he landed at Atsugi air base on 30 August 1945, demanding: 'Prepare 80,000 tons of small oysters in 50 packages at once.'

There was a problem: there were not enough oysters. The two major oyster-producing prefectures in Japan were Hiroshima and Miyagi. Hiroshima was devastated in the wake of the atomic bomb and Kumamoto was not far from where the second bomb had been dropped at Nagasaki. Miyagi, in northern Japan, did not have enough oysters to meet the demand. The Japanese, therefore, came up with a pragmatic alternative – the Kumamoto oyster from Ariake Bay. These smaller Kumamoto oysters were unpopular with the Japanese because they were small, but for the Americans they were similar in size to their own, now almost extinct, Olympias.

Not long afterwards, the Kumamoto oyster died out at its native habitat in Kyushu – a combination of commercial impatience (they take longer to grow to edible sizes in warm waters), pollution and possibly the side effects of the bomb. Today, all Kumamoto oysters come from the west coast of North America and are re-exported back to Japan.

The little dark-grey, wavy-shelled oyster developed a cult following, and although originally deemed just a sub-species of the larger Pacific, genetic research at the University of California elevated it to species status. Kumamoto sperm cannot fertilise Pacific eggs, but the opposite cross-produces viable hybrids. Thirty years after their introduction, the

DNA was tested to create a pure brood stock and separate out its identity completely from the Pacific.

Genetics & Washing Lines

Washington became an important centre of scientific knowledge. Perhaps the most important and controversial breakthrough became shrouded in a mystic jargon of its own – the diploid and triploid.

In 1983 Professor Kenneth Chew developed a non-sexual oyster. More than half the oysters produced in some farms today are sterile. Many oysters in jars and cans will be sterile. They grow faster because they do not spawn and can be harvested all year round.

Triploids are genetically altered so they have three sets of chromosomes in each cell instead of the normal two. Normally, an egg will drop one of its chromosomes as it grows, but Chew developed a process to inhibit the growth of the sex glands. The oyster fattens like a eunuch – an unusual fate for a bisexual creature.

Chew tried to patent his work. The court turned him down but the landmark case led the US Patent Office and the US Court of Appeals to declare that genetically altered, more evolved animals could be patented – a ruling from which consequences and implications unfold in the development of genetically modified foods of all kinds. Once again the oyster found itself at the start of a historic moment in human history.

From the west coast, also, came a new approach to cultivation. Historically, oysters were always bound to the floor of the estuary, so the best naturally came from shallow waters where the optimum cocktail of sun and plankton was available. Now oystermen began to stretch lines out to sea on which they would bag and hang the oysters near the surface in deep water. Modern aquaculture developed the idea, especially in Canada, Alaska and north-western France, from where it has been encouraged in Ireland to suspend oysters in bags fixed out at sea. This allows new waters to be brought into production and allows the oystermen to suspend the oyster near the surface where the plankton levels will be higher. Previously, New Brunswick used to only sell to the local Quebec markets, but now, using suspension techniques, the oysters there are fattening as quickly in three years where they took seven years before, and as a result it has become one of the major producers in North America. Line suspension also has an advantage of taking the oyster away from shoreline pollution. The change has allowed more northerly waters to flourish and bring on new generations of oysters and perhaps a new chapter.

Epidemic at Wesleyan

The poor and the sick leave few reminders of their passage on this earth. Their epitaphs read smallpox, cholera, typhoid, Aids, plague etc. Their tombstones are fire, famine, flood, drought, war. So with the oyster, except instead of the air that we breathe, it is the waters that harbour disease, pestilence, pollution and virus. Diseases have wiped out whole colonies, whole estuaries, sometimes to the point that they become death zones, despite the efforts of the oyster cultivator. Many diseases probably came from us and have been given straight back to us unceremoniously, like typhoid and cholera.

Native American Indians moved from bay to bay to protect the beds and the fishing from their own waste and pollution. Settlers had other ideas. They urbanised the land and destroyed the beds which fed them. The trains could take oysters to the cities, but the traffic the other way was also human. The new slums spilled their sewage and garbage back on to the oyster beds. New York killed its own oyster beds. Gowanus Bay, where the Dutch had fetched foot-long oysters in the 1650s, was polluted and closed to oystering in colonial days. By the mid-1800s Jamaica Bay was also off limits, as thousands of gallons of raw sewage poured in from the Five Towns and Jamaica itself.

Knowledge at the time about diseases like typhoid and cholera was sketchy. Cholera was not scientifically identified until 1865 and a vaccine not patented until 1900. Typhoid was not vaccinated until 1909.

Oyster brokers brought their cargo from the clean waters and parked up in the polluted bays of cities like New York and Boston to be nearer to market. They would submerge the oysters again to 'give them a drink', which made them plumper and paler and more marketable … and deadly. The oysters just sucked in the salmonella et al. from the raw sewage.

Epidemics arrived as if from nowhere and everywhere. On 5 November 1894 the local *Courant* newspaper reported 'The Epidemic at Wesleyan': 'A member of the faculty and twenty-three students are down with fever. One student has already died. Five are convalescent, and of those who had gone home five have been pronounced cases of typhoid fever.'

The water wells were checked and found to be clear. The milk deliveries were checked; each faculty had milkmen from different farms which also served the town of Middletown which was unaffected. Finally, the source was narrowed down to a bad batch of oysters served at three fraternity dinners. The *Courant* broke the story: 'Oysters Were the Cause':

Twenty-five percent of the members of the college who attended the three initiatory suppers where raw oysters were served were ill with symptoms of typhoid fever as were several visiting alumni. Two students who did not attend the suppers were ill with typhoid, but investigation has proved that they also ate raw oysters from the same shipment.

The Sad, Appalling Story of Typhoid Mary

In these early days of bacteriology and public health, it must often have felt like science was trying to pin down acts of God. The sad, appalling story of Typhoid Mary, a cook called Mary Mallon, is still enshrined in the spirit of public health legislation today.

In August 1906 the well-to-do coastal resort of Oyster Bay on Long Island was hit by typhoid. The disease was common in the slums and poor urban areas of New York, but not in this exclusive, upper-middle-class enclave. Oyster Bay was fashionable. Only the wealthiest New Yorkers could afford to holiday there, including President Theodore Roosevelt. The victims were well-to-do too. Charles Warren was president of the Lincoln Bank, and yet his wife, two daughters and their maids were sick, possibly dying.

The owner of the house they rented brought in a sanitation engineer, George Soper, to investigate. Soper checked the usual suspects: the drinking water, the indoor toilet, the cesspool, manure pit and the local fish. There was no trace of typhoid. There was only one clue as to the cause of the outbreak. Mary Mallon, a 39-year-old Irish immigrant, had been taken on as the house cook shortly before the epidemic broke out. She had since left. Soper checked Mallon's employment records; since she had arrived in America, there had been outbreaks of typhoid at every place she had worked.

The trail went cold until another upper-class outbreak of typhoid – this time on Park Avenue itself – led to her capture.

Confronted, Mallon refuted all charges and threatened Soper with a carving fork. It took five public health workers to subdue her. She was arrested and tested. She was a carrier and quarantined in isolation on an island in New York's East River. Mallon had probably been exposed to typhoid early on in her life and developed immunity for herself, but she was still able to pass it on to others. After three years locked away she was released, on condition that she did not work as a cook again. She was neither supervised nor retrained.

In 1915 there was a third outbreak, this time at Sloane Maternity Hospital in Manhattan. The cook was called Mrs Brown, only it was an alias Mallon had given herself to find work. She was exiled to solitary confinement on North Brother Island, where she was kept for the rest of her life. She died on 11 November 1938. She had lived in isolation for twenty-six years.

All told, Mallon gave typhoid to forty-seven people, three of whom died.

In the slums of New York, however, one in ten died from typhus, and doubtless in many cases the oysters would have been the carriers. The modern-day norovirus − responsible for 90 per cent of today's food poisoning explanations − is of the same family, in that it is transmitted from person to person or by poor hygiene. It is not an oyster disease, it is a human disease; the oyster just gives it back to us.

Parasitic Protozoans: Dermo & MSX

To an oysterman the threat of human diseases is less of a problem − oysters can be transferred to clean waters and will purify themselves. For an oysterman, much worse are oyster diseases.

Oyster diseases have catchy names like 'dermo' and 'MSX' − both of which attack the Native American oyster, but not the Pacific in the same way. Neither are harmful to humans but they have decimated east coast Native American oysters. Science gives them these modern names where historically they were just called black deaths or, wonderfully catch-all in Australia, winter disease and summer disease. Dermo is *Perkinsus marinus*, a parasitic protozoan that has brought the oyster industry on the Chesapeake to its knees. By 1988 production was less than 1 per cent of a century before. Virginia had 400 shucking houses in the 1950s; at the time of writing it has fifteen.

The dermo hydrolyses the proteins in an oyster. It has swept Maine round to the Yucatan Peninsula, where oysters seem to be more resistant away from the Chesapeake. One cause may be global warming. Dermo flourishes in warmer waters. In drier years the lack of rainfall allows the salinity in the estuary to rise. Heat and salt are conditions the dermo likes.

Dermo has been known off the Gulf of Mexico and in other southern waters since the 1950s, and was spotted in the Chesapeake as early as 1954. Something in the waters changed in the subsequent years. The dermo disables the oyster's immune system, which causes emaciation, gaping, shrinkage of the mantle away from the outer edge of the shell and retarded growth. Mortality rates are 90 per cent and more, although it can take a few years to take hold. A single oyster can safely filter a single dermo, but the vast numbers that will grow on an infected oyster cadaver create an epizootic.

In January 2005 the environmental consultant Wolf-Dieter Busch petitioned the American National Marine Fisheries Service to list the Native American oyster as an endangered species because of what was happening at Chesapeake. His petition was turned down. The oyster was deemed an invertebrate and as such other estuaries complained that protecting it nationally would affect business. Had it been defined as a vertebrate it could have been protected. The committee concluded: 'The many problems in the Chesapeake Bay, including the plight of the oyster, have been the result of more than a century of fishery, land use, and environmental mismanagement by both the public and private sectors.'

MSX has the grand – so grand it could almost be a computer game – scientific name Multinucleated Sphere X, or more of a mouthful, *Haplospordium Nelsoni*. It is a single-celled protozoan parasite that first attacks the oyster's gills, then moves on to the digestive system and eventually infiltrates the entire body. It will kill 95 per cent of the oysters it attacks.

MSX first appeared in Delaware Bay in 1957, and spread to oyster populations in Chesapeake Bay in 1959. Since then, outbreaks have occurred in Long Island Sound and along the coast of Maine. Like the dermo, it likes the warm waters of summer and high salt levels.

The Canadian beds were ravaged at Bras D'Or. The blame was laid on ships offloading low saline ballast water carried from Baltimore to increase their stability. Shipping has dramatically altered the ecology of more remote venues around the world. Ships from Australia and Asia offloading ballast waters in the same way have introduced new species. In one survey on forty ships, eight completely foreign species not found in New Zealand before were uncovered, and another eighteen foreign species already established were revealed. Conversely, the Pacific oyster may have been introduced to Africa and other parts of the world by shipping rather than man and can survive where the native oyster cannot.

Deadly Vibrio

Only one oyster condition is actually directly harmful to humans. *Vibrio Vulnificus* lives in warm waters and is related to cholera. You can catch it as easily as swimming with an open wound but its spread is restricted to the Caribbean and Mexican Gulf. In healthy people it can cause vomiting, stomach pain and diarrhoea, but for anyone with a weak liver and lowered immune system it can be fatal. It also creates a very unpleasant skin condition. Fifteen people a year die of it.

Film director turned restaurant writer Michael Winner was infected by an oyster on New Year's Day 2007 and very nearly lost a leg. Others have not been so lucky. Darrell Dishon, a Lebanese businessman, was to get married in Florida when he succumbed and his fiancée had to agree to the double amputation of his legs while he lay in a coma. Dishon was diabetic. He later died of complications.

In the summer of 2009 the American Food and Drug Administration tried to ban the sale of fresh oysters from April to October. The move was blocked by the Louisiana oyster businesses who feared it would bankrupt them completely. They argued that fifteen deaths a year was statistically a minor risk.

Temperature is crucial. The vibrio only thrives in temperatures over 81°F. Summer fishing is often only carried out at night as a result. Cooked or processed oysters are safe. For the most part oyster grading takes care of any risk of diseases. Top grade oysters are defined as pure for immediate consumption. Grade B would be the oysters sent for purification by being kept in clean water pumped through ultraviolet for forty-two hours. Grade C would mean the oysters being re-laid in cleaner waters to purge. Anything beneath that and the beds are closed.

Cancelled Due to Lack of Funds

In Europe there have always been diseases. In the Thames nearly half the oysters were destroyed by one outbreak just after the First World War, which may have been an alien incursion or neglect while minds were elsewhere. Other factors beyond disease certainly affected the Thames, notably the use of TBT (tri-butyl tin) to paint ships' bottoms, which killed oyster larvae and stunted the reefs' growth. The British government was pressured by the nascent yuppie yachting lobby to delay the introduction of the ban until many years after it was introduced in France and Canada. People who owned yachts were a more important political lobby than the men who harvested the catch.

In the 1920s and 1930s the Thames kept up a semblance of prosperity. Then nature intervened. The winters of 1929, 1940 and 1947 were so cold the Thames froze, killing millions of oysters. The great surge tide of 1953 smothered the Essex and Kent layings with mud. And finally, the hard winter of 1963 killed 85 per cent of the prime stock in Pyefleet and 90 per cent in the Colne. The Essex oystermen's annual general meeting of 1964 was cancelled due to lack of funds.

The Whitstable Royal Oyster Fishery Company had not made a profit since 1928. At the annual general meeting in 1975 it was revealed that it had debts of £40,000, owned equipment worth £342, a fallen down warehouse and a couple of beach huts. At Faversham the beds were killed by the run-off upstream from a paper mill.

And then there was a new disease, a parasitic protozoan bonamia, which erupted in the 1980s and decimated stocks across European beds, developing just as the oysters reached breeding age. It was especially virulent around the English east coast beds. Where it is fatal to an oyster, it is harmless to humans.

Bonamia was first seen in northern Brittany in 1979, then the Netherlands, Spain and Ireland. It may even have been imported from a laboratory in California. There it is called Microcell Disease because the symptoms could only be seen with a microscope. It does not just kill the oysters but infects the beds, making them sterile.

The native Essex oyster was diseased or deceased, or hopefully is in hibernation to return miraculously at some point in the future. Most oysters sold in Colchester since have been imported. Maldon still has the biggest oyster beds in the south, but today these are mostly Pacifics – which are not so susceptible – with only a few surviving natives that can still be found at the Shed among the boats at West Mersea beach. A native oyster today will likely have been spawned elsewhere and only brought to Essex for the last months of its life.

Pollution with heavy metals killed the Scottish beds. Ultimately the shipbuilding that began to support the oystermen outgrew the trade and halted it. The native Scottish oyster was declared extinct in the 1950s although some have been found recently and there are moves to try to revive it.

In Loch Ryan stocks declined to the point that the fishery was handed over to the Scottish Marine Biological Association in 1957 to see if sustainable oyster growing could be revived. It has slowly been brought back into production by the Colchester Oyster Fishery and then Loch Ryan Shellfish. An EC grant has been authorised to clean up the waters in the loch. It has become a last refuge for the native oyster in difficult times.

At Helford in Cornwall, after careful husbandry since the 1920s, the entire stock of 8 million oysters was wiped out by bonamia in the early 1980s.

The Solent has the greatest natural surviving southern resource of native oysters – which in Mayhew's time were called Miltons and were far too prized to ever be sold on a London street – but these are mostly the subject of research and the trade is still small. These deeper beds have stayed free of bonamia but the oyster boats have to fight for space alongside expanded yachting interests and massive oil tankers that ply over the same beds. Here there are four tides a day, which makes it ideal for raising oysters, but also ideal for running an efficient yachting harbour. Historically the beds date back to pre-Roman times, and possibly the Romans even started cultivation here, but they have never been developed in the same way as the Thames, probably because there was not the market locally for them.

As in England, native French oysters were hit by a black death of the 1920s, and then more recently Martellia in 1974 and bonamia in 1979 and 1984; they are now a fraction of what they used to be. The native round oyster has been decimated. Only 5 per cent of the native flat oyster deposits remain.

The Portuguese oyster was ravaged from 1949 by a terminal virus called Gill Disease, or *Maladie des Branchies*, and eventually the last link back to the *Morlaisen*'s cargo succumbed completely in the 1970s.

The French took a draconian and audacious decision to import the Japanese Pacific oyster directly from Japan, and second-generation cultures from British Columbia in Canada. The first consignment arrived on a DC-8 on 16 May 1971, arriving at Bordeaux, and was taken by van to Charente-Maritime. Two months later the larvae were thriving. Now, 98 per cent of French oysters are Pacifics. Even the Belon is unlikely to be a flat, round native oyster, though it may be, but the Pacific fattened in the Brittany waters.

Like us, the oyster has to fight for its place on the planet.

News of the World

Probably at any point in history a snapshot of events in the oyster world would throw up as much drama and scandals as a Sunday tabloid. Back in the Neolithic, the oyster bugle might have had headlines like 'New Cove Found Round the Head', 'Boat for Sale' or 'Roast on Sunday'.

There are records back in 1778 of Cornide in Spain despairing at the state of Spanish beds off Galicia. Today there is no shortage of news.

The news wires jingle with stories of arrests for poaching each year. A Scottish Heritage Trust appraisal of oystering north of the border identified poaching as one of the key obstacles to developing the industry, because in remote, unguarded communities the right to hunt and gather is taken for granted. On the Solent there are persistent allegations of industrial levels of poaching. In France, the high price and demand at Christmas makes the oyster a coveted target. Five people were arrested in Southend for poaching oysters, which was just as amazing to discover that oysters had returned to that part of the Thames as their arrest.

In France the government announced that it was scrapping tests for oyster safety on mice as it was old fashioned and unscientific. Sales of oysters have been banned where two out of three mice in the tests died within twenty-four hours, although the discredited test has seen mice die even where there were no toxins. It is being replaced with a biological test.

If Africa does not figure largely in this story it is because records are scant, but there are oysters and certainly the first instances of slavery mention Africans being transported east to dive and harvest pearls in the Red Sea. In Senegal there is a prize-winning project to teach local women how to harvest oysters from the mangroves without destroying the swamp. In Gambia the season has been shortened to three months to allow the beds to revive. The Zanzibar Woman's Pearl and Shellcraft Co-operative visited New York last year to promote their Mabe pearl business and learn new skills in jewellery making. Their pearls come from the Fumba Peninsula on Menai Bay. The best-quality pearls sell for $40 in a country where the average income is under $1,000 a year. The pinctada margaritifera, or black-lipped oyster, more common to the South Seas, are also found at Mafia Island.

The first oyster farm in South Africa was founded in 1946 as the Knysna Oyster Company on the Knysna River estuary by a retired wine merchant. More than 60,000 people attend the ten-day oyster Mardi Gras every July, raising more than 1 million rand for local charities.

To the north, in the United Arab Emirates, 90 per cent of the national income once came from pearls from oysters before oil distracted the economy and lured the divers to other jobs. Faraj al-Muhairbi, now aged 75, recalled how pastoral Arabs became fishermen for four months each summer. 'There was a day when I dived 350 times from sunrise to sunset,' he remembered. The industry was undermined in the 1950s by cultivated pearls from Japan. At Ras Al Khaimah a new pearl farm was opened in 2005 on the Persian Gulf, producing cultivated yellow-glowing pearls.

The massive hurricanes that have slammed into the Mexican Gulf coast this century have dumped huge piles of sediment on the oyster reefs destroying more than half of them. Hurricane Ike hit Galveston on 13 September 2008, and nearly 8,000 acres of oyster reef was swamped in Bolivar Peninsula mud. One part of President Barack Obama's regeneration programme has funded the restoration in Texas by laying fresh rock as a barrier against future surges. Seven million dollars was allocated by the federal government to repair damage from Ike: $2.7 million on oyster reef restoration; $1.4 million on stone dumping; $1.3 million for oyster boats to scrape the reefs clear of mud. Galveston beds have been officially closed for two years to recover.

In St Lucie, Florida, the oyster has been extinct for fifty years but 30 million shells have been replanted to try to revive the beds. On the west coast, at Tomales Bay, Marin County, there is another problem. While the native Olympia oyster was over-fished to extinction, other species have moved in that prevent it from re-establishing itself, particularly the oyster drills that can drive a hole in an oyster shell and suck it dry. Changing the ecosystem does not always mean you go back to the good old ways.

The biggest disaster, but also perhaps potentially the biggest success story so far in the regeneration of oyster country, is the Chesapeake, where efforts at restoration have been extensive and have gathered support from all levels – in some contrast to its historic rivalries. More than 750 million oyster spat have been put back into the Magothy, Severn, South, Patuxent, Lower Chester rivers and Eastern Bay, grown at the University of Maryland Center for Environment Science's Horn Point laboratory in Cambridge. The population is a fraction of its level a century ago. Since 1994 more than $60 million has been poured into the bay in terms of young oyster stock and shell. The Chesapeake is another Obama priority. Reefs are only opened to fishing when half the oysters are considered to be 4in or more in size. The real prize is longevity. A reef with older oysters is likely to be more fertile and more disease resistant. An old oyster is a valuable commodity.

Along the Great Wicomico River, on the west shore of the bay, more than 85 acres of oyster bed have been restored. An estimated 185 million live native oysters are now living in the reef complexes.

The roll call of American producing rivers that are no longer healthy enough to sustain an oyster industry is getting longer. They include Narragansett Bay, Peconic Bay, Great South Bay, Barnegat Bay, Chincoteague Bay, Mobjack Bay, York River, Raritan Bay and San Francisco Bay. As for the Hudson River and New York, Agent Orange was found dumped on the beds there dating back to the Vietnam War, which says all you need to know about that state's environmental stewardship.

Estuaries that can still support the oyster are increasingly further north, especially in Canada, like Caraquet Bay, New Brunswick; East and West Rivers and Malpeque Bay, Prince Edward Island. Of the famous east coast American bays, Wellfleet Harbor; western Long Island Sound from Norwalk to Milford; Oyster Bay and Northport Harbor; Rappahannock River; and Pamlico Sound survive.

Post-hurricane Katrina, the southern beds are recovering at Mobile Bay, Mississippi Sound, Galveston, Matagorda and San Antonio Bay. But at the time of writing this the Gulf of Mexico is being swamped with oil following an explosion on a BP oil rig. In California, Drakes Estero and Humboldt Bay still produce, and further north at Grays Harbor. The estuaries in British Columbia, and increasingly importantly Alaska, carry on and thrive.

Nature Conservancy has estimated that 85 per cent of the world's oyster reefs have vanished and may be functionally extinct. It blames destructive fishing, overdevelopment along coastlines, upstream pollution and vandalistic agriculture leading to the poor water quality.

The pollution of lochs in Northern Ireland has been severe enough to prompt the World Wide Fund for Nature to suggest that thirteen out of sixteen indigenous marine species, including the oyster, are under threat of extinction.

The Politics

One hundred years ago the oyster was the single most valuable item in the global marine economy. The once mighty industry that sustained the coastline economies is now just a glint of what it was – say, 1 per cent, a cataclysmic decline. In Maryland, where as recently as 1973 20 million pounds of oysters were taken from the rivers in a year, by 2000 that same figure was just 63,000. When the gene pool plummets to those kinds of levels, extinction becomes a reality. There is not the diversity to sustain the population.

In Britain, two world wars helped wipe out most of the knowledge that sustained our oyster culture for millennia. The space the oyster beds occupied was given over to councils to pour off their unwanted waste, for industry to dump chemicals and farmers to allow toxic run-offs into the waters. Moorings and shore management were given up to the richer fraternities of yachtsmen. There have been a great many valiant attempts to halt this decline, but other imperatives intervened. We have found other, although not better, ways to feed ourselves. We have found other, though not better, uses for the coastline. Roger Gachet's French book, *Everything You Need to Know about Oysters*, published in 2007, does not even deign to mention England at all except in a passing reference to Essex boats stealing Normandy oysters.

There is a political argument here. We know that decades of commercial fishing are undermining the stocks of wild fish in the sea. The North Sea is especially atrophied. What has happened in the deep sea is probably no better than what has happened inshore. Out of sight, out of mind. The very ships that bring foods and other cargoes from around the world may well also inadvertently be trashing our own marine environment and ability to feed ourselves. Vegetarians would say that it is more sensible to eat the crops and cereals that we grow than to feed them to animals which we then eat. Environmentalists would say it is more sensible to feed ourselves than to have to pay to haul foods around the globe.

The oyster, however, is not passive like an orchard. Unlike other natural resources, say gold, coal or iron, it might be possible to reconstitute the reefs for future generations – it is a regenerative resource.

The oyster offers an alternative perspective, another dimension. Creating an oyster 'farm' is not like pegging out a penned area for salmon or trout to be intensively reared like on a chicken farm. It is an attempt to create a clean, organic marine environment which has benefits beyond the oyster itself. All around the British coast there exists the possibility to revive oyster beds and the culture that goes with it. The first step in this would be to change the arcane laws governing estuarine ownership which have been in place since the Magna Carta, or before that with Canute's legend of trying to hold back the tides. Without ownership there can be no investment and vision.

The first benefits may be purely ecological – to clean up the filth that we have been busy dumping in the waters. Examples from the Chesapeake show that once reefs can establish themselves and oysters are allowed to grow into old age – twenty years or more – the benefits to the marine environment are manifest in attracting other species and fauna back to the estuary. We might have the beginnings of a new form of aquaculture. This encourages local fishing and tourism of the kind that has begun again in Whitstable, or in other guises in Padstow and Whitby. It is sustainable and inexpensive. It is green and translates into work, jobs, trade and business, and hooks up deprived isolated coastal communities with urban culture in terms of restaurants and tourism. And it is globally relevant and exportable. And it is needed.

As consumers it is an easy campaign to support. We need to buy oysters when we see them to create and support demand. They are, after all, one of the healthiest foods you can eat. We need to buy and wear pearls too because that is also a contribution to environmental aquaculture and sustainability. We need an equable redistribution of money back down to the estuary to clean up the coast environmentally and economically. And every time someone says they want to fly to the moon or Mars, we should ask if the investment might not be better spent here on earth, on the rock, a few feet below the surface of the sea on a sustainable, rewarding, constructive exercise in the kind of 'farming' that has been practised since the start of civilisation.

The UK government pretends to pay lip service to this argument, albeit in a roundabout way. At the Rio Earth Summit in 1992, 159 countries, including the UK, signed up to the 'conservation of biological diversity'. Two years later, the Biodiversity Steering group set out to identify declining species and habitats. By 1999, the native oyster had been identified as a 'priority species' and assigned a Native Oyster Species Action Plan.

It might be said it is not a very exciting action plan; it says the government will maintain and expand the existing geographical distribution and 'abundance' of the native oyster. So far it is perhaps more of an Inaction Plan. The Marine Act 2009 proclaims that it will 'support healthy functioning and resilient marine ecosystems'. We have, one suspects, the rhetoric without the rhythm or the rhyme.

The Scottish Natural Heritage, by contrast, has published a practical and far-sighted report on how the native oyster might be encouraged to return north of the border, including costings and strategy on specific areas. This year it received an EU grant to clean up Loch Ryan – to the public annoyance of the water company.

Some Economics: The Sherbet Lemon Argument

Robert Neild opened his book *The English, the French and the Oyster*, in 1995, with an obituary: 'Oysters are such a rarity in England today that they can scarcely be found outside a few bars in London.' Although that was accurate then, it is not the whole story. There are two things happening at once here. The native British oyster is under the same threat that it has been under for 100 years and unless we recognise that then it may well die out. The new science of aquaculture using the Pacific oyster is another more dynamic story altogether. Supermarkets have started to stock oysters again through arrangements largely with Scottish lochs, which could well become important breeding grounds.

More vigorous has been how the oyster has bypassed conventional trade and made cabaret-style appearances on restaurant menus. The historic trade of costermongers and even fishmongers may have died out. A number of surviving beds have opened their own restaurants: the Butley Oysterage in Suffolk was one of the first; then the Whitstable Oyster Company opened in the early 1990s and helped revive the dock front; the Crab Shack has taken over the management of the Abbotsbury beds; the oyster dealers, the Wright Brothers, have opened an oyster bar in London's Borough Market and secured the lease on the floundering Duchy of Cornwall beds in Cornwall. Most widespread is Loch Fyne, which began as a small tea shop beside the loch and has now furnished a small restaurant chain across England.

Other restaurants have revived interest: Sir Terence Conran's group brought back the symbolic crustacea bar at venues like Quaglinos; Marco Pierre White bought Wheelers at St James'; Mark Hix, former chef at the uber-fashionable The Ivy, called his new business Hix's Oyster and Chop house.

The restaurant economic is relevant because it undermines official figures which still presume the high street is full of fishmongers, butchers, bakers and candlestick makers. Old-fashioned trade wholesale prices are given in tons, bushels and gallons. So, for example, the Irish trade figures are given as 8,000 tons per annum which is worth €16 million to the economy. But that is a very basic economic that takes no account of the impact of the real infrastructure that delivers an oyster to the modern marketplace. If we could all buy oysters for £2 a ton we would be very rich indeed. In most restaurants that would buy you one oyster. Where does the rest of the money go? Not to the restaurant really. It is like money that no one can be bothered to count because no one knows how many oysters there are in a ton.

The calculation actually works out that with an average of twenty oysters to a kilogram, each ton is worth €40,000 as it passes through the economy. The real worth, therefore, of the Irish oyster industry, calculated as the amount that it ultimately generates from sales, is €320 million per year. Throw in the VAT at current levels of 17.5 per cent and that is real money of €56 million to the exchequer of whichever country they are finally sold in. In Ireland's case most go for export, so that windfall goes to another government. Obviously those that are sold in Ireland are worth considerably more in terms of the knock-on expenditure inside the economy. You do not have to work very hard to make a business case here. The same economic does not really apply to manufacturing because the component elements are all broken. From a national point of view, the oyster economic has a guaranteed contribution to the national treasury because it is a national asset.

It might be argued, and sometimes it is, that the treasury would get its €56 million in VAT whatever food people ate. It may as well be sherbet lemons. But the reality is that most people won't pay €2 for a sherbet lemon, nor has anyone as yet built a restaurant to serve sherbet lemons. You have to take another step back down the food chain to point out that lemons do not grow in this country (nor does sugar) so not only do they have to be imported but the value of having the orchard in this country is not there. The analogy with the oyster is the lemon orchard, not the sweet factory. If you own the orchard you have many potential outlets for your lemons. If you own a sherbet lemon factory you can only produce sherbet lemons.

You also know that in reality, if oysters were not on the menu at a restaurant then the starter might instead be imported prawns, imported foie gras, imported lettuce, imported mozzarella, imported whatever, which might not affect the VAT numbers but it would have a significant impact in that people in this country are left out of the economic cycle. We have no investment or involvement in the place we live. We become slaves to a new Rome.

The British political system is, in many ways, still pretty feudal. The baronies may have altered but power and taxation do not devolve down to coastal oyster towns such as Colchester or Southend or Faversham. Rather it evolves upwards to central government.

The Truth about the Fat Duck

The cleanliness and purity of UK waters is the responsibility of the Department of Environment, which takes its lead from the rather more concerned European Commission (EC). Management is vested in the private water companies. It is a long chain of command; the water companies have been regarded as a hot stock since privatisation. Europe has not been beyond waving a big stick. In 2009 Ireland was threatened by the EC with a court case that might have led to upfront fines of €48 million, and a further daily penalty of €40,000, for not implementing EC policy on water purity. These laws were brought in in 1991. Spain, Scotland and France have also been threatened with fines and the UK is only under suspended threat in the Thames. The position in Northern Ireland is even more shameful, where there are natural beds whose history goes back to the Neolithic which have been ravaged by pollution.

When customers at the three-star Michelin Fat Duck restaurant in Bray, Berkshire, began to fall ill in January and February 2009, another body was wheeled into action – the Health Protection Agency (HPA) – and the restaurant voluntarily closed. In all, 529 customers reported food poisoning over a period of six weeks. Predictably, the oyster on the £150 gastronomic tasting menu was cited, perhaps because unlike other ingredients it had more of a criminal record. Denials ran thick and fast and the case is still smothered in red tape, with the restaurant's insurers looking to claw back lost revenues. Restaurant, suppliers and the water company have all denied everything.

The HPA faced a similar investigation to that at Wesleyan College 120 years earlier, except here the evidence had been consumed and the restaurant had ordered a three-day deep clean of the whole building before the public health officials arrived. 'Delays in notification of illness may have affected the ability of the investigation to identify the exact reason for the norovirus contamination,' it announced. The horse had bolted.

The culprits were narrowed down to two dishes on the £150 tasting menu – oyster, passion fruit jelly, lavender and the jelly of quail, langoustine cream, parfait of foie gras. In total, 15 per cent of diners succumbed and most of them had eaten one of these two dishes.

Another source, considered by the inquiry as less likely, may have been the staff themselves – seventeen of the fifty-seven staff admitted to having been unwell at the time and six later tested positive for norovirus. The forensic trail led to Devon and an importer of razor clams from Holland, and to Essex, to oysters in the River Colne and the supportive evidence that three other instances of food poisoning had been reported locally. The oysters in the Colne were later tested and traces of norovirus were found, even though these oysters had not been purged yet.

Norovirus is not uncommon. There are 600,000 cases each year – and probably a lot more that are not reported – of which perhaps 10 per cent are food related; the rest come from contact – on hands, surfaces, utensils and even furnishings. It is one of the tenets of the great wash-your-hands slogans. It is not an oyster disease, it is exclusively a human disease; the oysters just pass it back to us from raw sewage in the waters. The real scandal is in the water, not the restaurant or the oyster, and would seem to be no different to the Thames and the waters around New York more than a century ago. The truth has just been concealed in modern scientific mumbo jumbo.

Turning the Sand to Stone

There are other signs that the oyster is not dead as yet. Fifty years after it was declared extinct, oysters have been found again in the Firth of Forth.

On the other side of the North Sea, at Sylt, the tidal flatlands have seen
an invasion of Pacific oysters in the past decade. A brood from a small
experimental farm escaped the confines of their breeding station and
spread, at first innocuously, until there was one oyster per square metre in
1995. By 2004 that had become 500, and by 2007 there were 2,000. The
sand had turned to stone.

Epilogue

Etiquette, Wines & the Best Oyster Soup in the World

There is a hierarchy in the opening of shellfish. The oyster sits at the top as the most regal and the most difficult. For a whelk, a small fork will do; for a winkle you get a pin and a cork to keep it safe. A clam, a cockle and mussels are steamed open.

Tomes have been written about how to open a raw oyster. All you really need, the first few times, is courage and a short stout knife or even a flat-faced screwdriver. The trick is the angle. Lay it cup-side down in a kitchen cloth in your hand. At the narrow end there is a small greyish hinge. Slip the point of the knife into this hinge at an angle of 40–45 degrees. If you push too hard you can stab yourself in an artery. It is easier than it sounds, or feels, before you find the right place of which there is just the one spot. Twist and lever enough so the blade can slip around horizontally to slice the sucker from the top shell. Wipe the blade clean of any dirt it might pick up off the shell … and get on to the next one. A skilled modern-day shucker can open three a minute.

Some oysters, a very few, are just too craggy for this technique; in these cases you have to revert to pliers to break into the outer lip and make a space to slip in the knife edge.

A good oyster is, for which the expression was originally coined, 'well heeled'. Grading systems have tended to collapse, but historically the English system was from five to one, with five being the largest. The French use the same system the other way round, where five is the smallest.

Oyster etiquette has also largely fallen into disrepair, from lack of use or else from sheer custom and bad practice. More often than not, certainly in

England, oysters are offered in ways that are inappropriate. The literature of gastronomy has its own highway code which is usually disregarded for practical reasons.

One myth is that oysters are at their best straight out of the sea. They are not. They need a couple of days to settle and absorb the liquor of the waters in which they have been kept before they reach their peak. Beachcombing your own oysters in Britain is probably not an overly clever idea these days, considering the state of the water in most estuaries. Equally, in the kitchen, an oyster needs time to settle after it is shucked. The first water inside the shell is just seawater – some people will even throw it away; give it some time and this will mingle with the oyster's own juice.

Serving oysters on ice has practical advantages. The shells do not scratch good china and spillages are contained. The tablecloth is saved. But they do not need to be served ice cold. Like white wine, they can be better at room temperature or warmer, as the many recipes for cooking oysters illustrate.

To be purist, you would say the first two or three should always be eaten naked, unadorned and free of condiment. No lemon. No Tabasco. No red wine vinegar. No shallots. No sausages. Nothing. The ceremony of these accompaniments is pretty ingrained but they are luxurious adornment; astringent tart flavours are not really sympathetic to the sweetness of an oyster, not at least in its raw sense. The point of an oyster is where it comes from. Once you have got the taste and flavour in your mind, then, and only then, logically consider what culinary navigation, if anything, might improve them.

Serving oysters with triangles of brown bread and butter is another culinary impostor. Butter is anathema to oysters. They reveal it for what it is – a smear of fat. Cooked is another yarn – cream and butter work well.

There are very few foods that wine writers ever accept as not really going with wine, and if they exist that will not stop enthusiasts trying to pair them off like some old spinster at the last-chance speed dating contest. The nutritional complexion of oysters is not too distant to that of milk, which poses the question more directly.

Oenologists suggest dry white flinty wines, but the weight of flavour and complexity of texture in an oyster usually far outweighs the skills of any vintner. The great wine merchant Joseph Berkmann said the best advice on choosing wines to go with foods is to follow the wine of the area from which it comes, where there is at least some historical evolved connection. So that suggests the Loire. But it also asks if maybe Calvados might work, which of course it will.

White wine does not usually go well with seawater either, so wine needs to be consumed like punctuation rather than accompaniment. The oyster is really doing the job in conventional dining of the aperitif. The oyster is the wine. It can set up the palate for a great wine, but that does not always mean they should be consumed at precisely the same time. It is not usual to drink good wine with the traditional accompaniments (even if you accept their validity) of lemon, Tabasco or vinegar, and accompaniments are always a good flavour signpost of pairing with wines.

Bubbles, on the other hand, offer a welcome distracting effervescence, so champagne, or sparkling New World wines, even cider or a *cidre bouche* from Normandy, all make sense. The bone dry biscuitness of champagne is possibly preferable to the appleness of the cider, but in a way, the dunking-biscuit-into-milky-tea analogy is not wide of the mark, and is echoed also in the American fondness for dry crackers with milky oyster soup.

In Islay, and the other Scottish malt islands, malt whisky is both splashed on the oyster and comes as a dram to the side, a practice that may have been the origin of the shooter. Warm sake works too.

Guinness has the texture. With Guinness there is an issue with quantity. What might work in a shot-glass portion size is too much in pints and half pints. On the size versus strength thesis there is always sherry, which has some of the viscous qualities of thicker drinks while the more deliberate flavour is robust enough to deal with the seawater overtones. The clean bitterness of a fino, and the comforting richness of the sweeter olorossos, is more of an equal than a companion – wives rather than mistresses – and were also companions along the west European coastal routes since the start of civilisation.

For cooked oyster dishes the match is with the seasonings, so the addition of some cream and butter for gratins opens the way for richer chardonnays; if wine is used in the sauce, then follow suit. For oyster and steak pie, or even stuffing a chicken, then the door opens finally for any good red wine. With chilli maybe go for a frothy beer.

The Best Oyster Soup in the World

This soup works in two stages. It takes less than twenty minutes but will improve the longer the first stage is left to stand. The second stage takes just long enough to wilt the spinach in the cream. You might use other vegetables like celeriac or parsnip but their job is sweetness and an accent, not centrality. Cream is a matter of taste. A small amount creates smoothness enough. If you prefer you can slake it at the very end with lemon juice or sherry vinegar to acidulate it rather than season it, which it does not need. The oysters are their own seasoning:

Slice a large leek thinly horizontally. Cut a good sized carrot into dice. Sweat the two in a generous amount of butter. Add a bunch of parsley still as a bunch. Add a bottle of white wine and simmer for 10 minutes. Shuck a dozen oysters and add them with their liquor to the stock and take off the heat and leave to stand. It will keep and improve for a day or more.

Bring the stock to a simmer again. Shuck four new oysters per person. Warm your soup plates. Remove the parsley from the stock. Add the new oysters to the soup. Add a handful of spinach per person. Add the cream. As the spinach wilts, about 60 seconds, and while the oysters are still plump, take off the heat. Serve in bowls with fresh bread.

Serves 4.

Enjoy.

Index